ADAMS VS. JEFFERSON

ALSO BY JOHN FERLING

A Leap in the Dark: The Struggle to Create the American Republic

Setting the World Ablaze: Washington, Adams, Jefferson,
and the American Revolution

John Adams: A Life

Struggle for a Continent: The Wars of Early America

The First of Men: A Life of George Washington

A Wilderness of Miseries: War and Warriors in Early America

The Loyalist Mind: Joseph Galloway and the American Revolution

PIVOTAL MOMENTS
IN AMERICAN HISTORY

Series Editors
David Hackett Fischer
James M. McPherson

Books in this series examine large historical problems through the lens of one particular event. Each volume gives attention to the experience of ordinary people, to deep historical processes, and to structural change in society. At the same time, these works examine the fundamental role of contingency in history and the importance of choices made by individual actors. In this way, the series seeks to combine new approaches in historical scholarship with the age-old idea of history as a narrative art.

ADAMS vs. JEFFERSON

The Tumultuous Election
of 1800

JOHN FERLING

OXFORD
UNIVERSITY PRESS

2004

OXFORD

UNIVERSITY PRESS

Oxford   New York
Auckland   Bangkok   Buenos Aires   Cape Town   Chennai
Dar es Salaam   Delhi   Hong Kong   Istanbul   Karachi   Kolkata
Kuala Lumpur   Madrid   Melbourne   Mexico City   Mumbai   Nairobi
São Paulo   Shanghai   Taipei   Tokyo   Toronto

Library of Congress Cataloging-in-Publication Data
Ferling, John E.
Adams vs. Jefferson : the tumultuous election of 1800 /
by John Ferling.
p. cm. — (Pivotal moments in American history)
ISBN-13: 978-0-19-518906-3
1. Presidents—United States—Election—1800. 2. Jefferson, Thomas,
1743–1826. 3. Adams, John, 1735–1826. 4. United States—Politics and
government—1797–1801. I. Title: Adams versus Jefferson. II. Title.
III. Series.
E330.F47 2004
324.973'044—dc22
2004007851

*To the faculty and staff
of the Irvine S. Ingram Library
for years of assistance
with countless projects*

Contents

Editors' Note

ON ANY SHORT LIST of pivotal moments in American history, the election of 1800 will always have a central place. The winner, Thomas Jefferson, called it the Revolution of 1800. Not all historians have shared his judgment, but the more we learn about this event, the more revolutionary it appears.

Jefferson believed that it was mainly a "revolution in the principles of our government," and truly it was so. The campaign of 1800 was a collision of three republican ideas: the oligarchic republic of Alexander Hamilton and the High Federalists, the balanced republic of John Adams (a balance between the few and the many), and the representative republic of Jefferson and Madison (in our terms, a democratic republic). Ironically, the tribunes of the democratic republic in 1800 were rich and well-born men of greater wealth than Adams and Hamilton. That would be so in many American generations.

The election of 1800 was also part of a structural revolution in American politics. The victorious party led a process of democratization in the abolition of property qualifications, the formation of closer ties between representatives and constituents, the development of party organization, and the growth of popular campaigning.

In all of these ways, the election of 1800 was not merely a revolution in political principles but also a deep change from one historical process to the next. During the decade of the 1790s, the American system had been moving in the direction of an oligarchic republic. In the elections of 1798, High Federalists made sweeping gains through the southern states as well as in the north, a consequence of the quasi-war with France. That movement was stopped with great courage and conviction by John Adams in 1799 and its momentum reversed in the election of 1800.

The voting in that year became a pivotal event in other ways. This was a realigning election, which established a new ruling coalition in New York, Pennsylvania, the southern and the western states. The Jeffersonian coalition had been unable to control the national government in the 1790s. It would dominate American politics for a quarter-century, from 1801 to 1825.

The contest that followed the election was also critical in its consequences. With great difficulty, Jeffersonians and Federalists established a precedent for the peaceful transfer of power between parties who detested one another. They affirmed the legitimacy of America's Constitutional system, which would fail only once in the next two centuries, during the slavery crisis. Many modern republics have gone a different way. One South American republic suffered more than 170 coups and revolutions in less than 170 years. The election of 1800 was a pivotal moment for political stability in the United States, a vital factor in economic growth, social development, and cultural identity. The election of 1800 was a pivotal event in all of these ways.

It was also a very close-run thing. A shift of merely five electoral votes would have reversed the result. The outcome might have been different if Adams had not decided to send a peace mission to France, if Hamilton had not decided to campaign against him, if Madison and Jefferson had acted in other ways, if Burr had chosen differently.

John Ferling tells this deeply interesting story in a graceful and fluent narrative that centers on these extraordinary men and the choices that they made. Rarely in American history did such a tightly centered event have such sweeping consequences for this great republic.

David Hackett Fischer
James M. McPherson

Illustrations and Maps

Illustrations

Maps

Preface

I TRY TO STAY INFORMED on political matters, but I've never considered myself a political junkie. Even so, politics has always seemed to have a place in my life, going back, I suppose, to one of the first snapshots of me taken by my parents. In it, my mother is holding me up to see Franklin Delano Roosevelt, who was riding past in a presidential limousine.

From an early age I remember neighbors and relatives talking avidly about politics. One of my grandfathers, John McCracken, told me about growing up in western Pennsylvania in a farm family that included several sons. His father did not have enough land to give to all his sons, so the family farm went to the eldest son, and eighty-acre tracts were purchased for the younger boys, which included my grandfather. He told me that the land he received, which was in West Virginia, near the Pennsylvania border, was purchased under a law for which Thomas Jefferson was responsible and which had made land readily available at cheap prices. I've never checked the land deeds, but I know that he believed the story to be true, and so at an early age I came to see that decisions made by those in high places could affect ordinary Americans.

My other grandfather, Wilbur Ferling, was the son of German immigrants and the first in the family to be born in the United States. He was a skilled artisan, a glass cutter in that thriving industry in the Ohio Valley early in the twentieth century. He endured the agony and uncertainty of the Great Depression, a time of austerity for him and an especially bitter time for my father, who was without steady work from 1930 through 1934. My grandfather talked fondly of New Deal programs that had restored security to his life, so that through him too I came at a young age to think that politics and politicians could have a salient impact on one's life and well-being.

My parents discussed politics from time to time, and though I didn't know it at the time, I realize now that they must have always canceled out each other's vote. My dad was a rock-ribbed New Deal–Fair Deal Democrat, while my mom remained faithful to her Republican upbringing.

Perhaps it was this background that cultivated my interest in history and led much of my work as a historian to focus on political history. My previous book, *A Leap in the Dark*, was a political history of the era of the American Revolution, and things that I encountered in the course of my work on that book led me to the election of 1800.

Much about that election intrigued me. Having come of age during the tumultuous 1960s, I was drawn toward the high-voltage atmosphere of the 1790s. I wanted to understand why activists such as John Adams, Thomas Jefferson, and Alexander Hamilton, not to mention thousands of ordinary individuals in the states, were so passionate about the politics of their time. It seemed obvious that those people had believed that the political choices that were to be made in the early years of the American republic would touch their lives, and those of their children and grandchildren, in profound ways. I wanted to discover their fears and aspirations for the new nation that was just taking shape.

But one thing above all pulled me toward writing this book. The prevailing sense for some time has been that politics in the eighteenth century was substantively different than modern politics. Supposedly, public officials were different as well, tending to be more detached and disinterested, more above the fray. That was not what I found when working on several previous books about early America, but I wanted to look again, this time through a more in-depth study. What I found once again, and what I hope comes through to readers of this book, is my sense of the similarity between politics and politicians then and now. Politicians then, as now, were driven by personal ambition. They represented interest groups. They used the same tactics as today, sometimes taking the high road, but often traveling the low road, which led them to ridicule and even smear their foes, to search for scandal in the behavior of their adversaries, and to play on raw emotions. They manipulated the political system to their advantage. They were conflicted with affection for and loyalties to foreign nations. Some were led by noble ideals, some were more self-serving.

Some of my views have changed, however, most notably with regard to Jefferson and Hamilton. I have come to a better appreciation of both. A book that I wrote a few years ago that compared Washington, Adams, and Jefferson during the American Revolution was extremely critical of Jefferson through his governorship of Virginia in 1781. While I would yet stand by what I wrote then, I believe that Jefferson changed immeasurably thereafter, and my view of him changed as well, as should be apparent in the pages that follow. Working on this book has led to a richer understanding of Hamilton and greater admiration of him, especially with regard to his colossal talent for leadership and his uncommon vision for truly profound change. Of the two, Hamilton may be the more fascinating. There were sinister overtones, I believe, to some of his inclinations. What is more, whereas by 1801 Jefferson had succeeded politically, Hamilton had failed egregiously.

Debts of gratitude accumulate in the time required to complete a book of this sort. In late summer of 1999 Peter Ginna of Oxford University Press and I happened to be in Boston at the same time, and we met on a warm afternoon near the Commons for a drink. He told me of his plans for a series that was to be called Pivotal Moments in American History, and he expressed the hope that it would include a volume on the election of 1800. I subsequently expressed an interest in such an undertaking, and the rest, as they say, is history. For a third time now Peter has shepherded a book of mine from inception to publication, and as always, his knowledge and guidance have been crucial ingredients in the transformation of a concept, and of a manuscript, into an immeasurably better finished product. For a third time as well, I am indebted to Furaha Norton and Helen Mules at Oxford for their ready assistance and care, not to mention their incessant cheer, in bringing a book into being. Laura Stickney did a wonderful job securing the illustrations. Nancy Isenberg provided immense help through her willingness to read and comment on the sections that deal with Aaron Burr. Philip J. Lampi of the American Antiquarian Society was more than generous in sharing his expertise on early American elections in general and the election of 1800 in particular. I benefited enormously from the work of Sue Warga, my copyeditor. I am grateful too that the staff of the Adams Family Papers at the Massachusetts Historical Society and William Fowler, the president of the MHS, have graciously granted permission to use numerous quotations from their unpublished collections. I am deeply in debt to Angela Mehaffey and her staff in the interlibrary loan office at the Ingram Library of the State University of West Georgia for their unflaggingly gracious assistance in meeting what at times must have seemed to be my unending requests. My wife, Carol, bears the real brunt of it, of course, and as always she has been understanding and supportive of my work, including the travel and the distractions that go with it.

February 2004   John Ferling

ADAMS VS. JEFFERSON

1

Election Eve, 1800

PRESIDENT JOHN ADAMS awakened early on the soot-black morning of October 13, 1800. He dressed hurriedly, not only to fight off the lancing autumn chill that penetrated Peacefield, his home in Quincy, Massachusetts, just south of Boston, but because he was to depart that morning for the nation's capital. His vacation was at an end, fourteen marvelous weeks of seclusion from treacherous politicians and political chicanery, detached even from the presidential election of 1800, though he was a candidate in that contest.

During the languid summer Adams had managed his little farm, a few indifferent acres that splayed out from the house, where grains were grown and four or five dairy cows and weary horses pastured. On occasion he worked alongside the hired hands, and he enjoyed daily hikes of three or four miles, but he spent most of each day in his dark study, where he read and reflected. Adams devoted as much time as was necessary to the presidency, reading every report sent to Quincy, but, truth be told, there was not much to do that summer and fall, as Congress was not in session and the members of his cabinet were in the capital tending to their respective departments.

Adams' mood that morning was bittersweet. He was delighted that his wife, Abigail, who planned to follow a few days later, would remain at his side in the capital until he returned to Quincy, whether in March, if he was defeated in the election, or the next summer, if he was victorious and embarked on a second term. At the same time, a dismaying heaviness weighed on his heart, as most signs indicated that he could not win reelection. Adams, who would turn sixty-five in the course of his journey, was not ready to retire. Defeat, he thought, would be ignominious, a humiliating repudiation of his presidency and an end to a public career that had begun nearly thirty years before, when he had been elected to the First Continental Congress. To lose this election, in short, meant that Adams would be sent home to die.

In 1800 people spoke of December 3 as Election Day. It was the day designated by Congress for the presidential electors of each state to assemble in their respective capitals and vote. The electors were popularly elected in five states. Elsewhere, they were selected by state legislatures, and as that process had been under way since the spring, observers had an inkling by October of the way things were unfolding. Nevertheless, until the electors met and voted, no one could be absolutely certain of the outcome of the contest.

Soon after Adams finished his breakfast of gruel on this brisk morning, his carriage, a two-wheeled chaise, pulled up at his door. In addition to the driver, John Briesler and William Smith Shaw were aboard. Briesler, a family servant, would care for the horses and ride ahead to arrange for accommodations. Shaw, the First Lady's nephew, had graduated from Harvard four years earlier, and in 1798 the president had hired him to be his secretary. He was a good listener and an energizing conversationalist, but he knew well enough to remain mum when Adams, who could be gruff and grumbly, did not wish to be bothered.[1] Once the coach was packed and Adams had climbed aboard, just as dawn spilled over the horizon, it pulled away with a shudder, amid great squeaks and groans.

The president had made the journey south from Quincy innumerable times since his first trip to Congress in 1774, but this time there would be an important difference. Always before, when he sat in Congress and for all but a single year during his vice presidency and presidency, Adams' destination had been Philadelphia. But over the summer the national capital had been moved to what was officially styled the Federal City in the District of Columbia, a place that already was universally known as Washington.[2] On this four-hundred-mile journey, the president's party likely followed his customary route to Philadelphia, initially heading due west, through Dedham and Framingham, and finally to Worcester, where they would have lodged that first evening. In the pink-blue glaze of sunrise the next morning, when fog yet hazed the landscape, they started out again, continuing west past worn farms with shaggy fields. On the third day, departing Springfield, they finally turned south, and in late morning they took leave of Massachusetts, plodding slowly into Connecticut, which required three wearisome days to cross. Travel was arduous and filled with heavy tedium. The carriage, which was unheated and without shock absorbers, bumped and swayed across slender rutted roads that were just a sudden storm away from turning to a fetid ooze. Charles Dickens, who rode America's roads a generation later, advised his readers to go by boat if possible, as even a brief journey was sufficient to make the jostled traveler think that every bone in his body had been dislocated. What is more, at day's end, the hungry and exhausted traveler often despaired of finding comfortable lodgings. Glum inns, redolent of the noxious scent of wet leather, stale tobacco, tallow, alcohol, horse blankets, and accumulated cooking odors, frequently awaited the sojourner, offering sparse quarters and barely edible cuisine.[3]

Adams' gig proceeded south through Hartford, Middletown, and New Haven, then westward, along the blue-gray Long Island Sound, through Milford, Norwalk, and Stamford, and finally—briefly—into New York State. Adams liked to avoid New York City, which even then could slow one's pace, and he probably crossed the Hudson River by ferry into New Jersey at Yonkers, several miles above Manhattan. Moving south again, they needed nearly four days to reach Philadelphia, and two more thereafter before Baltimore was sighted. Thirty-six miles remained to be covered to reach Washington. Adams made it in a single day, bumping through the dark and densely forested region, which appeared to be uninhabited save for occasional half-hidden windowless cabins occupied by haggard black families.[4] Gone were the intermittent villages of the northern states. It was as if at Baltimore the president had passed through a curtain that separated two different worlds. Below Baltimore, he was in the sparsely settled slave South, land of cash crops and great planters, and the home of his principal adversary in the election of 1800, Thomas Jefferson, the vice president of the United States.

Like Adams, Jefferson had spent the summer and fall of 1800 at home. In mid-May, when Congress adjourned, he had returned to Monticello, his mansion atop a tall hill overlooking Charlottesville in the remote Blue Ridge mountains of western Virginia. He left much of the management of his estate to his overseer, but there was plenty to keep the vice president busy. He tended his flower gardens and entertained a bit, and he supervised the labor of some of his chattels, especially the several teenage boys who toiled in the nailery not many steps away from his mansion.[5] But what held the greatest allure for Jefferson was the simple joy and solitude provided by his library. He spent most of each day in his study, churning out a voluminous correspondence, reading, reflecting, and during that summer writing a manual of parliamentary rules to guide those who in the future would sit in Congress. *Jefferson's Manual*, as it was simply called, has remained in use in Congress for more than two hundred years.[6]

Jefferson kept abreast of public affairs, reading several newspapers that were delivered to Monticello and conducting an extensive correspondence with political activists in several states. That summer too, at the request of a Richmond paper, the *Virginia Argus*, he jotted down some notes on his life and career for inclusion in a forthcoming campaign biography.[7] Now fifty-seven years of age, Jefferson looked back on roughly a decade of service in the Virginia assembly, nearly three years spent in Congress, two terms as Virginia's wartime governor, five years in France as America's envoy, almost four years as secretary of state in President George Washington's cabinet, and since 1797 a term as vice president. As summer turned to fall, Jefferson not only knew how the state elections were progressing but worked quietly to influence their outcome through his correspondence and by paying the mailing cost for pamphlets that assailed the opposition. By around the time that Adams started his journey south, Jefferson believed the news was good, although several states were incalculable and he would know nothing definitive until he learned the results of Election Day.[8]

Other news trickled into Jefferson's mountain lair. In August, he learned that a slave rebellion in Richmond—Gabriel's Insurrection—had been foiled on the eve of its implementation, and early in the fall, following the execution of several of the suspected ringleaders, he had written his friend James Monroe, Virginia's governor, urging that the remaining captives be spared.[9] The strangest news to reach Monticello that year arrived around Independence Day and afforded Jefferson the novel experience of reading of his own death. A Baltimore newspaper broke the story that Jefferson, "the man in whom is centered the feelings and happiness of the American people," had passed away after a sudden two-day illness.[10]

President Adams had left home in October, hoping to welcome Congress—due to assemble on November 20—to its new Potomac site with his State of the Union address. Jefferson, on the other hand, was in no hurry and did not depart Monticello until November 24. His coach was loaded and the carriage horses fed in the predawn stillness on that cold morning, while Jefferson dressed and ate breakfast. He would travel with a party of four or five attendants, all slaves, including his new coachman and valet, Davy Bowles.[11]

In the first gray light of dawn, Jefferson's carriage descended the hill, slowly bumping and swaying down the slope. He faced only an intra-state trek until he crossed the Potomac River into the District of Columbia, and it would be brief in contrast to the journey of the Adamses. His gig hurried through Charlottesville, heading almost due north past brown farms and undulating deer-colored forests. Sometime that morning he reached Gordonville, still in Albemarle County, where he paused to pay an outstanding bill at a gristmill. Then it was back on the road. The carriage gobbled up the miles, crossing into neighboring Orange County and beyond before stopping for the night. The party made more headway that day than on any subsequent day of its trek. Thereafter, in fact, the vice president moved at a snail's pace, taking four days to pass through Culpeper, Fauquier, Prince William, and finally Fairfax County. He spent the final night on the road at Brown's Tavern in Prince William County, barely fifty miles from Monticello, a distance that Adams' party would have consumed in a bit more than a day. On November 27, Jefferson breakfasted at Centreville, paused to oat the horses at Wren's Tavern in Falls Church, and in the half-light of early evening crossed the wide and placid Potomac by ferry into Georgetown, almost within sight of the new capital. He traversed the final mile or two in the gathering darkness before at last grinding to a halt at his destination, Conrad and McMunn's boardinghouse, at New Jersey Avenue and C Street, just a few hundred yards from Capitol Hill.[12]

In every presidential election since 1800 the parties have designated one candidate for the presidency and another for the vice presidential post. However, in the presidential contests of 1796 and 1800 each party nominated two presidential candidates. This practice was necessitated by the Constitution, which originally stipulated that each member of the electoral college was to cast two votes for president, "of whom one at least shall not be an Inhabitant of the same State with themselves." The Founders settled on this method at the tail end of the lengthy Philadelphia Convention. They had not wanted Congress to select the chief executive, fearing that the president would become the puppet of the legislature. Nor had they desired popular elections, partly from a belief that few candidates would have the national reputation to ensure that a popular vote would be decisive, and partly because the southern delegates were convinced that after George Washington no southerner would ever again be likely to be elected to the presidency. The notion of having each elector cast two votes grew from the belief that most electors would inevitably cast one vote for a man from their own state.[13] The Constitution additionally stipulated that the person receiving the largest number of votes, if a majority, was to be the president. The runner-up was to be the vice president. Operating under this system in 1800, the Federalist Party's members of Congress had caucused and nominated Adams and Charles Cotesworth Pinckney. Their counterparts, the congressional Republican Party members, nominated Jefferson and Aaron Burr.

Burr was in Albany, New York, that autumn and, unlike Adams and Jefferson, had no plans—or any reason—to come to the capital. He was attending a special session of the state assembly that had been called by Governor John Jay. Today Burr's career path seems convoluted, as he had held an important national office for six years, then returned to lesser state posts. This is not the customary way of getting ahead in national politics, although some have succeeded by following a similarly inverse course. Abraham Lincoln, for instance, spent a term in Congress, after which he held no national elective office until he won the presidency nearly fifteen years later. Franklin Delano Roosevelt returned home to serve as New York's governor after occupying a highly visible position in the executive branch under Woodrow Wilson. However, most who aspire to national prominence and power seek to go steadily upward, though all who play the game understand that setbacks in politics are not necessarily irreversible.

Burr was the youngest of the candidates in 1800, having been born in 1756, after Adams had graduated from college and while the thirteen-year-old Jefferson tended his prep school assignments. Burr alone among the aspirants was the descendant of well-known forebears. His maternal grandfather, Jonathan Edwards, was an acclaimed clergyman and theologian, his father the president of what soon would be called Princeton College. Both of Burr's parents died when he was an infant, and thereafter he was raised by relatives in New Jersey, Pennsylvania, and Massachusetts. He graduated with honors from Princeton at age sixteen and planned a legal career, but he had just begun his studies in Litchfield, Connecticut, when the colonists went to war with Great Britain in 1775. Burr, a thin, sallow youth of nineteen, volunteered to soldier and went on to serve with distinction for four years, rising from the rank of captain to colonel. Only Pinckney among the other candidates had also soldiered, but his record did not surpass that of Burr, who endured unspeakable miseries during the incursion into Canada in 1775, saw action frequently, including in the battles of New York and Monmouth, and suffered through several scarce winters. Although he was never wounded, his health steadily deteriorated, perhaps due to stress or deprivation, or both, and he left the army in 1779.

Two years of recuperation followed before he was able to resume his legal studies, and it was not until 1782, a few months after the decisive allied victory at Yorktown, that Burr opened a law office in Albany. At almost the same moment he married Theodosia Prevost, ten years his senior and the widow of a British officer who had died in the West Indies. The instant the British army abandoned New York City late in 1783, Burr moved his bride and four children—his six-month-old daughter and three stepchildren from Theodosia's previous marriage—to the city and took up residence at 3 Wall Street. His law practice flourished, and in time he acquired Richmond Hill, a stately mansion overlooking the Hudson River that had been the residence of Vice President Adams when New York City was the national capital in 1789–1790. Burning the candle at both ends, Burr lived a sumptuous lifestyle, as if he wished to make up for the time lost in soldiering and studying. He filled his home with elegant furnishings, stocked the finest wines, amassed an admirable library, hired a retinue of servants, and entertained lavishly.

Until he was in his thirties Burr had evinced little interest in politics. He had been elected to the New York legislature in 1784 but served only a single term, although he distinguished himself by playing an active role in an unsuccessful campaign to abolish slavery in the state. Thereafter, he briefly dropped out of politics, a course likely prompted by his economic woes, for by the late 1780s his sybaritic habits had plunged him into debt. He devoted his energies to his legal practice and to time-consuming land speculation forays

Aaron Burr, attributed to Gilbert Stuart. Burr was about thirty-six, and likely already a member of the U.S. Senate when he sat for the portraitist around 1792.

in a futile attempt to escape his parlous financial situation. By 1789 his interest in public affairs had reawakened, perhaps because he saw politics as a remedy for the anguish that pervaded Richmond Hill, where his wife was debilitated with frequent migraine attacks, chronic bouts of black depression, and what she herself characterized as episodes of insanity. Burr began his fitful ascent by accepting the post of state attorney general. Two years later the state legislature ousted Philip Schuyler, the father-in-law of Alexander Hamilton, and appointed Burr to the United States Senate in his stead. When Theodosia died of cancer midway through his term, politics became the focal point of his life. He worked tirelessly to build a strong political base in New York, and in 1796, with the first contested presidential election looming, he openly sought the nomination of the Republican Party, traveling to Virginia to win friends and calling on Jefferson at Monticello. Burr was nominated, though he finished fourth among the four candidates. Furthermore, as the Federalist Party captured control of the New York assembly, Burr, whose Senate term was expiring, could not be reelected.

When Burr came home to New York City in March 1797, he had no thought of resuming his legal practice. He remained active politically and soon was elected to consecutive terms in the New York legislature, where he once again played a leadership role in the abolitionist cause, this time winning passage of a gradual emancipation law. Otherwise, he appears to have been driven largely by self-interest. As he remained mired in debt, reportedly owing nearly $80,000, the equivalent of the lifetime earnings of four tradesmen, his support of land purchase laws and the termination of imprisonment for debt was self-serving. Some of his activities may have been shady. For instance, he refinanced Richmond Hill with help from Dutch bankers, whose interests he surreptitiously advanced in Albany. Not surprisingly, his conduct aroused suspicion, and in 1799 Burr was defeated overwhelmingly in a reelection bid, although his setback was due less to scandal than to the fact that the Federalists were in the ascendancy, riding the crest of a war scare with France. Nevertheless, Burr was resilient. A few months after his defeat, he was the key figure in orchestrating the Republican Party's successful campaign in 1800 to recapture the New York legislature, a great victory that paved the way for his renomination as a Republican Party candidate for the presidency.

Of the candidates in 1800, Burr is the most difficult to understand, in part because he revealed so little of himself, but in large measure because most of the surviving assessments by his contemporaries were colored by his controversial behavior during and after this election. What seems clear is that Burr was a striking figure, at first blush quite likely the most dazzling and captivating of the four candidates. He was only average height—he stood five foot six, about an inch below the median height of native-born Americans—and his body was small, even wispy.[14] Many thought him handsome, and indeed in the Gilbert Stuart portrait, for which he sat when in his mid-thirties, he bears a resemblance to a middle-aged Henry Fonda, a Hollywood leading man. Ten years later, in 1802, the artist John Vanderlyn captured the same qualities, depicting a subject who radiated a pleasant and attractive countenance beneath long, thick gray-black hair that was receding dangerously. In both portraits, and according to numerous observers, Burr's features were dominated by great, expressive hazel eyes and an air of earnest urbanity. Many were struck, too, by his gentlemanly bearing—some thought it an aristocratic manner—as well as by his self-assurance and, above all, an unconcealed pride in his superior intellect. Some thought him graceful, most found him to be friendly and agreeable, and all regarded him as a delightful conversationalist. Burr brought to public life better-than-average oratorical skills, a talent honed in countless courtrooms where he gradually jettisoned the pistonlike delivery and overbearing habits of his youth, substituting instead a slow, circumspect manner that convinced listeners that careful deliberation and reasoned reflection underlay his every word. Yet for all his compelling qualities, aspects of his demeanor caused him harm. For instance, when Burr came to Virginia in 1796 to court support, some who met him not only discerned an active and scheming mind but concluded that he was not passionately committed to any political principle. Winning laurels and holding power, they suspected, were his only real objectives. They were not alone in this judgment. Throughout his career, many detected in him a frenetic ambition, an insatiable, indomitable craving for more wealth, material possessions, power, and acclaim—more of everything, a gluttonous avidity that they assumed drove him relentlessly.[15]

That fall, while Jefferson and the First Family traveled day after day in the exhilarating chill of autumn, and foretastes of winter bore down on Burr in Albany, radiantly balmy days held sway in Columbia, South Carolina, where General Charles Cotesworth Pinckney took his seat in the state senate.[16] Born in 1745 at Belmont, a plantation five miles north of Charleston, Pinckney was the son of a distinguished lawyer who was also noted for his business savvy and enlightened outlook, having regularly defended religious dissenters and helped underwrite the costs of schooling for free blacks. Pinckney's mother, Elizabeth Lucas, was even more talented. The daughter of a British soldier, she had moved with her father from Antigua to the low-lying rice country of South Carolina, where over time she pioneered the production of indigo, a significant cash crop for her adopted colony during the quarter century before the War of Independence. At age eight young Pinckney—C.C. to his friends—was taken to England by his parents after his father was appointed the colony's agent, or representative, in London. There, intermingling with the sons of England's elite families, young Pinckney received a formal English education at Westminster, a noted prep school, and then at Oxford's Whiggish Christ Church College. He capped his studies by reading law at Middle Temple, a part of the Inns at Court, the empire's sole law school, before studying briefly at the Royal Military Academy in Caen, France.

After sixteen years abroad, Pinckney, now twenty-four, returned in 1769 to a South Carolina that was torn asunder by the colonial protest against Parliament's American policies. Pinckney devoted his energies initially to establishing his legal practice, although during his first year home he was elected to the colonial assembly. At first he played little role in the popular protest, and indeed in 1773 the Crown named him acting attorney general for the province. While he said little about imperial affairs, Pinckney played an active role as a colonial assemblyman, often pushing for reforms. His pet project was the establishment of a college for South Carolina, which was finally realized only in 1801, and he worked hard to improve Charleston's library and to upgrade the colony's militia system. In fact, he quickly became an officer in the Charleston regiment. As his thirtieth birthday approached, Pinckney—whom contemporaries described as burly and strong, with dark eyes and a friendly though not handsome countenance—began to court Sally Middleton, whose father owned twenty plantations and over eight hundred slaves. The couple married in the fall of 1773, just a few weeks before the Boston Tea Party.

Soon thereafter war with Great Britain loomed. Pinckney responded by keeping a foot in each camp. He served the protest movement by playing an active role on South Carolina's Committee of Correspondence and in town meetings, where he sided with the drumhead justice dispensed toward suspected Tories. In the late spring of 1775, having learned that war had erupted in Massachusetts, Pinckney regularly drilled his militiamen. All the while, however, he continued to act as royal legal officer. After spending most of his youth in England, Pinckney's ties to the mother country were deep, but his roots in South Carolina were also extensive. Not only had his family come to the province a half century before his birth, but virtually all his vast wealth was tied up in Carolina land. Pecuniary considerations were crucial in his ultimate decision to support the American rebellion, but so too were Britain's menacing policies. Parliament's attempts to tax the colonies may be the best-remembered of its new colonial policies after 1763, but it was merely part of a larger design that aimed at tightening London's control over the American provinces. Part and parcel of ministerial policy was a reduction in the colonists' influence over royal governors and magistrates, a step that threatened the traditional authority of many genteel old families, such as the Pinckneys. Part of the provincial aristocracy, they expected to share in running South Carolina, but as 1776 approached, the Pinckneys—like many other aristocratic clans—understood that their authority was under siege in London. Some evidence also exists that by then the family bitterly resented the British ministry for denying C.C.'s father the position of chief justice of South Carolina, giving it instead to a well-connected English insider. Independence was the answer to Britain's myriad threats, although a break with the parent state would be a leap in the dark, and especially so for those at the top, who had so much to lose. Pinckney decided that his best chance at possessing both wealth and power lay in breaking with Great Britain, and that was the course he ultimately chose, though he was the last of the four presidential candidates to finally make up his mind.

Charles Cotesworth Pinckney by Charles Fraser. This portrait shows Pinckney near the time of the election of 1800. He was about fifty-five when the portrait was painted. Never sleek and charismatic, Pinckney drew men to follow him through his intelligence and virtuous character.

He declared for independence only in July 1776, subsequently remarking that he had "entered into this Cause after much reflection, and through principle, [and because] my heart is altogether American." Once Pinckney made a commitment to the new nation, he was unwavering in his support and repeatedly risked his life for its survival, asserting that "Death . . . is the greatest felicity a

patriotic soldier can hope for." He served as a captain in a South Carolina regiment that defended Charleston against a British invasion in 1776,
although he confessed that he "was only a spectator" to the battle.[17] Later
he soldiered under General Washington, seeing action at Brandywine
and Germantown in the autumn of 1777, and still later he campaigned
in Georgia, Florida, and South Carolina. Three years later he was a briga-
dier general in the Continental Army, and when Charleston surrendered
in May 1780, he was taken prisoner. As was customary at the time, cap-
tive officers received preferential treatment, and Pinckney was permitted to spend what might loosely be called a "confinement" at his cousin's
plantation, Snee Farm, near Charleston, where he was even allowed to
keep his body servant. It was a time of tragedy for him, as his only son,
yet an infant, died of smallpox near the end of 1780. Pinckney was not
exchanged until the summer of 1782, nine months after the decisive
Franco-American victory at Yorktown, but he remained on active duty
until Charleston was abandoned by the British army at the end of the
year. Further tragedy soon tempered his joy at winning the war. In 1784
Sally died after a lengthy illness. Pinckney waited two years to remarry,
then wed Mary Snead, the daughter of a prominent Charleston merchant, who brought a dowry valued at £14,000 to the union. She became
the stepmother of C.C.'s three daughters.[18]

Pinckney spent the immediate postwar years in Charleston, resuming his legal practice and speculating in land and mercantile transactions, including two canal companies. He had lost his fortune in the
havoc of war, but with peace he soon prospered again. By the mid-1780s,
a time when a skilled craftsman in Philadelphia or New York would have
struggled to make £100 a year, Pinckney earned up to £4,500 annually
from the law alone. Soon he returned to the state legislature, which in
turn sent him to the Constitutional Convention in Philadelphia in 1787.
He came north, he later said, with "prejudices" against the northern states,
but his experience at the convention led him to believe that the northern representatives in Philadelphia were as "liberal and candid as any
men whatever."[19] Never an original thinker, Pinckney spoke infrequently
in the convention's debates, save when the issue of slavery surfaced. He
was a vociferous defender of the interests of slave owners, making it clear
that he would not sign a constitution that restricted slavery or the slave
trade. He fought to have each slave counted as one person in apportion-
ing seats in the House of Representatives, a step that would have enhanced South Carolina's political clout. Otherwise, like most delegates,
Pinckney supported measures to enhance the strength of the national

government. A representative of interests in Charleston, a ship construction hub as well as a commercial entrepôt for vending rice, naval stores, and lumber to the Caribbean, Iberia, and throughout the United States, Pinckney wished for a strong federal government that could aid in the expansion of American commerce and help slave states suppress insurrections by their bondsmen. Clinton Rossiter, the esteemed historian of the Constitutional Convention, characterized Pinckney's service as a "single-minded devotion to the interests of his class, state, section, and way of life."[20] He signed the Constitution and played a key role in its ratification in South Carolina, telling his fellow delegates to the state convention that the doctrine of state sovereignty was "a species of political heresy, which can never benefit us, but which may bring on the most serious distresses."[21] Once ratification was achieved, Pinckney shunned national office for years, pleading that his family's financial ruin would follow if he remained absent from his law office, although he attended his state's constitutional convention in 1790 and sat in the South Carolina legislature. He declined President Washington's offer to become secretary of war in 1794 and the following year refused his entreaties to be secretary of state. However, in 1796—at age fifty and at last financially comfortable once again—he accepted Washington's call to serve as the United States' minister to France.

However, the French government spurned Pinckney, and when he returned home in 1798 France and the United States were on the verge of war. He alighted in Philadelphia that autumn to discover that he had been appointed second in command of an army raised during the war scare. Washington, who described Pinckney as "spirited, active, and judicious" and also as "brave, intelligent and enterprising," feared that the South Carolinian would refuse to serve under Hamilton, who had held lesser rank during the war and had been named commander of the army.[22] Amazingly, Pinckney not only acquiesced in Hamilton's superior position but volunteered to serve beneath Henry Knox, who, as the commander of the artillery in the Continental Army, had outranked him in the late war. Either his propitiation was an act of republican sacrifice, the likes of which few had seen since revolutionary zeal and idealism crested in 1776, or he had grown politically ambitious and gambled that his deference would win favor within the Federalist ranks.

It was probably a bit of each. Pinckney was an old-school republican. The principal change he had wanted from the American Revolution was independence. An elitist whose social sensibilities had been reinforced by his lengthy residence in England, Pinckney yet expected respect from his social inferiors—whom his mother had called "cottagers"— and never saw the least reason for altering social practices that had long existed in the mother country and America. He wanted nothing to do with democracy, which he believed led inexorably to chaos. Instead, he favored a republicanism in which property-owning white males chose public officials, who in turn governed without consulting public opinion. Despite his views, Pinckney was neither haughty nor pretentious. In fact, he was accommodating, generous, and well-rounded. He was devoted to the sport of horse racing, served as a vestryman for three churches, and acted as the curator for a small museum of natural history in Charleston. People saw him as dependable, honest, and unselfishly patriotic, and some spoke of him as the "unknown soldier," the faceless patriot who was among the lesser-known Revolutionary generals.

In 1800 Pinckney was fifty-four. His hair had long since grayed, and he had grown pudgy. His appearance was quite ordinary, and indeed no one ever claimed that his was a charismatic persona. More than anything, he evinced an air of accomplishment that induced many to see him as steady and reliable.[23]

In the space of a single generation, the America that these four men wished to govern had undergone a striking transformation. The little nation had grown rapidly, its population doubling since 1776, to 5,250,000. There now were sixteen states, Vermont, Kentucky, and Tennessee having joined the original thirteen. Thousands were moving into the trans-Appalachian West, a place where virtually no American citizen had dwelled only fifteen years earlier, and thousands more flooded into what remained of the un- settled frontier, or backcountry, everywhere east of the mountains. The American Revolution, and the war that made it possible, had ushered in changes that would have been unimaginable in the colonial era. The monarchy was gone, and so too were royal officials of every description, from customs agents and judges to military officers. Many states had disestablished the established church of the colonial era, and unprec- edented religious freedoms prevailed. As an egalitarian spirit grew, ever larger numbers were suspicious of every kind of social distinction. A greater percentage of the population could vote and hold office than during the colonial years, and in general the conviction prevailed that more opportunities existed than ever before for upward mobility. In- deed, a man from a humble American family could become president of the United States, as John Adams had demonstrated. Change was in the air, and it is likely that most Americans would have agreed with the Scottish traveler Charles Nisbet, who came to America in 1787, looked around, and pronounced that the American Revolution had created "a new world."[24]

Yet despite the changes, most inhabitants of the new nation lived lives that bore striking similarities to those of their American counterparts of a century before. Most Americans still lived on farms, rising before the first ruddy light of day to work their fields or tend the house and retiring to bed soon after darkness gathered in the evening sky. Like their predecessors, most lived in sparsely furnished plain houses about the size of today's two-car garage, sharing the dwelling with several children and sometimes with an aging parent or unmarried sister. For the most part, northern farmers raised grains or, if they lived near a city, looked after dairy herds. Farmers in the upper South, in states such as Virginia or Maryland, increasingly were switching from tobacco to wheat, while those along the coast in the lower South, in South Carolina and Georgia, planted rice. In the backcountry, and throughout trans-Appalachia, virtually every husbandman produced corn and sundry grains.

The percentage of the population that dwelled in urban America had remained about the same for the past three or four generations. In 1800 only about one person in twenty-five lived in a city with a population of a thousand or more. Philadelphia was the largest city, with a population of sixty-nine thousand. Only four other urban centers—New York, Baltimore, Boston, and Charleston—topped twenty thousand inhabitants. Many of the men who dwelled in towns were skilled artisans, plying one of the three hundred or so crafts that were practiced in America, such as tanning, weaving, or smithing. Many unskilled workers toiled in the cities too, laboring on the waterfront, shipping out to sea, digging ditches, and sweeping chimneys. Professionals—lawyers, physicians, and clergymen, chiefly—inhabited every city as well. Almost all of the nation's newspapers were published in its cities, and the cities alone were home to the few museums and libraries that existed. However, one feature that soon was to be customary in nineteenth-century cities had not yet appeared: there were no smokestacks. By any definition, the United States was still in a preindustrial age.

One American in six was enslaved in 1800, roughly 900,000 human beings. Slavery remained legal everywhere save for Massachusetts and Vermont, although every other northern state—with the exception of Delaware and New Jersey—had recently provided for the institution's gradual termination. Approximately 150,000 free blacks also lived in the United States. Between half and three-quarters of all northern blacks were free in 1800, as were nearly 10 percent of the African Americans who resided in the upper South. But private manumissions were declining as the eighteenth century waned, and by 1800 the hopes of many that slavery was nearing extinction had given way to the realization that the institution of bonded labor was healthy and growing throughout the South.[25]

President Adams was the only candidate in 1800 who had never owned a slave. Jefferson and Pinckney owned scores of chattels, while in the past Burr, oddly, had been a slave owner even while striving to abolish slavery in New York. For three decades or more Adams had possessed the financial means to own slaves, but he wished no part of the repugnant institution and refused even to hire chattels to work his farm at Peacefield. Now, as the presidential carriage clattered into Washington, he saw slaves everywhere, toiling at the river's edge, working at construction projects, struggling with the cargoes of overladen wagons, and transporting their owners about the emerging city. Just at noon on November 1, Adams at last glimpsed the new President's House, signaling the end to his wearisome journey. His rattly carriage pulled off unpaved, furrowed Pennsylvania Avenue and ground to a stop with a resounding shudder before the house that Adams was to inhabit.[26]

Workers were everywhere, and so was the effluence of their efforts. The wagon-rutted lawn—in reality merely an overgrown brown field—

Washington, D.C., about 1803. This watercolor was painted by Nicholas King, a surveyor, showing the Patent Office at Eighth and E Streets on the right and the President's House, the white structure on the knoll to the left center. If this representation is correct, farm animals and even hunters roamed the unpaved streets of the new capital.

was littered with piles of sand, lumber, brick, barrels, and boxes. Inside, the not-quite-completed mansion was redolent with the fullness of a score or more of scents, from dried lumber to wet plaster, bricks and mortar, fresh paint, and fusty insulation. Yet what Adams confronted was not untypical. This capital city, which had not even been imagined ten years before, was being constructed from scratch even as its initial federal occupants arrived. The commissioners had decreed several months before that Washington was ready for occupancy. Not everyone agreed, including Abigail Adams, who upon reaching the capital two weeks after her husband pronounced the District of Columbia to be "romantic but a wild . . . wilderness at present." She characterized Georgetown, next door to the new capital city, as "the very dirtyest Hole I ever saw." She wished that Philadelphia had remained the capital, she said, but it was her fate to endure Washington, though for how long was unclear.[27] What happened on Election Day would determine the length of her residency in Washington.

2

"An Affection That Can Never Die"

Adams and Jefferson

VICE PRESIDENT JEFFERSON did not call on President Adams when he arrived in the capital late in November 1800. Nor did Adams invite the vice president to the President's House. Once these two had been close friends. As late as 1791, in fact, Adams had spoken of a bond of fifteen years "between Us without the smallest interruption."[1] They had worked together easily while serving in Congress, and later, while in Paris on diplomatic assignments, their friendship flowered to the point that Abigail Adams called Jefferson "the only person" with whom her husband "could associate with perfect freedom and unreserve."[2]

Jefferson had believed that Adams possessed the attributes necessary for extraordinary statesmanship, including honesty, a rare ability to persevere in the face of foreboding hostility, formidable intelligence, and remarkable disinterestedness. Adams, Jefferson added, was "profound in his vision . . . and accurate in his judgment, " and his tireless energy ensured that he would get things done.[3] Jefferson saw blemishes in Adams, noting that he was vain and irritable, somewhat naive, and unduly cynical. Nevertheless, his virtues easily outweighed his faults, Jefferson had concluded in 1787. Adams was a gregarious and warmhearted soul, he said, and advised Madison that he "is so amiable, that I pronounce you will love him."[4]

At first blush it seems odd that an affinity ever existed between Adams and Jefferson, given their mismatched temperaments and disparate lifestyles.

Adams was the eldest son of a middling farmer in Braintree, Massachusetts, near Boston, who moonlighted in the winter as a shoemaker to make ends meet. Jefferson was the eldest son of a wealthy Virginia planter who owned thousands of acres and more than a hundred slaves and sat in the colonial legislature. Adams was raised in a strict Calvinist household where he was taught the virtue of subordinating the individual will to the greater good of the community and to respect authority figures. Jefferson was raised in the Anglican Church but never suggested that it was important to him during his formative years. He was more impressed by his father, an outdoorsman who rose to the status of planter through surveying and land speculation. Peter Jefferson accumulated a large library and through self-education rounded the rough edges of his persona, gradually coming to be acclaimed in Virginia for his skills as a cartographer. It was the reflective, cerebral side of his father that young Jefferson most wished to emulate.[5]

Both boys were sent to school early on. Because he grew up in a New England village, Adams lived at home and attended a preparatory school in Braintree. Jefferson, who was raised in the sparsely settled Blue Ridge Mountains, was sent away for his early schooling. Each became an excellent student and eventually flourished in college, Adams at Harvard, Jefferson at William and Mary. From an early age Jefferson appears to have avidly wished to be distinguished from others in the planter elite, patricians whom he dismissed as "aristocratical, pompish, clanish, indolent . . . and disinterested."[6] He longed to stand out not just for his intellect but for his progressive way of seeing things, and he hoped to use his intellectual skills to make a useful contribution to his society. Jefferson made the most of college, later describing himself as having been a "hard student." Several of his classmates remembered that he contrived a rigid system of study and permitted nothing to distract him.[7]

Adams had to choose a career, but it was not essential that Jefferson do so, as he stood to inherit roughly 5,000 acres and numerous slaves on his twenty-first birthday. Nonetheless, for somewhat similar reasons both young men chose to practice law. Adams, who even as an adolescent unabashedly hoped that someday he might gain renown, came to see the law as the best vehicle for realizing his ambitions by facilitating his rise to important public positions.[8] He completed a legal apprenticeship in 1758, at age twenty-three, and opened a law practice in Boston.[9] After three years he was on his feet, and that enabled him to begin a courtship of Abigail Smith, a clergyman's daughter in nearby Weymouth. They married three years later, in 1764, and over the next eight years Abigail gave birth to five children, four of whom lived to adulthood. Meanwhile, Adams worked obsessively to get ahead, but it was a labor of love, as he relished the challenge of matching wits with a skilled opponent and of swaying jurors. He rose steadily, until after a dozen years in practice he had the reached the pinnacle of his profession in competitive Boston, a standing that was recognized in 1770 when he was asked to defend the British soldiers charged in the Boston Massacre.

Driven by what he called a "little spice of ambition," Jefferson also turned to the law. He took it for granted that someday he would hold his father's assembly seat, but he longed to be more influential in public life than Peter Jefferson had been, a goal that he might achieve by winning recognition as the foremost legal mind in Virginia. Still another passion drove him. A most unusual boy, Jefferson even in adolescence dreamed of building a mansion high atop a towering hill near his boyhood home. He needed capital to construct his mansion and to fill it with a magnificent library and exquisite furnishings, and he viewed the law as the means to those ends. Like Adams, Jefferson was twenty-three when he began to practice law, but unlike Adams, he did not make a lengthy career of this calling. Jefferson succeeded in the law, but he never enjoyed its practice, which he came to see as repetitive and intellectually stultifying. He also grew to think of attorneys as lazy parasites who subsisted off the malice and avarice of others. He abandoned his legal practice the moment he was financially secure, after a career of only five years.[10]

When London's new colonial policies triggered an American protest after 1765, Adams at first played only a modest role. He was not persuaded that the colonists faced a dire threat until 1773, when several purloined letters written by Thomas Hutchinson, the royal governor of Massachusetts, were published. Those missives laid bare discussions among royal officials about curtailing American liberties.[11] But more than that led to his political activism. After sixteen years of practicing law, Adams felt unfulfilled. Not only was he unknown outside of legal circles, but everywhere the leaders in the protest movement, men such as Samuel Adams in Massachusetts and Patrick Henry in Virginia, had eclipsed lawyers in visibility and popular esteem. No less ambitious for fame than when he was an adolescent, Adams in midlife was drawn into politics.[12]

Jefferson was more active in the early period of the American protest, but he had all but disappeared from Virginia politics by the time of Adams' great transformation. At age twenty-five, in 1768, Jefferson had won election to his father's old seat in the House of Burgesses, and he immediately supported resistance against ministerial policies. But he was preoccupied with the construction of Monticello, and in 1770 he commenced his courtship of Martha Wayles Skelton, a young widow with a son who lived with her father near Williamsburg. Two years later—on New Year's Day 1772—the couple married. Jefferson did not attend the assembly sessions that spring, and during the next two years his attendance was spotty at best.

Whereas Adams sought fulfillment through politics, Jefferson looked for and found happiness outside the public sphere. Jefferson had not enjoyed a happy youth, and late in life he remarked that he had no wish to repeat his childhood years, a joyless stage that he looked on as akin to a "colonial subservience." Jefferson displayed many signs common to those who feel abandoned, perhaps the result of having lost his father, whom he revered, while only in his early teens and of never having established what he regarded as a warm, loving relationship with his mother. Young Jefferson was self-centered, reclusive, and unable to establish even the slightest relationship with any young woman. Alone and single, he built his mansion, anxious to sequester himself in his solitary outpost, 867 feet above the sea of humanity at its foot. Consumed with despair, Jefferson described himself in this period as lonely and unhappy, and confessed that he longed for a family through which he might discover the domestic bliss that he had never known.[13]

Jefferson found what he was looking for when he met Martha Skelton. Marriage was such an unmitigated joy for Jefferson that he soon withdrew even further from the world beneath his sylvan retreat, seeking to revel in a serenity that he had never previously known. He had found fulfillment and contentment in his mountain lair, and he anticipated a long life of unconstrained and uninterrupted love and repose. At age thirty in 1773, the year that Adams at last committed himself to political activism, Jefferson was drifting away from public life, seldom attending the meetings of the Virginia assembly, preferring to remain at home, in the bosom of felicity, where he would build, farm, read, reflect, and write. Neither work nor public life appeared to be in his future.[14]

Yet when the imperial crisis heated up the following year in the aftermath of the Boston Tea Party, Jefferson was wrenched back toward public life. As war loomed, Jefferson, like Adams, quietly decided that only independence could secure the interest of Americans. For both, independence was essential for escaping British tyranny and corruption, but for Jefferson a break with Great Britain also offered the possibility of bringing far-reaching change to Virginia. In addition, pecuniary considerations shaped Jefferson's course. A tobacco planter who suffered from the necessity under imperial law to send his products to British markets, he knew that independence would usher in potentially lucrative free trade. Furthermore, as the owner of frontier lands, Jefferson was nettled that the ministry was forestalling the settlement of the western region. Both Adams and Jefferson additionally understood that their opportunities were limited simply because they were colonists, and that an ambitious young man living in British America quickly reached the perimeter of possible advancement. Indeed, the highest legal and political offices were reserved for well-connected, home-grown Englishmen, as Charles Cotesworth Pinckney's father discovered.[15]

Adams attended the First Continental Congress in the fall of 1774. Jefferson was added to Virginia's congressional delegation the following summer. Adams was unknown outside Massachusetts when he entered Congress, but Jefferson came to Congress with a reputation as a gifted writer, and of the two the Virginian appeared the more likely to achieve prominence.[16] Yet it was Adams who blossomed into a leader. Adams had never imagined the eminence he would attain. In addition to his political inexperience, he feared that he lacked the physical attributes needed to lead others. He was not statuesque. At roughly five feet seven inches, he was only of average height, portly, pallid, and ungainly, and at age forty he was already balding. "By my Physical Constitution I am but an ordinary Man," he lamented, wishing that he could be like Washington, tall, agile, and able to impress others "like the Lion." Adams also admitted to several pernicious qualities. He was too formal. His visage was excessively stern, somewhere between a pout and a scowl. He was brusquely impatient with those of little talent or inadequate preparation. He loathed backslapping and flattery, lacked a facility for telling jokes, and was inept at small talk, once admitting that he could think of nothing to say when a conversation turned to what he believed were men's favorite subjects: women, horses, and dogs. And there was more. He not only assumed that it was his right to dominate every conversation but was utterly deprived of the virtues of holding his tongue and hiding his feelings. Radiating an imperious irascibility, Adams acquired a deserved reputation for cantankerousness.[17]

Amid his flaws, however, were virtues that led to his success and to greatness. Many acquaintances who persisted discovered that behind Adams' choleric demeanor was an unflinchingly honest, good-humored, and self-effacing individual. He won dear, lifelong friends at every stage of life, more true friendships in the real sense of the word than were enjoyed by Jefferson or most other activists of his day. Furthermore, he brazenly ached to succeed. The same high-voltage ambition that drove him to the pinnacle of the legal profession in Massachusetts pushed him to become a leader in Congress. He worked tirelessly to get ahead, serving on ninety committees—and chairing twenty-five—in a three-year span. He rose before dawn to tend to his correspondence, turned to committee assignments in the early morning, took part in the daily congressional session between 10:00 and 4:00, and spent additional hours in the late afternoons and evenings in yet more committee meetings. He also impressed his colleagues with his expertise in several key areas. Several congressmen noted that Adams was their most knowledgeable colleague in the areas of diplomacy and political theory, and once he became the head of the Board of War and Ordnance, he acquired a specialist's understanding of weaponry, naval craft, and military organization.[18] Adams' intellect was readily apparent. He possessed a facility for quickly grasping the essence of every problem and for divining the implications of strategic choices. He had a nearly unique ability, said a colleague, to see "the whole of a subject at single glance."[19]

In some respects, Adams was tailor-made for success in a legislative setting. He was neither deceitful nor weak and tentative. One colleague said he was "fearless of men," never shrinking from taking on any colleague or any issue. Fluent and persuasive, he thrived in the daily debates and possessed more than adequate skills as an orator, the legacy of his years in courtrooms. Some thought him a "sensible and forcible speaker," and one congressman was so moved by one of Adams' speeches that he gushed that "an angel was let down from heaven to illumine the Congress." Recognizing his impressive talents, another member of Congress declared that Adams "possesses the clearest head and firmest heart of any man in the Congress."[20]

By the time Jefferson took his seat in Congress in June 1775, Adams was emerging as the leader of a faction that covertly dreamed of independence. While Adams took charge, Jefferson played a secondary role. Jefferson was more experienced in legislative halls than Adams, and he looked more like a leader, at least according to Adams' inventory of essential physical attributes. Tall and slender—Jefferson stood six feet two inches, with long, sinewy arms and legs—he was recognized as a superb horseman, a quality seen then as athleticism is today. Although few thought him handsome, Jefferson was pleasant-looking, with deep-set, nondescript hazel eyes, sandy red hair that he tied back and almost never powdered, numerous freckles, and a ruddy complexion. While he carefully chose fashionable attire, Jefferson otherwise was given to such habitually poor posture, slumping when seated and seldom standing fully erect, that observers often remarked on his lack of grace, and one even described him as resembling an innocuous farmer. Although surpassingly amiable, he was timorous and withdrawn, and new acquaintances had to penetrate his defenses to discover his reserve of humor and charm. He was modest, indulgent, considerate, and unsurpassed as a conversationalist in the company of those with whom he was comfortable. He listened to others, always a winning trait, but he was also well informed on a myriad of subjects and had a penchant for provocative, even shocking observations.[21] Jefferson appeared to possess abundant leadership qualities, but he was not interested in playing such a role. He planned to serve only briefly in Congress before returning to Virginia, to be near his family and, after independence, to reshape his state as it escaped British control. In addition, Jefferson lacked the temperament for legislative leadership. He thought it repugnant to cajole some colleagues, truckle to others, and daily importune and pester those about him. He recoiled from debate and contention, once confessing his "love of silence and quiet" and "abhorrence of dispute."[22] He was never comfortable as an orator—Adams once said that he never heard Jefferson utter more than "three sentences together" on the floor of Congress—and in a public career that exceeded a quarter century, not one observer ever claimed to have heard Jefferson effectively deliver a speech.[23]

Jefferson functioned well in small groups and found his niche in committee work, where with three or four colleagues he could discuss problems and set his trenchant mind to pondering thorny matters. However, his pen was his greatest asset. Good writing was unfairly easy for Jefferson, and his colleagues in Congress often turned to him to draft important statements. A virtuoso with words, he invariably produced easily read and readily comprehensible drafts that usually included some memorable phrases. His pen was equally as useful for its intrinsic propagandistic value as for its literary flair. He wrote a narrative for Congress on the causes of the war that one historian characterized as a "cartoonlike version of the imperial crisis." Yet it resonated with general readers.[24] When at last Congress was ready to break with the mother country, that body named Adams and Jefferson to the committee charged with preparing the statement that declared independence, and the committee in turn unanimously requested that Jefferson draft the document. Busy with sundry responsibilities, and never imagining that the Declaration of Independence would long be remembered, Adams did not want

The Declaration of Independence by John Trumbull. The five members of the congressional committee given responsibility for preparing a statement on independence are shown in Trumbull's painting presenting their work to the president of Congress. Adams, the figure on the left, is at about five feet seven inches the shortest of the five. Jefferson is the tallest at six feet two inches. Benjamin Franklin stands to Jefferson's left.

the assignment.[25] He learned soon enough that he had tragically miscalculated, and thereafter jealously begrudged Jefferson his magnificent achievement, pouting that his friend had "run away with all the stage effect . . . and all the glory of it."[26]

Jefferson penned a majestic draft that captured the hopes of Americans who shared the dream that independence, in the words of Thomas Paine's *Common Sense*, would be the opportunity "to begin the world over again."[27] Adams did not think in those terms. He subsequently remarked that the American Revolution had been made in the fifteen years before the outbreak of the war in 1775, the period when the colonists' "filial affections" toward Great Britain terminated. As far as he was concerned, severing ties with Britain was the crux of the matter.[28] He did not want great change. Indeed, he feared "mighty Revolutions," convinced that they inevitably "sett many violent Passions at Work."[29] Yet Adams sought some change. He embraced republicanism, the belief that power ultimately rested with the citizenry, and made clear his opposition to monarchy and aristocratical rule.[30] He especially hoped that the long-shuttered windows of opportunity would be opened with independence. He once remarked that the most that an ambitious young man in colonial Boston could aspire to was someday to own a handsome carriage, become an officer of exalted rank in the militia, and sit in the provincial assembly.[31] He wanted more. He wished for a society in which the meritorious could rise, and he yearned to terminate the governance of the British "Dons, the Bashaws, the Grandees, the Patricians, the Sachems, the Nabobs," who exercised power over the colonists as if it was their inherited right, monopolizing for themselves the best of everything, and denying talented provincials the opportunity to fulfill their potential.[32]

Jefferson and Adams harbored different dreams for the American Revolution. Whereas Adams envisioned the people, through government, fostering a greater good, Jefferson wished to ensure that individuals would be liberated from governments.[33] He sought the least possible government—"energetic government is . . . always oppressive," he remarked—and was ever more distrustful of government the further removed it was from local control.[34] When Jefferson returned to Virginia after independence, he sought to reform the state. He wanted to make land available to landless white males, move toward freedom of religion, provide at least some free education to all white males, and reform Virginia's criminal code and treatment of criminals.[35] He subsequently postured as having been a steadfast foe of slavery throughout the American Revolution, but that was mostly hyperbole.[36]

After independence Jefferson sat in the state legislature, and in 1779 he reluctantly agreed to what would be the first of two terms as governor. His tenure as chief executive was calamitous and nearly ruined his chances of ever again holding public office. Virginia was invaded twice while he was governor, and Jefferson was nearly captured in June 1781 when a British cavalry column raided Charlottesville. He was forced to flee for his life, and he remained in hiding for several days.[37]

Popular outrage toward Jefferson swelled in the wake of these disasters, and Virginia was rife with talk of a legislative inquiry into his conduct. Had that probe occurred, it easily might have resulted in career-ending censure, but Jefferson was spared that ignominy by the triumphant siege at Yorktown in October. After the British surrender, and with victory in sight, passions cooled. Few any longer had the stomach for going after him. Jefferson had tried and failed, but at least he had tried. What is more, he had loyally supported the American Revolution and had authored the magisterial Declaration of Independence. Even more, Jefferson was out of office, his second term having expired just as he took flight in June, and he had vowed never to return to public life. "I have taken my final leave" of politics, he said in a heartfelt pronouncement, adding that he planned to retire "to my farm, my family and books from which I think nothing will ever more separate me."[38]

Adams, meanwhile, had spent much of the postindependence period abroad. He left Congress at the end of 1777 and spent all but six months of the next eleven years in France, Holland, and England. His service came at enormous personal sacrifice, as at one point he was separated from Abigail for four years, but it was capped with his participation on the diplomatic commission that hammered out a glorious war-ending treaty for the United States.[39] With peace, Adams was asked by Congress to seek commercial treaties throughout Europe, and he was soon joined in this undertaking by Jefferson, who was appointed at war's end to undertake a similar assignment.

This was not a post that Jefferson had ever imagined he would occupy. True to his earlier pledge not to return to public life, Jefferson had remained at Monticello for nearly two years after June 1781. Drawing on the succor provided by his family, he was contented and likely planned on blissfully living out his days as a self-indulgent nabob who occasionally authored a piece for publication. However, his life turned upside down late in 1782 when Martha died following childbirth. Inconsolable, Jefferson plunged into such a black depression that his friends feared he was suicidal. Eventually he began to cope with his desolation, in part through the assistance of James Madison, who got him away from Monticello by pulling strings to secure his election to Congress in 1783. The realization that he could once again have a public life was crucial to Jefferson. So too was his absence from his home, with its sad, haunting memories. He remained away for most of the next seven years, for in 1784 he sailed for France to join Adams on the mission to negotiate commercial accords.

Jefferson and the Adamses lived near one another in Paris for nearly ten months, until the former was named United States minister to France and Adams departed for London in May 1785 to serve as the first United States minister to Great Britain. The two had grown close during their stay in the French capital, and Abigail bonded with Jefferson as well. They spent many evenings together, dining and talking, and Jefferson additionally lavished time and attention on the Adams children who were in Paris, nineteen-year-old Nabby and seventeen-year-old John Quincy, taking them to concerts and Paris' fashionable shops.[40] Jefferson likely found

John Adams by Mather Brown. Adams sat for this portrait in London a few weeks after taking up his responsibilities as the U.S. Minister to the Court of St. James in 1785. He was fifty at the time.

Abigail to be the brightest and best-educated—albeit informally schooled—American woman that he had ever met.[41] When she moved to London he wrote often, missives that radiated his deep respect and loving friendship. He missed her husband just as badly, telling John that their separation "has left me in the dumps." After the Adamses had been away for a year, Jefferson crossed the bleak and windy English Channel to vacation with them. Adams presented Jefferson to George III, who snubbed him, a gesture that only stoked the Virginian's enmity toward Great Britain. Later, Jefferson and Adams took a lengthy garden tour of England, visiting places such as Caversham, High Wycombe, and Stow, and touring William Shakespeare's historic residence in Stratford-upon-Avon.[42]

For both Adams and Jefferson, residency abroad was pivotal. By late in the 1780s Adams had been away from the United States for nearly a decade, but through a voluminous correspondence he had managed to keep abreast of the state of affairs at home. He knew that the war had nearly been lost through the weaknesses of a powerless central government. He was also aware that in the postwar period powerful interests had grown ever more restless with a central government that lacked the power to tax and regulate commerce, to open the trans-Appalachian West, to find new channels of trade, and to cope with domestic unrest. By early 1787 he knew too that a meeting was set for that summer in Philadelphia to consider ways to strengthen the powers of the central government. Adams was excited. He understood not only that this was a critical moment in which great forces were gathering that might give shape to America for generations to come, but that Europe too hovered on the brink of a precipice, with significant change likely. As a youth he had prayed for something like this in his lifetime, and in 1776 he had exalted at his good fortune to be alive "at a time when the greatest lawmakers of antiquity would have wished to live."[43] Now, seemingly, another great historical epoch loomed, and this gathering vortex drove Adams to think and write.

The result, the *Defence of the Constitutions of Government of the United States of America*, published in 1787, was a labored inquiry on constitutionalism in France and the United States.[44] France was an obvious subject. It was a powder keg about to blow. Adams presciently suspected that the French reformers who talked much of limiting monarchical powers and establishing republican government were a dreamy, ill-informed, and poorly prepared lot. Even before France came unglued, Adams predicted that these misguided reformers would set in motion a train of events culminating in "Confusion and Carnage" and despotism. That was bad enough, but he also feared that the events in France would have ominous consequences for the United States. If the French blundered from bad to worse, republicanism everywhere might be discredited. Furthermore, should the botched efforts of the reformers plunge the nation into a maelstrom, France might be unable to honor its alliance with the United States, leaving the infant American republic to cope alone with sulky, and mighty, Great Britain.[45] But Adams also had immediate concerns about the United States. He feared that it was too much of a democracy, a system of governance that historically had ended everywhere in tyranny and chaos.

His starting point was the belief that America would grow to resemble Europe, and sooner rather than later. Every nation, he reflected, ultimately witnessed a concentration of social, economic, and political power. Wealth, including inherited riches, ambition, and natural inequalities in talent resulted in time in the formation of a predominant elite, or an aristocratic class. In Adams' view, aristocracy had been the great scourge of natural rights in Europe, as the elite used their multiple weapons to keep the populace in shackles. Unless safeguards were built into the American constitutional system, his countrymen would in time face the same fate as their counterparts on the Continent. Adams took the creation of a strong and independent executive branch to be the primary solution to the problem of controlling the aristocracy. The executive, he insisted, would be the solitary official who represented all of society and who had the institutional ability both to protect the people from the oligarchy and to safeguard the nation from the destabilizing "parties, divisions, tumults, and war" that would be waged between the haves and the have-nots, or the "gentlemen" and "simplemen," as he sometimes put it.[46]

Adams limned his strong executive as the very "essence of government," nothing less than the "father and protector" of the nation and its citizenry. His ideal chief executive would possess the authority to negotiate a path between all selfish interests, whether that of the narrow elite or malevolent popular movements, in order to act for the greater common good. But to truly be the linchpin, the spring that kept the system on course, the executive must be strong, independent, and—it went without saying—prudent and sagacious: "more wise, more learn'd, more just, more every thing" than any other official.[47] Independently of the Philadelphia Convention—neither Adams nor anyone else had any idea what was occurring within that conclave—he had proposed an office strikingly similar to the presidency that emerged in America's new Constitution.

Soon thereafter Adams came home. He had been away far too long, but what drove him to return was the hope of claiming an office in the new national government. When Jefferson learned that his friend was sailing, he hurried to see him one last time, and when he heard that the Adamses had landed safely in Boston in mid-1788, he wrote to reassure them "of my constant friendship." Adams responded by expressing "an affection that can never die."[48]

Although John and Abigail were unaware of it, a profound transformation had also overtaken Jefferson. His outlook changed substantively in the course of stay in France, but in addition he had undergone a transfiguring personal experience. Jefferson had arrived in Paris still in the clutches of ineffable sadness. His mood brightened as spring blossomed in 1785, and he voraciously explored the city and frequented its emporiums. By the next spring, now comfortable with the language and fascinated with Paris and its delectable opportunities, Jefferson was even happier, and it was then that he crossed the Channel to visit the Adamses.[49] Three months after he returned to Paris, in the summer of 1786, Jefferson met Maria Cosway, and the romantic within him was released. Of English lineage, Maria had been born and reared in Italy, where her father ran an inn. While an adolescent, she studied in Rome with several of the leading artists of the day, and soon thereafter her paint-ings were avidly collected in fashionable circles in London.[50] She was beautiful and blond, worldly and accomplished, and Jefferson immedi-ately fell in love with her, despite the fact that she was married and in Paris with her husband, a marginal English artist. She was twenty-seven, Jefferson was forty-six. She was unhappily married, he was an anguished widower. In many ways Maria resembled Jefferson's late wife, save that she had been formally educated and was cosmopolitan in a way that no woman in eighteenth-century Virginia could hope to be. Seeing her as if through a lambent haze, Jefferson soon described himself as a "mass of happiness," and later said that during his six weeks with Maria "every moment was filled with something agreeable."[51] Richard Cosway took his wife back to London in October, temporarily ending the tryst, but the Cosways returned to Paris in the summer of 1787, and Jefferson and Maria enjoyed three additional months together.

Their second affair appears to have been terminated by Jefferson more than by Maria's return to London in October 1787. In a remarkable missive that has come to be known as his "head and heart" letter, Jefferson told Maria of his love for her but then appeared to say that he could never again be married or even hope for a deep, ongoing re-lationship with anyone. Having been hurt too many times by those he loved, he had concluded that the "art of life is the art of avoiding pain" and that the "most effectual means of being secure against pain is to retire within ourselves." To this, he added: "I am born to lose every thing I love."[52]

Jefferson never again saw Maria, who was confused and hurt by his extraordinary admission. She may have wished to leave her husband for him, and perhaps it was this desire that brought Jefferson to push her away. Or he may have given so much of his heart to her

Thomas Jefferson by Charles Willson Peale. Jefferson was forty-eight and had been secretary of state for about one year when this portrait was painted in 1791 in Philadelphia.

because he did not feel threatened by her. After all, she was married and the resident of a foreign land, seemingly making a long-term, entangled relationship impossible. Maria responded to Jefferson's letter with missives of her own that by turns were dismayed, angry, cool, and distant, while Jefferson, as if unaware of the hurt he had caused, wrote numerous letters to her over the next couple of years that burned with passion, and maybe second thoughts. He confessed that he missed her and that his love for her remained "unchangeable." She was, he wrote, "all peace and goodness." Employing language that takes on a special meaning once one understands his sense of abandonment, he told Maria that she was an "asylum for tranquility" and that he longed "to take refuge every day" in her arms. He reminisced about her effulgent aura and the dulcet times they had enjoyed together. He told her how he "wish[ed] much for you," and frequently pleaded with her to "love me much, and love me always." When he first contemplated returning home, he asked her to sail with him. They would tour the country together, and he hinted too that she must come to Monticello. She demurred, but as the time for his departure neared, he wrote frequently—business letters aside, Jefferson sent more letters to Maria than to any other person during the final weeks before sailing—to tell her how he longed to see her again. Anxious at the prospect of an Atlantic crossing, he confided, "When wafting on the bosom of the ocean I shall pray it to be as calm and smooth as yours to me."[53] Yet he never asked her to leave her husband or to marry him, and that together with the wall that he erected about his heart doomed whatever chance existed for their relationship. Jefferson wanted more than a carnal affair, but as he discovered, he was incapable of ever again submitting to a deep, loving, intertwining relationship in which he fully gave himself to another. In the course of making that discovery, however, he reached a pivotal understanding of himself, and in so doing came to terms with a crucial truth: while he could not live with another person, he now could live without his deceased wife. That knowledge freed him to get on with his life in a productive albeit emotionally austere manner.

While Maria touched his soul, Jefferson's life and travels in Europe had a crucial impact on his outlook toward public affairs. He was abroad for five years, residing in Paris but visiting London, Milan, Genoa, Amsterdam, and Cologne, and exploring the rural countryside in several nations and principalities. Like Adams, he was shaken by what he beheld, but whereas his friend proposed coping with the evils he discovered by creating a stronger government, Jefferson more than ever came to believe that humankind's best hope lay in the diminution of government's reach.

Jefferson was appalled by the powerlessness of most inhabitants in Europe. On the Continent, he said, "every man . . . must be either the hammer or the anvil." A few possessed great power over all others. The majority controlled nothing, and especially not their own lives. The unhappy plight of Europe's humanity confirmed what Jefferson had long believed about the dangers of government, for he was observing a people who suffered a suffocating dependency on those above them in a hierarchical society. The top spot in that hierarchy was the monarchy, and in Jefferson's mind monarchical rule symbolized all that was wrong with the venality, exploitation, and despair that he encountered throughout Europe.[54] But he understood too that widespread misery also sprang from a privileged aristocracy that crushed the peasantry's opportunity for self-betterment, and from the church, the vehicle used by kings and noblemen to bind the citizenry in the shackles of ignorance, superstition, and subservience. Stunned by the hopelessness of Europe's rural population, Jefferson was no less horrified by the implacably shabby conditions in which urban workers lived. Although he had dwelled in Philadelphia for nearly a year and had visited New York and Boston, nothing prepared him for the depth of squalor that he witnessed in Europe's cities. What Jefferson was observing was a Europe in the first throes of a financial transformation, forerunner to the Industrial Revolution. Jefferson sensed that the impecunious urban workers, like reeds in a storm, were tossed about unsparingly by the cyclonic impact of decisions reached in faraway stock markets, great banks, and monopolistic companies possessed of awesome power. The "extravagance" of the few in this modern economy, he wrote, was in many ways "a more baneful evil" for the impoverished than the iron fetters of political despotism. All these things aroused in Jefferson an adoration for his own country and its "equality, liberty, laws, people & manners. My god," he exclaimed, "How little do my countrymen know what precious blessings they are in possession of, and which no other people on earth enjoy."[55]

Like Adams, Jefferson perceived that great changes in France were on the horizon. But whereas Adams feared the worst, Jefferson, expecting that sweeping republican reforms were in the offing, exulted that the French "have been awakened by our revolution." When the French Revolution came, Jefferson celebrated the downfall of the ancien regime. He predicted that France soon would have a constitutional system much like that which flowered in the United States in 1776.[56] What Jefferson did not tell anyone in America was that, despite his status as the United States minister to France, he was meeting surreptitiously with the marquis de Lafayette and other reformers—the very sort that Adams denigrated as callow fools—advising them and even assisting in the preparation of a bill of rights.[57] Jefferson expected the reforms to be put in place peacefully, and was startled by the intransigence of those with power. Nevertheless, when the reformers who pushed for a constitutional monarchy appeared to have succeeded in bloodlessly gaining their ends in June, Jefferson sighed that the crisis was over. Three weeks later the first violence of the French Revolution erupted—the storming of the Bastille, not far from his residence. Once again, Jefferson presumed that the revolution was over.[58]

As these stirring events unfolded in the summer of 1789, Jefferson was packing his bags for what he believed would be a brief hiatus in Virginia. Months before he had requested permission to leave France, thinking that he would return to his post in Paris within six months.[59] Two things drove Jefferson to come home. His daughter Martha, who had accompanied him to France, was approaching her seventeenth birthday. He wanted her to marry a Virginian and wished to take her home and announce her availability. In addition, Jefferson had known for fifteen years that he was in debt, but it was only in the course of his stay in Paris that he first understood the magnitude of his dilemma. Two years after Jefferson married Martha, her father, John Wayles, died, and Jefferson consented to inherit his land, slaves, and debts. It was a conscious decision, one that at the time did not seem imprudent, though some risk was involved. Jefferson presumed that he could liquidate some of the debt by selling the land he received. He gambled too that tobacco prices would rise when the Anglo-American difficulties were resolved, enabling him to meet the remainder of his indebtedness. Instead the protracted War of Independence had wrecked the land and tobacco markets. All the while, the interest on his debt grew. By 1789 Jefferson, though not yet in a panic, had begun to ask nervous questions about the complexities of his quandary. He also had come to believe that his return to Monticello would enable him to organize and supervise operations for a couple of months, and that his profit margin would increase to the point that his debts would be manageable.

Congressional authorization for his departure arrived shortly after the attack on the Bastille, and on a warm September morning in 1789 he sailed home on the *Clermont*. Two slaves, James and Sally Hemings, accompanied him, as did his daughters, Martha and Maria, who had joined him in Paris in 1787. Debt or no, Jefferson was loaded with the legacy of five years of consumption. He shipped home 116 crates loaded with clothing, art, musical instruments, plants, tea, food, wine, twenty chairs, fourteen tables, four mirrors, two beds, clocks, vases, candlesticks, porcelain, draperies, wallpaper, and especially books. Fully one-eighth of the boxes were packed with books for the magnificent library that he was building at Monticello.[60]

Jefferson and Adams left behind a Europe that was changing and returned to an America that had changed in profound ways. When he sailed, Adams wrung his hands over what might occur in the Old World, but he radiated optimism at the new United States Constitution, especially as he believed it would succeed in restraining the emerging aristocratic elite within the new nation.[61] Jefferson sailed rejoicing in the sweeping reforms already implemented in France. They were the "death certificate of the Old Regime," he said, and would be to the benefit of the United States, as the leaders of the French Revolution shared a kindred spirit with their republican cousins across the Atlantic.[62] However, doubt clouded Jefferson's outlook toward the political reformation in his own nation. He regarded as bogus much of the hysteria that had brought on the Philadelphia Convention, though he agreed that the Articles of Confederation were due for an overhaul. But when he saw the new Constitution, Jefferson immediately expressed consternation. There "are things in it which stagger all my dispositions," he remarked, and nothing more than its departure from "the good, old, venerable fabrick" of a weak, decentralized national government that had existed since 1776.[63] Nevertheless, like Adams, he saw things that he appreciated, including the division of powers between the small and large states in the two houses of Congress. All in all, it was a blend of good and bad. "I do not know which preponderate."[64] Time would tell, and no one knew better than Jefferson how unforeseeable the future could be.

3

"Dark and Menacing Evils"

Creating the New National System, 1786–1792

ON A WINSOME SEPTEMBER EVENING in 1788, just weeks after Adams' return to America and about a year before Jefferson sailed home, Alexander Hamilton sat at his desk in his residence on Wall Street in New York to write General Washington. His message was simple: Washington should accept the presidency in the new national government, disregarding his pledge, made at the end of the war, to never again hold public office.[1] Hamilton had a personal stake in getting Washington into the presidency. He badly wished to be part of the first administration and to design the program that would battle the economic distress that had lingered for a decade.

Understanding that Washington feasted on acclaim, Hamilton advised that the general would expose his reputation to greater hazard by refusing to serve. To spurn his countrymen's entreaties, Hamilton warned, was to risk arousing a sense that he had deserted them.[2] Soon after he received Hamilton's missive, Washington consented to serve. In February 1789 every member of the electoral college cast one of his votes for Washington, making him their unanimous choice to be the first president of the United States. Adams, who received the second greatest number of votes, though not a majority, was elected vice president. Several weeks after he was sworn in, Washington named Hamilton his secretary of the Treasury.

Hamilton had a long history with Washington, going back to the bleak winter in 1777 when he joined the general's "family" at Continental Army headquarters. Few, if any, figures of his day overcame such formidable odds to reach the epicenter of power. Hamilton was born on Britain's Caribbean colony of Nevis in 1757, the illegitimate son of Rachel Lavien and James Hamilton, an indifferent Scottish drifter. At age eight he moved with his mother to St. Croix, a Dutch-controlled sugar island where the slave population was twelve times that of the free population.[3] While James Hamilton languished out of sight elsewhere in the West Indies, Rachel operated a small store. Though never destitute, the family hardly prospered, and at times Alexander was pressed into work in the little business. In 1768,

Alexander Hamilton by John Trumbull. Hamilton was thirty-five and completing his third year as secretary of the Treasury when he sat for this portrait in Philadelphia in 1792.

when he was eleven, Rachel died in an epidemic of yellow fever. She died intestate, and the Dutch courts ruled that Alexander and his older brother were ineligible to inherit any of her modest estate, due to their illegitimate births. Soon thereafter Alexander went to work full time, clerking and keeping books in Christiansted for a mercantile firm with business ties to New York.

Hamilton desperately wanted more than a lifetime as a clerk. In the first letter that he is known to have written—at age ten—he announced that he wished to achieve an exalted place in society.[4] It was his good fortune that he was blessed with sufficient qualities for upward mobility. Ambitious, formidably bright, and incredibly industrious, he excelled in school and the countinghouse. What is more, heaping measures of daring, cunning, and brazenness enabled him to display his attributes to powerful men. Both his employer and his minister took him under their wing, the former contributing money from his own purse for Hamilton's education, while the latter raised funds from among his Presbyterian parishioners. At age fifteen Hamilton began his dizzying ascent, sailing alone for New York to begin college. For a lad in early adolescence who had never before been away from home, the voyage from the Caribbean to the mainland colonies was an act that laid bare his aspiring and courageous nature. It also revealed his desperate ardor to escape to a larger stage, where greater opportunities existed. In 1772 he enrolled at King's College (now Columbia University) and soon distinguished himself as a student and an activist. Before his eighteenth birthday young Hamilton engaged a New York Tory in a vexatious pamphlet war. Furthermore, when war erupted in 1775 he abandoned his studies to soldier, and the following year he saw action in the battle of New York, retreated across New Jersey with Washington's ragtag army, and fought again at Trenton and Princeton.

Soon after those stunning victories, Washington advertised for an additional aide-de-camp. Someone nominated Hamilton, who was interviewed and, predictably, made a favorable impression. Barely twenty, he may have looked older, as is common among battle-weary soldiers. Furthermore, after being on his own for five years, he must have radiated a self-assurance uncommon for someone his age. But his quick intelligence and earnest demeanor were more likely the reasons that he got the job. Hamilton moved into headquarters in March 1777, putting himself in Washington's slipstream. Much later, in fact, he acknowledged that Washington had been "an Aegis very essential" to his advancement.[5]

Hamilton served Washington as an amanuensis and by performing administrative duties, and in the evenings, when the day's work was completed, he and other aides often socialized with their commander, relaxing with a glass of wine. Some aides impressed Washington more than others. Hamilton dazzled him. The younger man was glib, polished, and articulate, with an informed and reasoned opinion on a vast array of subjects, including the disadvantages of a weak national government and what might be done to combat the mounting economic malaise that had set in after 1778. Hamilton was young enough to be the childless Washington's son—the general even called him "my boy"—and the commander may have imagined that he saw in this young man a mirror image of himself at the same age: a dashing, eager, intelligent, stouthearted young warrior who needed only the aid of an insightful benefactor to achieve great things.[6]

Hamilton was not fettered to a desk at headquarters. He was in harm's way in the engagements at Brandywine, Germantown, and Monmouth, where he had a horse shot from beneath him, and in between he endured the miserable winter at Valley Forge. In 1781, impulsive for glory, he begged Washington for a field command, and when the commander obliged at Yorktown, Hamilton successfully led his infantry brigade on a perilous nighttime assault to capture an enemy redoubt, prompting Washington to laud his "firmness and bravery" under fire.[7]

After five years of service, Hamilton left the army soon after Cornwallis' surrender. Now twenty-six and married to Elizabeth Schuyler, the daughter of General Philip Schuyler, he was ready to launch a civilian career. Although licensed to practice law (after only three months' study), he turned first to politics and was elected to Congress in 1782. He came to Congress intent on pushing what historians now call the Nationalist agenda, the program of those who sought to strengthen the powers of the national government. Vesting the national government with sovereign authority over the states had not been the aim of most Americans when independence was declared. Nothing in the Declaration of Independence or in the instructions from the colonial assemblies to congressmen suggested a need, or a desire, to create a powerful United States government.[8] Just the opposite, in fact. Most Americans feared strong and remote governments. Indeed, only a few years before the war every colony had spurned the proposal of the Albany Congress, a conclave of several provinces, to create a national government for the colonies. None had been willing to surrender its authority to a central government. Thus it was hardly a surprise that the Articles of Confederation, finally ratified by the states by 1781, divested the United States government of real power, denying it even the authority to levy taxes or regulate commerce. Instead, it created a union of equal, independent, and virtually sovereign states.

No one knew better than Hamilton how dearly the United States had paid for having an impotent national government during the last, desperate war years. The economic collapse took the infant nation into what one congressman called a "Wilderness of darkness & of dangers."[9] With the national government powerless to find revenue, the war was nearly lost. The army could not be supplied, and soon it was virtually immobilized. Morale buckled among civilians, who were nearly driven to want by runaway prices. Washington and Hamilton understood by 1781 that independence might be lost unless a decisive victory could be won during that campaign season.

With Washington warning that the American Revolution and the new nation were "verging . . . fast to destruction," Congress in 1781 appealed to the states to permit the national government to levy an impost—a revenue tariff—on trade.[10] That would have secured the funds to supply and pay the army, but the move failed. Unanimous consent was required. Rhode Island voted it down.[11] Nevertheless, the nation was saved a few months later by the victorious siege at Yorktown. Victory notwithstanding, the Nationalists tried again to secure a national impost in 1782 and 1783. The move originated primarily in the northern mercantile states, where the most powerful merchants were convinced that even in the postwar period, their commercial interests required the support of a strong national government. Hamilton was in the thick of this campaign, bursting onto the national scene with *The Continentalist*, six newspaper essays that mooted the economic crisis with unmistakable clarity and an air of certainty. He warned that the Union was doomed unless the "WANT OF POWER IN CONGRESS" was remedied, and additionally proposed a federal system, a sharing of authority between the national government and the states, so that the central government would "neither be independent [of] nor too dependent" on the states.[12] The tocsin he sounded was the first warning that powerful interests would bolt from the Union if the national government was not given greater powers. Soon thereafter Hamilton entered Congress and became a leading force in the second attempt to secure an impost. However, it too failed to gain the unanimous consent of the states.[13]

Peace eliminated all hope that the Nationalists could achieve their ends, at least for the moment. Hamilton left the feckless Congress in July 1783, and when the British army quit New York City at year's end, he moved his family to his newly acquired residence at 57 Wall Street and flung open the doors of his legal practice. He prospered at once, mostly representing wealthy merchants, large landowners, and scores of downtrodden loyalists who sought protection from anti-Tory legislation. He was also actively engaged in seeking to help another oppressed group. Treated as an outcast himself in his West Indian youth, and having observed the awful conditions faced by chattel slaves on St. Croix, Hamilton at an early age came to loathe slavery. Throughout his life his writings were free of racist cant, and in a letter written in 1779 that was remarkable for the time he observed that the "natural faculties" of Africans were "as good as ours." In 1785 he joined with thirty-one others to organize the New York Society for Manumission of Slaves. While he failed in his attempt to induce his cohorts to liberate their slaves, he and the others signed a petition to the state legislature that denounced the foreign slave trade and implicitly branded slavery itself to be a dark stain on the character of "a free and enlightened people."[14]

Although not yet thirty, Hamilton had come into his own by the mid-1780s. He had succeeded so rapidly in the law that after only two years in practice some believed that only one or two among New York City's thirty-four other lawyers were his equal.[15] Nor could many attorneys match his income. Soon Hamilton and his rapidly growing family—by mid-decade he already had a son and daughter—lived quite comfortably. What is more, his new social status left him well connected with the city's elite. Hamilton appeared to have the Midas touch. He put the lie to Adams' belief that physical appearances were everything. Adams, in fact, subsequently re-ferred to Hamilton as "the little man," though the two were probably the same height, five feet seven inches.[16] When Adams and others described Hamilton as small, they were referring to his slight physique. His body more nearly resembled that of an adolescent than a hearty man, and it drove Hamilton to seek ways to compensate. He habitually stood ramrod straight, not only to appear taller but as if he wished to remind others of his soldier's background, and he dressed to be seen, always wearing the most fashionable clothes, often in the boldest hues. He exhibited polished manners and a loquacious charm, and there was a nimbus of zest and panache about him. Yet, while convivial, he also exuded both a combat-iveness and a strutting omniscience, and more than a touch of arrogance. It was as if he not only was convinced that he was the superior of each per-son within his presence, but wanted to be sure that all others understood that they were inferior to him. Many thought his gimlet eyes—deep-set and bewitchingly blue—were his strongest physical asset, but all agreed that his keen intellect was formidable and that his mind appeared to be acute and coldly realistic. Physically and intellectually there was a pulsat-ing dynamism to his makeup that seemed to serve as a force field that com-pelled others to him. Animated by an almost maniacal energy, Hamilton seemed always to be active and lively, moving, thinking, talking, planning, imagining, arguing, explaining, radiating a restless impatience with not having his way, and a determination to somehow, some way, win through, most often by seizing the offensive and driving his adversaries into a de-fensive posture.[17]

What Hamilton wanted was what he had always sought. He had never forgotten the indignities and thousand humiliations of his misbegotten childhood, nor the obloquy wrongly visited on his mother. He ached to be somebody, to be deferred to for his status and acclaimed for his achievements. But there was more. He believed passionately in the United States. Hamilton, who was foreign-born, felt no loyalty to any one state. His service had been to the American Revolution and the nation it brought into being. Furthermore, he now was in league with commer-cial interests whose enterprise did not stop at state lines and who sought profits in North American and Atlantic markets. A continentalist, as he had styled himself, Hamilton dreamed of an expansive United States that someday would grow to be rich, powerful, and secure, and he yearned for a substantive role in bringing his dream to fruition. In this vision his grandiose ambition and Nationalist passion meshed.

Many shared Hamilton's concerns. Some thought an ineffectual Congress was humiliating. Others wished for a strong central government that could spread American hegemony or, more simply, provide security from Europe's great powers. Many of the most conservative Americans anguished at the transformative changes unleashed by the republican Revolution. Affection for Great Britain and its venerable ways had vanished with breathtaking suddenness, inducing Jefferson to quip that most Americans made the transition to independence with the same nonchalance that they might have displayed in changing their coat.[18] In addition, within a few years of 1776 suffrage had been broadened almost everywhere in America, the bars to holding office had been lowered, and backcountry districts were more equitably represented in the state legislatures. Nor were the alterations limited to politics. A spirit of egalitarianism took root and, in the words of the historian Gordon Wood, "tore through American society and culture with awesome power."[19] Abandoning displays of deference toward their social betters, commoners no longer bowed, doffed hats, and stepped aside when greeting a gentleman or lady of rank. It was becoming commonplace for all adult white males to be addressed as "Mr.," as titles such as "Esquire," fashionable among the gentry before 1776, rapidly passed from the scene. These changes unsettled many of the socially and economically prominent, such as the Virginia planter who fretted that "the spirit of independency was converted into equality," leading each man to believe himself "upon a footing with his neighbor." Worse, he added, each of his neighbors "conceives himself, in every respect, my equal."[20]

Many from what once had been the traditional elite were additionally unsettled at the sight of men seated in the state legislatures who before 1776 would have been unlikely to have held a county post or an office in even the tiniest village. These upstarts were denigrated by some as shallow, gauche, and lacking the virtue "to pursue the common good of society." What especially troubled some Nationalists was that the newcomers to power often sympathized with dramatic change. To many, in fact, they represented an emerging democracy. Not only did they champion the interests of middling yeomen and urban artisans, these new men advocated annual elections, popular elections for previously appointive offices, and the secret ballot. Often they supported land taxes that fell hardest on the largest landowners, and many embraced fiscal unorthodoxy, urging debtor relief and inflationary policies that were designed to drive up wages for laborers and to increase farm prices, and of course made it easier to pay fixed debts.[21]

The Nationalists were strongest in the North, but some southerners also chafed miserably under the impoverished national government, especially those who were eager to open the trans-Appalachian West. Many southern farmers anxiously wished to move across the mountains, and many affluent southern speculators who owned—or hoped to purchase—frontier acreage were no less eager for the exodus to begin. However, British troops yet occupied the region and funneled arms to the Native Americans beyond the mountains, making settlement dangerous and, for many, unthinkable. Southerners were equally avid to open the Southwest—present-day Tennessee, Alabama, and Mississippi—but Spain controlled the Mississippi River, and one of Madrid's first postwar acts had been to close to the United States the southernmost one hundred miles or so of that waterway, denying access to the sea to western settlers. For as long as Spain enforced this policy, few settlers wished to migrate to this area, where they would remain dirt poor.

Matters came to a head in 1786, a pivotal year in America's history. Two events that year stirred the Nationalists to action and changed the United States forever. The first arose from negotiations between the United States and Spain. Madrid offered to open Spanish ports to the United States, an ambrosial tender to the economically strapped North, but in return it demanded that the United States renounce navigation on the Mississippi River, an unthinkable step for most southerners. Each of the eight northern states was prepared to accept Spain's conditions. Each of the five southern states said no. As the votes of nine states were needed to ratify a treaty, talks were broken off, but the imbroglio had sown deep sectional tension and bitterness. The South knew that the North had been willing to block its interests in the southwestern region, but just as surely it had frustrated the yearning of the northern states to open a new line of commerce that might have restored prosperity. The hurt visited on the North was immediate, and soon talk of secession was rampant.[22] No one was more alarmed by the threat than James Madison.

Born in 1751 into the largest slave-owning family in Orange County, Virginia, and not coincidentally the most prominent clan there, Madison excelled as a student and graduated from Princeton College. He chose a legal career, but for three years after he was licensed to practice, he remained idle, adrift, living a purposeless life and coping with emotional woes that included hysterical, hypochondriacal fears and obsessive anxieties. The American Revolution gave meaning to his undirected existence, and he turned to politics. Luckily for him, the political system had not yet been democratized, and the first public positions he held were secured through his family's influence. Once started, however, he rose quickly, and in 1780, on the cusp of his thirtieth birthday, he was elected to Congress by the Virginia legislature. Few congressmen likely thought the fragile and boyish-looking Madison would ever become a legislative leader. He was utterly deficient in the skills that had catapulted others to prominence. Timid, withdrawn, and wispy, he lacked Washington's commanding stature and majestic presence, Franklin's gregarious wit and charm, Adams' oratorical gifts, Jefferson's glib conversational skills, or Hamilton's and Burr's facile and dashing manner. Nevertheless, within three years Madison was an important figure. He doubtless benefited from the diminished quality of the congressional personnel by the early 1780s, but Madison was not without winning qualities. His manner was

James Madison by James Sharples, Sr. Madison was about forty-five when he sat for Sharples in 1796 or 1797. At the time he was actively encouraging Jefferson to stand for president.

inoffensive, and indeed he was artful in convincing others of his guilelessness. None was threatened by him, and no one thought him irresponsible. Colleagues were struck by his intellect as well as by his diligence. In addition, having never married, Madison—who now was in his early thirties—never went home. He was always present, always on the job. In a sense, he was married to his post. Politics had become the focal point of his life. Living all this time in a boardinghouse, in a spare chamber not much larger than a college dormitory room, Madison immersed himself in the affairs of Congress and its members, getting to know everyone, winning the trust of his peers, and gaining a reputation for erudition, rationality, prudence, and getting things done.[23]

Changed by the onset of the American Revolution, Madison's outlook similarly was transformed by the war and the myriad problems that carried over into peace. Initially an advocate of a system of virtual state sovereignty, Madison's horizons were broadened during 1780 and 1781, a tempestuous time when Charleston fell to the British army and Virginia's vulnerability to British raids became readily apparent during Jefferson's governorship. Aware that the South needed assistance that could be provided only by an efficient national effort, Madison gradually moved toward the notion of granting Congress greater powers. His transformation into an unabashed Nationalist was completed by the crisis of the Union that was brought on by the abortive Spanish-American negotiations in 1786.[24]

Madison understood that the Union was crucial for protecting American security and opening the newly acquired West. A strong and sovereign national government that was capable of disallowing state laws would have the additional advantage, at least in his eyes, of reining in the mushrooming "leveling spirit" that fueled democracy and aroused fiscal irresponsibility. In the spring of 1786 Madison retreated to Montpelier to read and search for the means of constructing a powerful, but constrained, national government. He sought some way to balance safe governance with "energy and stability in government," to erect a government that could act vigorously, yet not tip toward despotism. He also sought a means to assure that the national government would be in "safe" hands, as the colonial governments once had been. He wished it to be the bastion of the conservative elite—those whom he called "individuals of weight"—who could protect against what he also called the "dark and menacing . . . evils" of democracy.[25] His challenge was to find the means of putting all this together in such a way that the interests of the propertied elite would be safe from those who were lower in the social and economic strata, and that the minority South would be safeguarded from an energetic national government certain to be dominated by northern interests. Initially, Madison had more questions than answers. The one thing he knew for certain was that change was inevitable: either the national government would be strengthened or the Union would come to an end, and the breakup of the Union would bring on menacing uncertainties.

From Madison's agonized brooding came a plan for a reconstructed national government in which authority would be separated and balanced between a judiciary, a strong executive, and a bicameral legislature armed with powers of taxation and the regulation of commerce. With so many branches, such a government would constitute a firewall against rapid and drastic change, while its extensive election districts would function as a filtration system to weed out upstarts and ensure that the "most considerate and virtuous citizens" (he never ran short of euphemisms for the elite) predominated. Above all, the national government was to be sovereign. Having little use for the states, his national government was to be "arm[ed] . . . with a negative *in all cases whatsoever* on the local Legislatures."[26]

His was a formula for palliating the northern mercantile interest and social conservatives everywhere, but he also wanted safeguards for certain minorities in which he was interested, the propertied elite and southern slave-owning planters. Madison also realized what others had overlooked: the vast size of a republican United States would stymie profound change. In a nation ten times or more the size of France, such a plethora of interests would exist that no single faction could hope to predominate. Inevitably, the multitude of factions would have to coalesce, forging coalitions in order to attain power. Extremists—democrats and social levelers in his time—would be politically disarmed, making it terribly difficult for them to bring about real change.[27] Madison had envisaged radical change to prevent radical change. He had sought a means of saving the Union and preserving what had hitherto been achieved in the American Revolution. However, the means that he found came with a steep price: the peaceful attainment of truly meaningful reform would be painfully gradual at the very least, and might be impossible.

The Nationalist movement was bigger than Hamilton and Madison, but during the disunionist scare in 1786–87 they played crucial roles in galvanizing the campaign for a stronger national government. Ultimately, they brought off the Constitutional Convention. In this they were aided by a second seminal occurrence during 1786. An insurrection by debt-plagued farmers threatened with the loss of their farms erupted in western Massachusetts that autumn. Massachusetts suppressed the uprising, but the most conservative citizens throughout the United States were badly shaken. They knew that had Massachusetts been unequal to the challenge, there would have been nowhere else to turn for assistance in reestablishing order. Certainly the infirm national government could not have kept order. "Good God!" Washington cried when he learned of the violence in New England. Reluctant to speak out earlier against the Articles of Confederation, he thereafter signed on to attend the Constitutional Convention—the cyclonic impact of which should not be minimized—and cranked out letters warning others that there were "combustibles in every State, which a spark may set fire to."[28] The potential firebrands of which he spoke included debtors everywhere, disillusioned settlers in trans-Appalachia, and in his neighborhood sullen slaves.

Benjamin Franklin pronounced the Constitutional Convention "*une assemblée des notables.*"[29] Better, it was a conclave attended by notable Nationalists. Neither yeomen, artisans, nor foes of centralization were present, but Nationalists came, cognizant that this might be their last chance to achieve their ends and to save the Union. Furthermore, they came prepared to make compromises with interests from other sections. In the course of four contentious months the delegates drafted a charter for the strongest central government that they dared to recommend. Their goal was what their foes called "consolidation." Much of the authority previously vested in the states was to be consolidated in the national government, whose will was to be the "supreme law of the land." It was to have the authority to tax and regulate commerce, and it could enforce its laws through coercive means if necessary. The states, meanwhile, were to be forbidden to restrain interstate commerce, coin money, impair contracts, or permit the payment of debts with anything but gold or silver legal tender.[30] The national government would not have total authority over the states. Rather, a federal system along the lines that Hamilton had presciently envisioned in *The Continentalist* in 1781 was to be erected. The states were to be left with whatever authority was not given explicitly to the national government. To achieve all of this, concessions had to be made among the Nationalists. The South, for instance, agreed to the principal demands of the northern commercial and financial interests. These northern interests in turn not only conceded to the South federal protection for slavery but through the "three-fifths compromise" permitted southerners to count 60 percent of their slave inhabitants in determining the apportionment of representatives in both the House of Representatives and the electoral college. As a result, the South, where 41 percent of the nation's white inhabitants dwelled, would initially have 47 percent of the seats in the House of Representatives and a similarly enhanced clout in choosing presidents. The northern delegates swallowed this reproachful giveaway with deep misgivings, seeing it rightly or wrongly as the price it had to pay to secure ratification.[31]

The campaign for ratification that followed was bruising, and there was no shortage of foes of the presumed ills of centralization. These Anti-Federalists railed at the intended emasculation of state authority, a step, said one, that was "totally subversive of every principle which has hitherto governed us."[32] The Anti-Federalists were probably a majority in at least four states, but they failed to prevent ratification. Most Americans were prepared for change and wanted to believe that a constitution that was supported by luminaries such as Washington and Franklin offered hope for a prosperous and secure future.[33] Furthermore, twice in recent memory the American people had fought long, desperate wars, the French and Indian War in the 1750s and the War of Independence. This generation wanted a government that could act with sufficient energy to resolve long-standing national ills, protect American security, and if need be effectively wage war. But it also believed that consolidation must be accompanied by adequate safeguards for the protection of individual liberties.[34] The Constitution was ratified in the summer of 1788, and President Washington was inaugurated the next spring. Hamilton took up his post in September 1789.

Secretary Hamilton was bent on making the United States safe from foreign threats, capable of protecting its commerce, and sufficiently strong to secure, perhaps even expand, its boundaries. Understanding that national power and manufacturing soon would go hand in hand, he longed to use the resources of the national government to aid the establishment of mills and factories. But his first problem was to cope with the $76 million debt that the nation and states had accumulated during the war, and for this revenue was needed. Hamilton favored an impost that would fall equally on imported items from all nations, as well as an excise on distilled liquor.

Taxation alone could not achieve all that Hamilton had in mind. Private investment was essential, and the lion's share would have to come from abroad, as the United States was virtually destitute of capital. Hamilton expected that most of the needed capital would be supplied by British investors. He also wanted the national government to assume the debts of the states, a step that would set in motion the liquidation of those debts while at the same moment it incontestably demonstrated the ability of the new national government to accomplish something that was beyond the capability of most states. This was merely the beginning of Hamiltonianism. The revenue derived through the impost would in part be applied to debt reduction, but it would also help capitalize American entrepreneurs, jump-starting the economy and industry. What is more, he had discovered through the British model a way to increase wealth. He wished to refinance the debt—foreign, national, and state—by issuing new securities to replace the old. The sale of new national securities would immediately produce capital to be applied against the debt, and the certificates themselves would constitute a lucrative investment. Furthermore, the possessors of these securities would be tied inextricably to the new national government, whose survivability alone guaranteed their investment. One thing more: Hamilton sought a rapprochement with London, ending the strain in Anglo-American relations that stretched back a quarter century to the violent colonial protest against the Stamp Act in 1765. Amicable relations with the former mother country, he was convinced, would reap numerous dividends: Britain's imports would increase, its ports would be opened to American merchants, and its capitalists would be enticed to invest within the United States. It was breathtakingly innovative, the product of a true visionary who—it can now be seen with the benefit of hindsight—was constructing what was to be the superstructure of America's modern economic system.[35]

Hamilton began in January 1790 by asking that the debt be funded and the central government assume the state debts. That alone was an audacious scheme that aimed at the transformation of the American economy into capitalism, for his plan would infuse the economy with capital.[36] No one was surprised when opposition crystallized swiftly, but what was startling—especially to Hamilton—was that it was Madison who mobilized the attack on funding and assumption in the House of Representatives. Hamilton averred that the callow Madison was "very little Acquainted with the world," but for the most part Madison acted to mend political fences at home—where his zealous Nationalist leadership had cost him dearly, preventing his election to a Senate seat that he coveted—and as a means of securing the national capital for the South.[37] His goal was to rally sufficient southern opposition to stalemate Hamilton's proposals, after which he hoped to effect yet another sectional compromise along the lines of the many that had been reached at the Constitutional Convention. The deal that he now envisioned was for the northern commercial interests to get the Hamiltonian financial program and for the Chesapeake to get the national capital.

Jefferson was crossing the Atlantic while Hamilton drafted his plans. When he arrived in Virginia, he found an invitation to join Washington's administration as secretary of state. It was not what he had in mind. He was anxious to return to Paris to observe the French Revolution and perhaps be reunited with Maria Cosway, for whom his heart smoldered. Nevertheless, he accepted Washington's tender and came to New York in late March, two months after the fight over Hamilton's recommendations had begun.[38] Jefferson played little role in that battle, as he was unfamiliar with the issues and intrigues that were playing out. Trusting Madison's judgment, he became involved only at the last minute, participating in the negotiations that Madison had envisioned. Madison got what he wanted. He and Jefferson delivered enough votes from the Virginia delegation to enact Hamilton's economic program, while Hamilton arranged for the assent of a sufficient number of northern congressmen to pass the Residence Act, which moved the capital to a location on the Potomac that was to be selected by President Washington.[39]

Jefferson soon questioned the wisdom of the bargain, as he grew to believe that there was more to Hamilton's plans than met the eye. His concerns were additionally aroused by his discovery that during his lengthy residence abroad drastic changes had occurred in the outlook of some among the most conservative northerners, new ways of thinking that led him to fear for the future of republicanism. At every turn during his brief stay in the capital in the spring and summer of 1790, Jefferson heard comfortable New Yorkers express their "preference for kingly over republican government." It was not long before he was convinced that "we have among us a sect" that believed that the English constitution was "perfect [for] human institutions" and should be in place in the United States.[40] He was especially disappointed to find that these reactionary ideas had presumably taken hold of Vice President Adams as well. While Jefferson was yet in Paris, Adams had urged Congress to create a royal-sounding title for the chief executive: "His Highness the President of the United States of America, and Protector of the Rights of the Same."[41] Jefferson was aghast when he learned of Adams' proposal, calling it the "the most superlatively ridiculous thing I ever heard of."[42] He additionally discovered that Adams, much like Europe's royal officials, had taken to being driven about the capital in a handsome carriage drawn by a large team of horses and attended by a retinue of liveried servants. Jefferson was dismayed but initially shrugged off his old friend's outlandish behavior, attributing it to his having spent too many years abroad. Soon enough, Jefferson thought, Adams would come to his senses. However, late in 1790 the vice president published a series of newspaper essays entitled "Discourses on Davila," in which he expanded primarily on the need for a strong, independent executive. In the final installment Adams defended monarchy as "the true answer, and the only one" for many nations, though he did not advocate the establishment of a monarchy in the United States.[43]

The Davila essays convinced Jefferson of Adams' apostasy. Even so, their relationship remained friendly, and in private they argued about their philosophical differences, heatedly at times. In one exchange, Jefferson called Adams a "heretic," and the vice president, who thrived on provocation—historian Joseph Ellis noted that Adams "regarded an argument as the ideal form of a conversation"—did not take umbrage.[44] But in 1791 Jefferson crossed the line and the seemingly unbreakable bond between the two was severed. Early that year Jefferson sent a friend a copy of Thomas Paine's recently published *The Rights of Man*, with the inscription "I am extremely pleased to find it will be reprinted here, and that something is at length to be publickly said against the political heresies which have sprung up among us." To Jefferson's horror, his commendation of Paine's magisterial treatise appeared as a preface to the Philadelphia edition of the book, which was published late that spring. Every politically articulate American knew that Jefferson had meant to include Adams among the heretics. The vice president, who was happy to dispute endlessly with Jefferson in private, felt betrayed, thinking his friend had stabbed him in the back in public. Jefferson was mortified as well, for he had never intended for his private remark to be circulated. He attempted to make amends, apologizing to Adams and explaining what had occurred. But Adams would have none of it. The friendship that Jefferson and Adams had thought would never die perished that spring.[45]

Hamilton caused Jefferson the greatest concern. By late 1790 Jefferson suspected a concurrence of Hamiltonianism and royalism. Madison surely had filled him in on what he had gleaned of Hamilton's private thinking during the Nationalist battles in the 1780s, including a recapitulation of a remarkably unabashed pro-monarchist speech that the New Yorker had given at the Constitutional Convention. In addition, Jefferson learned some things at first hand, having personally heard Hamilton extol the merits of the British system. Jefferson was coming to believe that the "ultimate object" of Hamilton and his followers was to "prepare the way for a change, from the present republican form of government, to that of a monarchy, of which the English constitution is to be the model." Indeed, he had grown certain that the Hamiltonians were "panting after . . . [and] itching for crowns, coronets and mitres," and that the economic revolution that the Treasury Secretary envisioned was part and parcel of a transformation to the British way of things.[46] Jefferson saw too that funding had unleashed a speculative craze in New York and other commercial hubs. A hot mass of feelings, Jefferson exclaimed that America was being transformed into a "gaming table." Already, he contended, the new national government was imperiled by the financial mania. A "corrupt squadron of paper dealers," whom he labeled as "stockjobbers" driven solely by pecuniary interests, had surfaced within

Congress, and the day was coming when they and their kind would have the resources to sway a congressional majority. Furthermore, Jefferson cautioned, their gamester ethic would corrode the traditional frugality and industry that had defined the American character. Jefferson believed Hamilton and his compatriots were taking America for a ride along the same sordid path that adulterated Europe had traveled. During 1790 the notion took shape in Jefferson's mind that unless Hamilton was stopped, America someday would be dominated by huge financial institutions. Commercial avarice would dominate the national mores, and ever larger chunks of the American population would become the propertyless denizens of vast, squalid cities. This, Jefferson believed to the very marrow of his bones, was no way for free people to live. Indeed, those who lived in such a checkered society would not be free, and as they lost their independence, republicanism would be relegated to the scrap heap of the past.[47]

Jefferson never wavered in his judgment of Hamiltonianism. The conclusions that he reached in 1790 presaged the decade of fiery partisanship that lay ahead, for Jefferson saw his disagreement with Hamilton not merely as a difference between men or a clash over policy but as a deep ideological rift. This was a view with which Hamilton concurred. Indeed, it was this sense of a titanic struggle between rival ideologies that in large measure brought to the politics of the 1790s a passion only occasionally equaled in America's political history.[48] What loomed, virtually all activists understood, was a political war to shape the American future, possibly for all time, as it was widely presumed that what was put in place in the first days of the new Republic would not be easily changed by subsequent generations. Perhaps too, as the historians Stanley Elkins and Eric McKitrick theorized, the politics of the 1790s took on a supercharged quality because those who participated were revolutionaries.[49] It was not just that Hamilton, Jefferson, Madison, and those in Congress and the state governments had played active roles in the American Revolution. They had a revolutionary mentality. Not only were they audacious, they were visionaries. They beheld an American vista for which they had been willing to die after 1775. For them, the politics of the 1790s was about the ultimate realization of their often grandiose dreams, and it meant that the political battles of the decade were almost literally fought on a battlefield.

Filled with foreboding by Hamiltonian economics, Jefferson sought to learn more about his fellow cabinet officer. He cobbled together an informal network of friendly congressmen and capital insiders who were to report to him whatever Hamiltonian scuttlebutt they heard.[50] Through these sources, and by what he read in, and into, Hamilton's published reports, Jefferson soon concluded that his rival posed a grave danger to the American Revolution and the independence that had been achieved through years of hard fighting. In Jefferson's estimation, the Hamiltonians, believing that the Revolution had gone far enough, had supported the creation of a powerful national government at least in part to inhibit further reforms and to salvage the social and political superstructure of the Anglo-American world that had existed before 1776. In addition, Jefferson pulsed with agitation at the prospect of the inextricable tethering of the United States to British commerce, the cash cow of the impost, for he feared that it would reduce the new republic to the status of a British puppet state.[51]

By the time Jefferson and Madison moved with the government to Philadelphia late in 1790, their relationship had changed. Looking on Jefferson with worshipful esteem, Madison had accepted his friend's assessment of the threat posed by Hamiltonianism. Jefferson in turn had come to see Madison's congressional leadership in the funding and assumption battles as ill-conceived, designed not to stop Hamilton but as a contrivance through which to secure the nation's capital. By that autumn Madison followed Jefferson. Even so, the tandem was unable to prevent the enactment of Hamilton's next program, the creation of the Bank of the United States. The loss of that battle early in 1791 was a transforming experience that led Jefferson to several important conclusions: Washington could not be trusted to rein in Hamilton; Hamilton had won thus far by capitalizing on the lack of organized opposition; some who were Nationalists were not committed Hamiltonians; some in Congress would have opposed Hamilton in 1790–91 had they better understood the ramifications of his schemes; and many who had been in the Anti-Federalist camp during ratification were eager to resist the further consolidation of power in the national government that was part and parcel of Hamiltonianism. Believing that most Americans yet abhorred a powerful national government, Jefferson resolved to organize the torpid opposition. His object was not the creation of a political party, but merely the election of an anti-Hamilton majority in Congress in the elections of 1792, now a bit more than a year away.

Three days after Washington signed the Bank Bill, Jefferson took the first steps to establish a newspaper dedicated to a ceaseless and unsparing opposition to Hamiltonianism. By the autumn of 1791 the *National Gazette* was rolling off the press. It was edited by Philip Freneau, a college chum of Madison's who possessed noteworthy literary and satirical

skills and—even better—the fortitude to go after even the most formidable adversaries. Jefferson set him up as a counterweight to John Fenno's
Gazette of the United States, which was little better than a house organ
for the Treasury Department and which in the eyes of the secretary of
state broadcast a message with eerie similarities to the rant of the Tories
during the American Revolution.[52] Simultaneously, Jefferson wrote to
activists in several states to ascertain their abhorrence to "scrip-pomany,"
his term for capitalism, and to inquire about their willingness to "come
forward and help" organize an opposition movement.[53]

A few weeks later Jefferson and Madison departed Philadelphia for
a trip to New York that they described as a "botanizing tour." They spent
a portion of their time scrutinizing flora and fauna, but most observers—
including Hamilton's spies, who kept a close watch on the Virginians—
suspected a political component to the journey.[54] The Treasury secretary's
intelligence was dead on target. Jefferson and Madison mostly kept to
the backcountry, where butterflies and bluebirds could be found, but
also where a brooding resentment against the urban elite was pronounced. It was here too that the Anti-Federalists had been strongest
three years earlier. In dusty farm villages and on grand estates Jefferson
and Madison sought out local leaders.[55] Jefferson's trek betrayed a telling grasp of politics—not only a sense that the popular will could be
mobilized but the knowledge of how to begin to organize those who
hoped to halt the further expansion of national power.

Soon after returning home, Jefferson urged Madison to take up his
pen in the growing newspaper barrage against Hamilton. Jefferson subsequently claimed, probably accurately, never to have engaged in newspaper polemics in the 1790s. He disliked the drudgery of composing
quarrelsome treatises and abhorred the time they took from other, more
fruitful and enjoyable pursuits. He also loathed confrontation. His style
was to find others to do unpleasant things for him. Madison, who found
it nearly impossible to resist his friend's blandishments, consented and
churned out at least nineteen sulfurous pieces for Freneau's paper in
1791–92. His essays divulged the seismic shift that had occurred in his
thinking over the past two years. He portrayed Hamilton's adherents—
mostly "men of influence, particularly the moneyed" class, he said—as a
self-serving, anti-republican elite that thought the people incapable of
self-government. Assuming that the citizenry "should think of nothing
but obedience, leaving the care of their liberties to their wiser rulers,"
these elitists believed that the people need know only one word: "*Submission.*" They exercised power "less to the interests of the many than of

"A Peep into the Anti-Federal Club." This 1793 etching is the earliest known anti-Jefferson cartoon. It portrays Jefferson leading a meeting of the "Anti-Federal Club," an assortment of dissolute and visionary characters. The devil, on the left, expresses "pleasure" at what the Jeffersonians are up to.

a few, and less to the reason of the many than to their weaknesses." Their ultimate objective, he insisted, was that the "government itself may by degrees be narrowed into fewer hands, and approximated to an hereditary form." Indeed, Madison exclaimed that his foes had taken large strides toward making two-thirds of the new national government—the Senate and presidency—into "hereditary orders."[56] To fight this threat, Madison announced the need to create a political "party." He was the first in the growing opposition to Hamilton's schemes to use the word *party*, and he allowed that it might properly be called the "Republican party."[57]

Always aggressive, Hamilton countered with immeasurably harsh discourses of his own. His fiery essays targeted Jefferson, not Madison. He knew who was ramrodding the emerging resistance, and he coolly recognized that Madison was the "General" while Jefferson was the "Generalissimo" of the enemy camp.[58] A shimmering malice, not present in Madison's essays, epitomized Hamilton's effort, as he raised questions about Jefferson's judgment by pointing out his failures as a wartime governor and ginned up reminders of the Virginian's flight from the British troops in 1781.[59] Hamilton's response was so visceral because he immediately understood the profound danger that Jefferson posed to Hamiltonianism. Like his adversary, Hamilton too had an intelligence network, and through it he learned not only that his Virginia nemeses had "predicted that the people would not long tolerate [his]" program but that they were "notoriously" intriguing to sway opinion against him. Two objectives drove his enemies, Hamilton allowed. On every issue they sought "to narrow the Federal" authority. In addition, Hamilton was convinced that Jefferson, a "man of profound ambition & violent passions," lusted after the presidency.[60]

In fact, Jefferson had no immediate designs on the presidency. But he was ambitious and enjoyed standing out. For Jefferson, a man with a vision every bit as palpable as that of Hamilton, the thought of being the great architect constructing the shape of the new United States had to have been intoxicating. The architect of Monticello who also aspired to design the new national capital, the composer of America's declaration of ideals, the would-be drafter of Virginia's constitution, the diplomat who was incapable of passively observing the French Revolution, was no mere meddler. His desires extended beyond merely stopping Hamilton. Jefferson would not have been Jefferson had he not dreamed of some-day occupying the presidency. Hamilton, who wished no less himself, and who possessed extraordinary skills in fathoming others, saw Jefferson with crystal clarity.

Pronouncing Jefferson's threat to be "of great moment to the public weal," Hamilton pledged to respond in kind as the elections of 1792 loomed. They would be the first since the ratification of the Constitution to be contested on a partisan basis. No alternative existed. Jefferson had made it necessary that he should "mount the hobby horse of popularity" and "ride in the Whirlwind." Like Jefferson, his object was to "direct the Storm."[61]

4

"War on Our Own Citizens"

Partisanship, 1793–1796

HAMILTONIANISM HAD DRIVEN THE POLITICS of Washington's first term. Foreign policy ignited the partisan fires that blazed like a raging inferno throughout his second administration and for the remainder of the decade. Indeed, the 1790s was one of America's most passionate decades. It was kindred in warmth and fervor, and especially in rage, to the 1770s, 1850s, 1930s, and 1960s, for activists of all persuasions understood that colossal choices in foreign relations were to be made that would dramatically shape the nation, if in fact the infant republic survived those choices.

Hamilton's economic program was in place before the congressional elections in 1792. Jefferson had hoped that those elections would be a referendum on Hamiltonianism, and as the results trickled in he was convinced that the Treasury secretary had lost his congressional majority. Candidates did not yet label themselves Republicans, but those who campaigned against broadening the authority of the national government scored victories "every where South of Connecticut," Jefferson crowed, leaving the "republican interest" to hold a slight "majority of the next Congress." Other signs also existed that Jefferson's partisan efforts had paid dividends. Feeling the heat, Vice President Adams abandoned his regal accouterments. He jettisoned his powdered wig, ceremonial sword, conspicuous coach, and liveried coachmen and moved from a sumptuous house perched above the meandering Schuylkill River to a plain, small room in a town house rented by the secretary of the Senate and his family.[1]

The only suspense in the second presidential election was whether Adams would get a second term as vice president. Four years earlier his nemesis had been Hamilton, who was so eager to ensure Washington's unanimous election that he had engaged in legerdemain to strip Adams of some votes. Inevitably, word of his machinations reached Quincy, and when Adams received less than half the number of electoral votes cast for Washington in 1788, he angrily blamed Hamilton for what he felt was an unpardonable slight.[2] However, in 1792 it was not Hamilton who posed a threat to Adams, but elements within the nascent Republican Party that sought to replace him with George Clinton, a seven-term governor of New York. Republican congressmen from at least five states caucused that fall and threw their support behind Clinton, an event sometimes seen as the formal birth of the party.[3] Hamilton meanwhile reached out to Adams, expressing his "respect . . . and attachment," and—Hamilton being Hamilton—providing instructions on how to behave. Among other things, he admonished Adams to spend more time in the capital.[4] Hamilton worked hard to line up support for the vice president, telling adherents that Adams, despite his "faults and foibles," was "honest firm faithful and independent—a sincere lover of his country—a real friend to liberty" and "stable government."[5] In reality, he supported Adams because he looked on Clinton as an "enemy of National Principles." In his worst flights of fancy Hamilton envisaged Jefferson sneaking in, with southern electors casting their second ballot as a bloc vote for him while northern electors divided theirs between Adams and Clinton. Seeing Jefferson as the greatest possible danger, Hamilton declared him to be "a man of sublimated & paradoxical imagination" who cherished "notions incompatible with regular and firm government."[6] In the end, Adams won easily, capturing seventy-seven votes to Clinton's fifty. Embedded within their vote totals was convincing evidence that the sectional split, so evident in the negotiations with Spain several years before, yet existed. Adams had won only seven votes in the South. Outside of his home state, Clinton captured merely a single vote in the North.

Washington was reelected without opposition and embarked on his second term with the expectation that foreign policy was likely to become his biggest headache. Rumors of impending war in Europe had swirled since the early days of the French Revolution, and while the United States was across the wide Atlantic from the Continent, European conflagrations always touched America. In June 1792 the "eventful moment in Europe" occurred, as the president put it, when France declared war on Austria.[7] For the moment, hostilities remained localized, but the genie was out of the bottle.

For three years the stirring events in France had been cheered by most Americans. The more radical believed that the French, like themselves in 1776, had set out to create a new world. The more conservative were hopeful that the inspired French reformers were putting their nation on the road to republicanism and a constitutional monarchy. While President Washington proudly hung a key to the Bastille—a gift from Lafayette—in his hallway at Mount Vernon, and Fenno's newspaper exalted in the revolutionary changes in France, Hamilton exclaimed that the French Revolution was the most electrifying occurrence since American independence.[8]

However, as tumult quickened in France, the more conservative Americans grew wary. In 1790 Washington for the first time deplored the riots and bloodshed, which he labeled "great enormities," and a year later he confessed his anxiety at the ongoing convulsions. Even so, he continued to pray that the "example of France" would lead to "strides towards liberty" elsewhere in Europe. Meanwhile, those Americans who had been most committed to seminal change during the American Revolution were not alarmed by the French paroxysms. Jefferson, for instance, declared that one could not "expect to be translated from despotism to liberty, in a feather bed," and he insisted that the liberation of Europe's subjugated masses hinged on the eradication of an absolute monarchy in France.[9]

Americans yet hoped for the French Revolution's success, especially when the war widened in 1792. Prussia joined Austria against France, and by summer the coalition armies advanced on Paris, threatening the revolution and with it all hope for the spread of republicanism. Then, just before Christmas, word reached the United States of a great French victory at Valmy, 150 miles east of Paris. Believing that the revolution had been saved, Americans erupted in spontaneous celebrations, including in Boston, where despite a blanket of snow the citizenry flocked outside to cheer at a parade and fireworks. Some Philadelphians, who felt linked in spirit with the French revolutionaries, took to calling themselves Jacobins, after the most radical faction in France.[10] Few went that far, but many would have agreed with Madison, who privately exclaimed that France's "enemies . . . are the enemies of human nature. We have every motive in America to pray for her success, not only from a general attachment to the liberties of mankind, but from a peculiar regard for our own."[11]

However, just as the victory at Valmy occurred, while the American elections of 1792 were playing out, the French Revolution turned very bloody. Well over a thousand were executed in Paris and perhaps four hundred more died in regional capitals in what came to be known as the September Massacres. Priests and political prisoners were targeted, but in the carnival thirst of frenzied retribution numerous criminals and beggars who had the bad luck to be imprisoned at that juncture were slaughtered by licensed executioners wielding axes and hatchets. The first phase of de-Christianization soon followed, accompanied by the spoliation of many churches and the desecration of sacred relics.[12] While Americans celebrated Valmy, the king—Louis XVI, the only European monarch to recognize the United States before Yorktown—was tried and in January 1793, about six weeks before Washington's second inauguration, executed together with the queen, Marie-Antoinette.

As news of the excesses trickled across the Atlantic, the first signs appeared of a dramatic turn in the outlook of America's more conservative populace. They thought the violence bad enough, but the French "democratical hurricane" (Adams' term) was worse, and unbridled egalitarianism worse still. Vibrantly sensitive to any evidence of the blurring of class divisions, the most socially conservative Americans recoiled in horror as the elite Frenchman's customary dress of knee breeches and silk stockings was eclipsed by the long trousers of the sansculottes, a fashion revolution that in an instant banished discernable signs of rank among males. The revolutionaries also adopted *citoyen* and *citoyenne* (translated in America as "citizen" and "citess") as forms of address for all inhabitants, abandoning the titles that had set apart the privileged nobility from those below. Some even thought it ghastly that the French substituted embraces and handshakes for formal bowing, practices that some traditionalists scorned as "hugging and rugging . . . addressing and caressing."[13]

Early in 1793 the European war took an ominous turn, changing forever how it was seen in America. Great Britain entered the conflict against France. London's belligerency exacerbated the divisions in American opinion. There were those who remained convinced of the inseparable ties that bound republicans everywhere and who feared that the destruction of republicanism in France would lead to its demise in America. As word of Britain's belligerency spread, an organization in Philadelphia that called itself the Democratic-Republican Society sprang into being. Within a year more than fifty similar societies, with approximately two thousand members nationwide, were in existence. Their membership was drawn mostly from among small merchants, editors, tradesmen, professionals, and some unskilled workers.[14] For many, the European war provided coherence to the otherwise tenebrous trends of recent years. They now beheld an epochal struggle for liberation in the western world. Hanging in the balance was the quest to fashion an independent republic in America and the French revolutionaries' dream of eradicating monarchical and aristocratical oppression throughout the Old World. In each instance, the same towering force stood sentinel against the spread of the rights of man: Great Britain.

On the other side were those who had never wavered from the earnest hope that the new American nation would be fashioned socially, economically, and politically on the model furnished by Britain. Those Americans recoiled from the Democratic-Republican Societies, which they believed posed a threat to hierarchy and deference. Above all, they understood that the societies intended to compel public officials to listen to, and act on, the popular will. They castigated the societies as democratic "sons of darkness" bent on undermining the social order. If successful, they would bring to power a new breed of man, the very sort that many Federalists in 1787 had sought to filter from office in the national arena. The most conservative saw the Democratic-Republican Societies as one with the Jacobins in France, and cautioned that democracy, once unleashed, led inexorably to "extremes of anarchy." To Fisher Ames, a congressman from Massachusetts, and doubtless numerous other conservatives, the solution was obvious: established authority must exercise "more energy to suppress" this evil.[15] While the Democratic-Republican Societies symbolized and contributed to the gathering passions that characterized American politics after 1793, the Anglo-French war was the driving force behind the political emotionalism. Yet the fundamental issue remained unchanged from the days of the battles over Hamiltonian economics: what shape—socially and politically—would the new American nation take?

The United States greeted the news of Anglo-French hostilities by proclaiming its neutrality, a position steadfastly embraced by the entire cabinet. However, pro-French Americans bridled at the supposed impartiality mandated by neutrality, fearing that Britain would be the beneficiary of such a course. In the spring the Republican press opened up on the president himself. Freneau and others blasted Washington, charging that his foreign policy was driven by Hamiltonian economics, which made it imperative that nothing interfere with British trade.[16] The foes of the Republicans—the Federalists, as they had taken to calling themselves—defended the president, who never wavered from his view that the United States needed a breathing space and that a long, divisive war would prove ruinous to the fragile young nation.[17] Most Americans agreed with Washington. Despite their warmheartedness for France, which stood alone and needed help, their more fervent hope was to stay out of Europe's wars. It was a conviction that antedated independence. In *Common Sense*, for instance, Thomas Paine had held out peace— "neutrality" actually was the term he used—as among the greatest benefits that would accrue from independence.[18]

Yet there were limits to what Americans would do to maintain peace, and London tested those limits in 1794. Word arrived in the spring that Great Britain had issued orders-in-council that prohibited commerce between neutrals and the French West Indies. All knew that Britain's action "must bring on a crisis," as Jefferson put it, for hundreds of American ships annually sailed to and from the French Caribbean.[19] By March nearly four hundred American vessels had been confiscated and many crewmen impressed into the Royal Navy on the premise that they were British sailors who had deserted. As the spring solstice neared, America's once thriving commerce dried up. Nor were these Britain's only affronts. Its troops remained on American soil, in the Northwest Territory, where they supplied the Native Americans. Twice Washington had sent military expeditions to bring the Indians to heel. Both had been routed. Now, while a third army commanded by General Anthony Wayne was being raised, word arrived in Philadelphia that Britain's governor-general of Canada had allegedly incited Indians south of the Great Lakes to take to the warpath and reclaim lands they had lost during the American Revolution. A firestorm of passion raced across the land. For the first time since independence, the country was swept by war fever.

By summer, maritime activity had nearly come to a halt in every port city, idling sailors and dockhands and sending out shock waves of implacable anguish among tradesmen, shopkeepers, and consumers up and down the coast. Yet in what may have been Hamilton's finest moment of artful political orchestration, his party never lost control of the situation. The Federalists took on the appearance of preparing for war by having Congress approve defensive measures, while behind the scenes Hamilton quietly persuaded Washington to send an envoy to London in quest of a peaceful settlement. Against this steamroller, the feckless Republicans—who never contrived an effective plan for responding to

London's threat—were helpless. They obviously badly missed Jefferson, who had left the cabinet in December 1793 and returned to Monticello, from which he had been absent for nearly a decade.[20]

Nevertheless, the Republicans made hay after the fact by painting the Federalists as the "English party." They heaped abuse on Washington's choice of an emissary, John Jay, the very diplomat who would have relinquished American rights on the Mississippi River during the negotiations with Spain in 1786. The tendentious western region especially exploded at the prospect of Jay negotiating with the British. He was reproached as a scapegrace and an Anglophile, and in many frontier communities he was hanged in effigy, sometimes with a copy of Adams' purportedly pro-monarchist essays tied about his neck. Several Democratic-Republican Societies also denounced both Jay and Washington. One society scathingly charged that the president, "like the grand sultan of Constantinople, shut up in his apartment," had grown so remote from the people that he was incapable of making good choices. Another maintained that in selecting Jay, Washington had "sacrifice[d] ... the interests and the peace of the United States."[21] The assault paid dividends in the elections of 1794. The Republicans—or at least those opposed to the Federalists—maintained their narrow majority in the House of Representatives.[22] What is more, although the Federalists won the New York City elections again that year, many mechanics jumped to the Republican Party, which tripled its previous year's vote total in the city's canvass.[23]

While Jay sailed, a domestic crisis exploded. Since before Washington's presidency, discontent had bubbled along the western frontier, and in no place more than the counties near Pittsburgh, where the inhabitants watched helplessly as their standard of living declined. Many reasons existed for their plight, including the national government's inability to open the Northwest and the Mississippi River. But the ire of the hard-pressed frontiersmen fell mostly on Hamilton's whiskey excise, as the corn whiskey they exported to eastern markets was their most dependable source of income. Jefferson had objected when the whiskey tax was enacted, warning Washington that the measure would be "odious" to those in the western areas. It would arouse "murmurings," he predicted, leaving the president with no choice but to resort to "arbitrary and vexatious means," including making "war on our own citizens to collect the revenue."[24] Washington, however, needed a national revenue. He consented to Hamilton's duty.

Crunch time arrived in 1794. Not one cent was raised that year in western Pennsylvania, as farmers refused to pay the tax and violently drove away revenue agents. With the Federalist press working itself into a frenzy over the defiance of the pernicious "ignorant herd" out west, and Hamilton, never more intractable, insisting that action be taken before the disorder spread and made it impossible to uphold federal sovereignty, Washington proclaimed the existence of an "open rebellion" and summoned thirteen thousand militiamen to suppress it. Together with Hamilton, the president rode on his powerful gray charger at the head of the army as it marched toward western Pennsylvania.[25]

The army combed the quiet, russet western hollows and forests that autumn but found few "whiskey men." Some had fled. Many others had availed themselves of a munificent amnesty offered by Washington. Furthermore, as Washington's army descended on the frontier, word arrived in the hills that General Wayne's force had just won a convincing victory over its Indian adversaries in the Battle of Fallen Timbers. In a flash, a crippling blow had been dealt to one of the sources of frontier disaffection, for Wayne's triumph virtually guaranteed that the Ohio country at last would be opened. Ultimately, Washington's army nabbed just 150 suspects in its dragnet, and merely a score of those were marched back to Philadelphia under scudding wintry clouds to stand trial. Just two desperadoes were convicted of high treason, an imbecile and a madman, and both were pardoned by Washington.[26]

Neither Madison nor Jefferson raised their voices against the federal show of force—Madison labeled the rebels "universally . . . odious"— and even some Democratic-Republican Societies denounced those who broke the law.[27] Nevertheless, having won their war, the Federalists lost their peace. In their hour of triumph, they overreached. Washington, who normally was unsurpassed in his restraint, even magnanimity, was unable to contain his simmering fury toward the Democratic-Republican Societies. His State of the Union message that fall included a bluster of rage against the societies, which he superciliously described as "self-created" bodies—his code for their democratic faith—and further accused them of being disunionists who fomented revolution.[28] Some Federalists immediately jumped on the bandwagon and sought to link the societies to the Republican Party.

The president's intemperate remarks offended many, none more than Madison and Jefferson. Madison thought Washington's truculent rhetoric was "the greatest error of his political life," and both he and Jefferson sadly concluded that the president had exchanged his constitutional role as "the head of a nation" for that of "the head of a party," the Federalist Party.[29] Jefferson was less bitter at Washington's animadversions than at his hypocrisy. He observed that the president had denounced those "whose avowed object is the nourishment of the republican principles of our Constitution," when he himself had headed the Society of the Cincinnati, an organization whose membership was restricted to Continental Army officers and their descendants, and which Jefferson described as "a *self-created* . . . [society] carving out for itself hereditary distinctions," meeting and corresponding in secret, and yearning to "confine . . . freedom to the few." Many Republicans also now saw the campaign to smash the whiskey men in a more sinister light. They were convinced that the ultimate goal of the Federalists was to suppress all dissent. More than ever, they were certain that they had been right to question the further growth of national authority and to organize a party that represented the popular will against an elite that demanded deference.[30]

The Whiskey Rebellion and its fallout were seen by many as part of a struggle to shape the new nation that dated back to 1776. The tempest that erupted six months later over the Jay Treaty was seen by many in a similar light. Washington received the treaty in March 1795. He was disappointed by it. As expected, it recapitulated the Treaty of Paris: Britain was to withdraw its troops, and Americans must honor their pre-1776 debts to British creditors. However, Washington had hoped that Britain would relax its commercial restrictions against the United States and recognize the right of neutrals to trade with belligerents. London had done neither.[31] Nor had it repudiated its policy of impressment. Britain's only concession was to provide compensation for the spoliations that had occurred during the past year or more. Although frustrated, Washington summoned the Senate into special session in June and submitted the treaty for ratification. It alone provided hope of avoiding war and securing the withdrawal of the British army,

George Washington by Gilbert Stuart. Known as the Vaughan-Sinclair portrait, dated 1795, when Washington was at the mid-point of his second term. He was sixty-three years old.

which in turn offered the promise of the rapid settlement of the Northwest. In addition, he thought, a flood of settlers into the trans-Appalachian frontier might serve as the lever for wrenching concessions from Madrid in the Southwest. Sensing as much, Washington had sent an envoy—he chose Thomas Pinckney, C.C.'s brother—to Spain.

The Federalists had a two-thirds majority in the Senate, precisely what was needed to ratify the Jay Treaty. As now was commonplace, the tally was along sectional lines. Northern senators voted overwhelmingly for ratification. Southerners and westerners were generally opposed.[32] As Washington deliberated signing the treaty, the Republican press pulsed with invective, including what the president labeled as "poison."[33] For vitriol and sheer magnitude, the partisan bombast was unprecedented, doubtless because both sides were keenly aware that war or peace hung in the balance, as perhaps did the success of the French Revolution and even that of the American Republic.

Washington, once unassailable, was targeted with ad hominem abuse. He was limned as the vain and dishonest *"grand lama"* of the United States. His principal aim, it was said, had always been to advance "the greatest good" of those who possessed "the greatest wealth."[34] For the first time too, the Republicans portrayed the Federalists as the literal descendants of the Tories. Unlike the loyalists, they had supported independence, but since 1776, it was charged, they had resisted the changes that many anxiously believed had been the great promise of the American Revolution. And, according to the Republicans, the Federalists, like the Tories, were monarchists and nabobs who yearned to shore up the old deferential and hierarchical social structure of the colonial past. For many, Federalist actions—funding, the Bank of the United States, the haughty dismissal of the Democratic-Republican Societies, the fawning before Great Britain, and the denunciation of the French Revolution— had come to be seen as all of a piece: Federalists marched arm in arm with Great Britain, bent on dashing the hopes of the two great revolutions of the eighteenth century.[35]

The Federalists fought back, none harder than Hamilton, who now was a private citizen, having left the administration soon after the Whiskey Rebellion was suppressed. Typically, his was a Herculean effort. Writing under the pseudonym Camillus, he churned out a fusillade of essays that he called "The Defence," all of it rendered in the tone of a Delphic utterance. No one was more impressed than Jefferson, who acknowledged his adversary's awesome abilities. "Without numbers, he is an host within himself," Jefferson admitted privately and ruefully.[36]

Washington soon signed the Jay Treaty. Hamilton alone had not saved the accord. In fact, his voluminous essays were so sophisticated that they likely reached only a small audience.[37] Washington's linkage with the treaty was of more help. Despite the vituperation directed at him, Washington remained the great icon in American politics, and most continued to trust his judgment. Furthermore, the Federalist press—which accounted for nearly three-fourths of the newspapers in the United States—saturated the land with a pro–Jay Treaty blitz. In addition, rancor toward Great Britain ebbed throughout 1795 as incidents on the high seas declined. By then too, those in the West saw the Jay Treaty with greater clarity. As frontier inhabitants came to understand that both the departure of the British army and a cherished sunbeam of peace hinged on the treaty's ratification, opposition to the accord waned. Moreover, during that passionate winter and spring of 1796 news arrived that Spain, in Pinckney's Treaty, had at last granted the United States free navigation on the Mississippi River. In the space of eighteen months, beginning with Wayne's spectacular victory, the United States appeared to have solved its previously intractable western problems.

This was Washington's finest hour since his daring strikes at Trenton, Princeton, and Germantown during the War of Independence. He had kept the peace and opened the western region. Acting as America's uncrowned monarch, Washington had used his office, renown, experience, and uncanny sense of the exercise of power to demonstrate the prudence of having supplanted the Articles of Confederation with an authoritative national government capable of resolving the great perplexities that had lingered since the end of the War of Independence.

When Washington had agreed to a second term, he intended it to be his last, and nothing occurred after he took the oath to dissuade him from retiring in 1797. Not only did Washington understand that there would never be a better time for laying down his public burdens, but throughout his public service he had wished to be seen as a patriot who selflessly sacrificed for the public good. By laying down his sword in 1783, when the job was done, Washington had won greater laurels than he ever had earned on the battlefield. Now, as he entered his eighth year as president, Washington once again was eager to relinquish his authority and return to private life, and doubtless expected to be acclaimed for his disinterestedness.[38] Thus, on the day before he turned sixty-four in February 1796, Washington instructed his farm manager at Mount Vernon to hurry along with a rebuilding project on the mansion, even if "you must engage . . . Negro carpenters." He wanted the job to be completed within twelve months. During that same week he met with Hamilton, who was visiting Philadelphia on business, and divulged that he would not accept another term. Hamilton was the first outside Washington's immediate family to know, but soon thereafter the president confided his intentions to a favorite nephew. He would, he said, perhaps with a twinkle in his eye, "close my public life the 4th of March [1797], after which no consideration under heaven that I can foresee shall again withdraw me from the walks of private life."[39]

5

"Quite at My Leisure"

Jefferson and Adams on the
Eve of the Battle in 1796

EARLY IN 1796 Washington told his cabinet that he planned to retire at the end of his term.[1] Adams already knew of Washington's plans, as Martha Washington had informed him a couple of weeks earlier. Having all along considered himself to be Washington's legitimate successor, Adams immediately informed Abigail that he would be a candidate in the election of 1796.[2] Jefferson appears not to have known what Washington had divulged to his closest associates, and if he did divine anything of the president's intention, he said nothing when he and Adams briefly resumed their correspondence that year.

Adams wrote to Jefferson in January, his first correspondence with the Virginian in years. He envied Jefferson's retirement, he began, then unctuously exclaimed that he too planned to leave public life when his term expired in fourteen months. It is unlikely that Jefferson believed this tripe.[3] Although he said nothing about the coming election, Adams coyly dilated on the "foul Fiend" of electoral degeneracy, and went on to descant on how he and Jefferson would be able to close their careers with their "Hearts pure and hands clean of all Corruption in Elections." It appears that Adams, who expected Jefferson to run against him, was obliquely exhorting his likely foe to renounce the base partisanship that had characterized the newspaper wars and, increasingly, local elections in recent years.[4] Jefferson did not take the bait.

Adams was certain that Jefferson would seek the presidency. Hamilton believed that Jefferson had been obsessed with the office from the moment he returned to America from France. Madison quietly plotted for a Jefferson presidency. Jefferson alone was uncertain about his political future.

Jefferson had wished to retire at the conclusion of Washington's first term, as the new national government was in place and stable and Washington had agreed to a second term. He could retire, Jefferson had remarked at the time, and it would be "no loss to the public, and a great relief to me."[5] However, word of Great Britain's belligerency changed everything. Washington asked Jefferson to remain on board until the end of 1793, and Jefferson consented. At Christmas 1793 the president yet again implored Jefferson to stay on into the coming year. This time Jefferson was unyielding. His "debt of service has been fully and faithfully paid," he said. For ten long years he had exchanged "everything I love ... for everything I hate," and during the previous thirty-six months, while he had been the secretary of state, he had been "Worn down with labours from morning till night." All the while, he added, his personal affairs had been "abandoned to chaos & derangement."[6]

Once he came home, Jefferson made no secret of his hope to never again leave Virginia, declaring that the "length of my tether is now fixed for life from Monticello and Richmond." He claimed to "have no fear of ennui from want of emploiment" in public affairs, and soon proclaimed that life at home was easy and sweet. "I am enjoying at home peace, peaches, and poplars," he told a correspondent, and even confessed to be "in a retirement I doat on, living like an Antediluvian patriarch among my children and grand children, and tilling my soil."[7]

Jefferson had left France four years earlier in the hope of putting his financial affairs in order. His parlous situation stemmed both from having inherited his father-in-law's debts and from his own obdurate acquisitiveness. In an age when most skilled craftsmen earned about £100 yearly, and perhaps £4,000 in a long lifetime of toil, Jefferson's debt in 1789 exceeded £6,500. It was a formidable challenge merely to stay abreast of the annual interest charges. When he joined Washington's cabinet, Jefferson, in an act of brash self-deception, believed he could live within his $3,500 annual salary as a cabinet official and pump every penny in profit from his agricultural enterprises toward retiring his indebtedness.[8]

Like so much in the world of Jefferson's personal finance, this soon proved to be whimsy. In fact, Jefferson had already dug a deeper hole for himself by the time he boarded the *Clermont* for the voyage from France.

He not only paid immense freight charges on the staggering number of goods he was shipping home but, believing that he soon would return to France, maintained his expensive living quarters in Paris. Jefferson being Jefferson, he also waged a losing battle after 1790 in making ends meet on his salary as a cabinet member. Whereas Vice President Adams frugally lodged in a modest room in downtown Philadelphia, Jefferson rented a grandiose home on the Schuylkill River, where he stabled four horses and kept five servants and a maître d'hôtel, at a cost that approached 10 percent of his annual income. During 1791 his expenditures exceeded his salary by $2,511. In the course of that year he spent roughly a quarter of his salary on clothing, furniture, and books. During the more than three years that he served in Washington's cabinet, Jefferson's indebtedness increased by about 10 percent.[9]

Nor did Jefferson's financial predicament improve during the three years following his retirement. His farm operations were profitable, though not so much as he had imagined they would be. Several problems confronted him. Half or more of what he had under cultivation was in distant counties and under the supervision of indifferent overseers. In addition, the great majority of his property, situated as it was on the slope of the Blue Ridge Mountains, simply was far from the most fecund in Virginia. He also suffered bad luck. Sandwiched between damaging freezes at the outset of 1795 and disastrous floods that autumn, a fungal disease struck his crops in the summer. He was driven to sell land and mortgage slaves, and he additionally instituted lawsuits to force payments from those who owed him money. Three years after coming home, Jefferson's indebtedness had increased by another 10 percent, to £7,800, leading him to confess that he now was kept awake at night with worry over the prospect of someday losing Monticello.[10]

Yet during these years at home Jefferson wrote letter after letter proclaiming his contentment. He had returned to his idyllic estate to pursue a quiet and easy lifestyle, and he appeared to be fulfilled. He was surrounded by family. His daughter Maria, who was fifteen when he retired, lived at Monticello, while his eldest child, Martha, came for long visits and in 1795 left her children, four-year-old Anne and two-year-old Thomas Jefferson—called "Jeffy" by his mother—with their delighted grandfather for most of the year. Twelve months after leaving Washington's cabinet, Jefferson told Adams that he had discovered "tranquility of mind," and advised that in large measure it was due to his escape from public office. In fact, he "look[ed] back with wonder and regret over my useless waste of time" in politics.[11]

Jefferson claimed that his days were so absorbed with farming that he had time for little else, including reading out-of-state newspapers or books or reflecting on public matters.[12] Allowing for hyperbole—he found the time to write 220 letters in 1794–95—there was considerable truth in his disclaimers. Farming and gardening consumed most of his time, and much of what remained was taken up by work on his mansion, for after 1794—indebtedness notwithstanding—Jefferson undertook the rebuilding of Monticello. His interest in redesigning his estate was quickened by his perusal of Parisian and Italian landmarks during his stay abroad, as well as by his discovery that the mansion had suffered from neglect during his long absence.[13]

As an unhappy youth in flight from the world, Jefferson had relished Monticello's seclusion. Now that he was a successful public figure who had spent most of the previous decade in Europe's and America's largest cities, Jefferson at times found that the isolation of his mountain lair weighed heavily. The carriages of numerous visitors rattled up his craggy hill, but most—including even Martha after 1794—came almost exclusively in the summer, when the roads were in peak condition. After only a year at home, Jefferson lamented that he missed seeing old friends, yet he did not wander during his retirement, making only a single extended trip, an inescapable journey to Richmond in June 1794 to tend to financial matters.[14]

Maria Cosway once had been his antidote for loneliness. Before departing France, Jefferson told her that he hoped to return by late spring 1790, and in a letter written aboard ship while waiting to sail, he spoke rapturously of a reunion, closing with his customary admonition: "remember me and love me." Jefferson waited six months after arriving home before writing, not taking up his pen until he heard from her. He replied with alacrity. By that time he knew—through friends, as Maria had not divulged the news—that she was pregnant. Even so, he told her that "all I could desire in the world" would be realized should she come to Monticello. Having told her in 1787 that his head overruled his heart when he contemplated their relationship, Jefferson confided in 1790 that "I have no desire but to enjoy the affections of my heart."[15] Months, then years, elapsed before he heard from her again. After three years he wrote a mutual friend to inquire about Maria, remarking: "I have heard she was become a mother, but is the new object to absorb all her affections?" Thirty days before he finally retired from Washington's administration, Jefferson learned that Maria had entered a convent in Genoa. He was staggered. He thought she "would rather have sought the *mountain-top*," he exclaimed.[16]

Early in 1795 Jefferson finally heard from Maria. She wrote that she had not avoided him exclusively, but that she had withdrawn entirely from the outside world during her four years in the Italian monastery. She had just returned to London, where for the first time she learned not only of the missive he had written in 1790 but of the inquiries he had made during the intervening years. Maria mentioned a desire to come to America, and asked: "Why Can I not come?" She wrote feelingly that, save for the joy brought by her daughter, she remained ineffably sad and envisioned Monticello as "a smal spot unknown to Misery, trouble, and Confusion." Her letter was guarded and encrypted, but having just now discovered that years earlier Jefferson—in similarly circumspect language—had with all his heart invited her to live with him at Monticello, she appeared to be discreetly probing his current feelings.[17]

Jefferson waited nearly nine months before responding, a sure sign that his feelings had changed, and in fact in his parsimonious letter he made it clear that she was not in his future. He rattled on unconvincingly about hoping to see her someday in Italy, but he neither issued an invitation to Monticello nor engaged in any lovelorn flights of fancy. He said only that he wished for her happiness and that "I have a most sincere and cordial friendship for you."[18] Undeterred by Jefferson's cool response, Maria replied with lyric sadness the instant she heard from him, and in a less guarded vein than previously. She kept a portrait of him on her mantel, she confided, and then plaintively expressed her hunger to come to Monticello.[19] Jefferson did not reply.

It now appears that at some point during this period Jefferson began an amorous relationship with Sally Hemings, one of his female slaves. She was born in 1773 to John Wayles—Jefferson's late wife's father—and Betty Hemings, a chattel at The Forest, Wayles' estate not far from Williamsburg. As a mother's status was passed to her child under Virginia law, Sally was born a slave. Soon after Wayles' demise, by 1776 at the latest, Jefferson brought Sally and her siblings, as well as her mother, to Monticello. All lived along Mulberry Row, the slave quarters, but otherwise the members of the Hemings family were set apart from the other chattels. The males were trained as skilled artisans, and none, male or female, was ever put to hard labor as field hands. In addition, all received special treatment when the threat of an epidemic loomed.

Sally was nine when Jefferson's wife, Martha—her half sister—died. She was eleven when her master sailed for Europe in 1784. When Jefferson summoned his daughter Maria to France in 1787, fourteen-year-old Sally was chosen by relatives to accompany her on the transatlantic voyage.

Sally lived in Paris for the next twenty-four months. With both his daughters away at school, there was little work for her, but Jefferson kept Sally on, hired a tutor to teach her French, and spent lavishly on her wardrobe. By the time Jefferson returned to America, Sally was nearly seventeen, a young woman in the eyes of most in that period, and only a few months shy of the age at which both of Jefferson's daughters married. It was subsequently alleged that she was pregnant when she sailed home to Virginia, but it is possible neither to confirm that rumor nor, if true, to identify the father of her child.

Given the preponderance of circumstantial evidence and recent DNA testing, many scholars now believe that Jefferson fathered several children born to Sally Hemings. He was single, virile, and young—he did not turn fifty until 1793, the year he left Washington's cabinet—and it is easy to see how he could have been aroused by Sally or deeply in love with her. A quadroon who some thought to be Caucasian—she was "mighty near white," according to one of the slaves at Monticello—Sally was later described as a beautiful young woman with abundant dark hair that cascaded well down her back. She may have resembled Jefferson's late wife, either in appearance or through quirks and habits. Furthermore, by 1789 she had traveled more widely, and likely was more cosmopolitan, than most free women in America. She had made two ocean crossings, visited London, resided in Paris, studied French, and lived in the Hôtel de Langeac, where Jefferson frequently entertained French and American notables.

Hemings conceived and gave birth to a child at Monticello in 1795, a daughter named Harriet, who lived for only two years. Harriet's birth, as well as that of five additional children borne by Sally between 1798 and 1808, were recorded by Jefferson in his Farm Book, a register of operations at his sprawling estate in which he routinely made note of the birth of dozens of babies to slave mothers. Jefferson, who had arrived at Monticello in mid-January 1794 to begin his retirement, had been home for a year prior to Harriet's conception. Although he was away from home more than half the time from 1797 until the conception of Sally's last child, he was present at Monticello at the time that each of those children was conceived.[20] What is more, Sally never conceived a child during any of Jefferson's frequent absences.

Sally told her children that Jefferson was their father, which in itself is not proof, although other factors suggest that what she said was true. Numerous visitors were struck by the resemblance that her children bore to Jefferson, and some among his acquaintances subsequently acknowl-

edged that he had a slave mistress. Furthermore, Jefferson, who liberated virtually no slaves in the course of more than a half century of own-
ing chattels, freed all of Sally's children, either by legal manumission or
by permitting them to leave for freedom. Nor was it unheard of for a
slave master to have a sexual liaison with a female he owned. Indeed,
miscegenation was part of the landscape at Monticello and countless
other southern plantations. Two mulattoes were part of the legacy of
Jefferson's father, and several residents of Monticello, among them members of Jefferson's family, tendentiously accused numerous whites who
lived on, or regularly visited, the plantation—including Randolph
Jefferson, Thomas' brother—of having been intimate with Jefferson's
female slaves. In addition, census reports, wills, and divorce petitions in
early national Virginia attest to the thriving practice of interracial sex.[21]
Finally, the results of recent DNA testing has established a perfect match
on the Y-chromosome markers among descendants in Jefferson's line
and those of one of Sally's sons. Although not certain proof, this scien-
tific discovery, in concert with the considerable body of circumstantial
evidence, points convincingly toward Jefferson's paternity.[22]

Jefferson's own words also provide reason to believe that he had a
lengthy love affair with Sally Hemings. In his remarkable "head and heart"
missive to Maria Cosway, Jefferson confided his inability to ever again
risk the surrender of his heart to someone who might break it.[23] Sally
Hemings not only lacked the autonomy to wield such authority but, as a
slave in racist Virginia, she had little hope of a better life beyond Monticello. She was most unlikely to abandon Jefferson, a reality that made
her a person to whom Jefferson could surrender his heart.[24]

Jefferson knew that public knowledge of a relationship with a female
slave would have been ruinous to his public career, but when he came
home in 1794 he had no desire to ever again hold public office and no
expectation of ever again doing so. Indeed, fifteen months after returning
to Monticello, he confessed that his political ambitions had "long since
evaporated."[25] He had retired in the belief that the Federalists had been
stopped and that the opposition press—which he had helped to establish—would aid in the continued corralling of the most extreme Federalists. At bottom too, Jefferson believed that his work was done, as he was
convinced that the American people loathed the reactionary "monocrats."

Ten months after returning home, Jefferson declined Washington's
offer to serve as a special envoy to Madrid, the post that Thomas Pinckney
assumed.[26] Soon thereafter he said that he could never be "reasoned out
of" retirement, and when the subject surfaced of his someday seeking

the presidency, Jefferson shut the door with the resounding remark that the "question is for ever closed with me."[27] Yet when Madison urged him to consider running for president in 1796—"I intreat you not to . . . abandon your historical task. . . . You owe it to yourself, to truth, to the world"—Jefferson's response was noticeably different.[28] "I by no means think of declining the work. . . . On the contrary, I wish with ardor to begin it," he remarked, although he appeared to suggest that private concerns might delay his return to the public stage for a few years. Nevertheless, for the first time he had left the door ajar.[29] Something had changed Jefferson's mind about returning to public life.

Jefferson's protests of disinterest always had a hollow ring. He had never been as politically unconcerned as he suggested, and in fact a small network of friends kept him abreast of public affairs. By early in 1796, moreover, the concerns that had troubled him earlier in the decade resurfaced. He envisaged a gathering crisis, an emergency nearly as great as the one that had prompted the American Revolution, and as in 1776, he believed the struggle at hand concerned the preservation of liberty. Once again he had come to believe that those who were committed to republicanism were summoned to "unremitting labors and perils."[30]

He told a European observer who sought to understand politics in the United States that two American political parties existed: "One which fears the people most, the other the government." By early 1796 Jefferson was convinced that the former, the Federalist Party, once again was gaining the upper hand.[31] In his estimation, those frightened by popular rule had dominated the Constitutional Convention and the early period of Washington's administration, instances when he had been absent and Madison supposedly had defended those interests that he held dear. Events that occurred after he retired, when Madison once again had been left to lead the fight, convinced him that his adversaries were back in charge. Even though a decided minority—the urban merchants and financiers were "a zero in the scale," Jefferson said—the Federalists since 1794 had succeeded in suppressing the Whiskey Rebellion, almost silencing the Democratic-Republican Societies and others who applauded the French Revolution, and ratifying Jay's Treaty. Jefferson by 1796 feared that the alliance with France would be terminated, and he was no less apprehensive that the Federalists thereafter would formally ally with Great Britain. Unless they were stopped, Jefferson—who now had grandchildren of his own—worried that those who wished "to confine" human rights "to the few" would shape the world that the next generation or two would inherit. This "British party" or "Anglican, monarchical and aristocratical party," as he variously labeled his rival, controlled the presidency, Senate, and federal judiciary, and it was bent on transforming America into the embodiment of Great Britain.[32]

There was little question in Jefferson's mind that Adams would be one of the Federalist Party's nominees in the election of 1796. As early as 1794—after the vice president had written his cordial letter wishing his former friend a happy retirement—Jefferson probed to learn whether Adams was in the camp of the extremist Federalists. The earth belongs to the living and no generation should be bound by the decisions of its predecessors, Jefferson told Adams. Stability is crucial and is reinforced by obedience to old laws and charters so that uniformity "becomes a national Habit," Adams responded. Jefferson deprecated Great Britain but prayed for peace. Adams concurred, saying that he too was filled with foreboding at the prospect of war, which would "rouse up a many headed and many bellied Monster of an Army to tyrannize over Us, totally dissadjust our present Government, and accelerate the Advent of Monarchy and Aristocracy, by at least fifty years." Never one to hide his thoughts, Adams soon took the initiative, telling Jefferson that the French Revolution was irrational folly and that a century would be required to repair the damage it had caused. Jefferson replied that he hoped the "age of experiments in government"—revolution—would spread to England. "I am sure, from the honesty of your heart," he told Adams, that "you join me in detestation" of the decadent former mother country. Adams answered that he fervently wished Britain could be spared the notorious volatility of a revolution, as it would bring misery to thousands of innocents.[33]

After swapping a handful of letters over two years—the final letter from Adams was written in April 1796—Jefferson appeared to have been reassured. While he and the vice president disagreed on many matters, Jefferson was convinced that Adams, unlike Hamilton, was not an extreme Federalist. Most importantly, he believed that Adams was too committed to protecting the independence of the United States ever to ally with Great Britain. Though he was more at ease, Jefferson's ardor for returning to public life waned as rapidly as it had sprung to life. Confident that his former friend's instincts were correct, Jefferson anguished only over whether Adams—should he become the chief executive—would have the liberty, or the strength, to withstand the fanatics within his party.

While Jefferson declaimed about remaining at home, Adams dissembled about going home when his second term as vice president ended. Jefferson initially meant what he said. Adams never for a moment considered not running for president in 1796. His unwavering ambition since returning from Great Britain had been to succeed Washington in the presidency. Why else endure the vice presidency, an office with no authority? Why else subject himself to a post that "renders me so completely insignificant," that made him feel "as in a Prison," and that imposed on him an eight-year siege in a "Scene of Dullness"?[34]

Since 1791, his third year as vice president, Adams had fallen into the practice of living in the capital only while Congress was in session. No single factor can account for his behavior, but his unwillingness to live apart from Abigail was high on the list. She came with him to New York in the spring of 1789 and accompanied him to Philadelphia in the fall of 1790, so during his first two years as vice president Adams spent only about six weeks at Peacefield. However, Abigail remained at home after May 1792. Health considerations dictated her decision—she was afflicted with rheumatoid arthritis, which made traveling a painful ordeal—but so too did her concern over the expense of maintaining two homes. After she refused to come to the capital, Adams never remained in Philadelphia for more than five months annually.[35]

Adams found the long months apart from his wife nearly unendurable. He spent day after day presiding over interminable debates in the Senate, and night after solitary night in his sparse rented quarters. His uneasiness at his separation from Abigail marked a striking change in his attitude. He now craved her company. Calling himself a "lone Goose," he repeatedly beseeched her to join him.[36] When she demurred, he poured out his soul in long, impassioned missives, confessing his love for her and vaguely—he was too straitlaced not to be circumspect—alluding to his smoldering sexual desires.[37] The change in Adams between midlife and senescence was startling. Like many men in their twilight years, Adams appeared to grow more passive and dependent, more in need of the nurture that only his wife could provide. On some level he may also have been anxious to atone for the hurt that he had caused her over the years.[38]

Each year Adams rushed to Abigail's side the instant that Congress adjourned, but he did not endure the arduous journey solely to share her company. Adams sought therapy in the tranquility of Peacefield. On three occasions between 1771 and 1783 he had fallen grievously ill, leading physicians to despair for his life. During those illnesses he had exhibited symptoms that included heart palpitations, rapid heart rate, weakness, night sweats, skin disorders, inflamed and protuberant eyes, insomnia, confusion, tremors, exceptional anxiety, and possibly a goiter. Today a patient who exhibited those symptoms would be tested for

Graves' disease, or thyrotoxicosis, the overproduction of hormones secreted by the thyroid. However, the disease was not finally understood until long after Adams' death, and eventually it was found to be an autoimmune disorder that is often triggered by stress. Before modern therapies existed, the disease usually proved fatal, but in some patients it went into remission. A small percentage lived for years, even sometimes experiencing repeated onsets of the disorder.[39] In Adams' case, the disease appears to have gone into remission after 1783 and never returned. Adams, in fact, may even have taken steps that prevented its recurrence. By observation he concluded that his health improved, and the affliction seemed to be kept at bay, when he regularly exercised and was free of acute stress. To recoup his strength after the 1783 affliction, he began to walk several miles daily and to ride horseback for long distances. After several weeks, he felt well. Moreover, the disease did not recur while he lived an easy, comfortable life as the United States minister in London. Thus Adams kept at his exercise regimen, and by 1792 his correspondence suggests that he envisaged the annual lengthy absences from the capital as flights from an unhealthily vexatious environment.

While at Peacefield, Adams worked in his study, exercised (if the weather was inclement, he threw open the windows in his library and briskly strode about the room for a few minutes), and often labored on his small farm.[40] Unlike Jefferson, who lived from the yield of his lands and considered himself a farmer, the vice president actually toiled alongside his yeomen, hoeing weeds, shoveling manure, pushing heavy loads of lime and seaweed in a balky wheelbarrow, digging ditches, cutting trees, mowing the meadow, stacking the hay, building low stone walls, transporting provender for the livestock, and gathering the harvest under a hot late summer sun.[41]

During these months at home the never-ending tempests, contests, and gamesmanship of the capital receded over a distant horizon. It would be too much to say that Adams ever was carefree, but he was happiest while home. He delighted in being with Abigail and reveled in the accessibility of his cherished library. He not only remained healthy but was free of what he called the "blue devils," pangs of melancholy that tormented him while he lived in solitude in Philadelphia.[42] Unlike Jefferson, financial worries did not lie heavily on Adams. He owned Peacefield, a house in Boston that he had lived in for a time prior to the War of Independence, and 362 acres (mostly in Quincy, though some parcels were elsewhere) that included pasture and meadow lands, valuable tracts of salt marsh, and some properties that were purely for investment.[43] He earned $5,000 annually as vice president, in addition to the income he derived from rental fees—the yearly rental on his house in Boston netted him valuable income—and government securities that he had acquired following the enactment of Hamilton's program.[44] Adams was by no means wealthy, as were Washington, Jefferson, and Madison, but he was comfortable.

While at home, Adams' worries were mostly about his children. Nabby, who lived with her husband, Colonel William Smith—a wartime aide-de-camp to General Washington and, after 1785, the secretary of the American legation in Great Britain—was caught in an unhappy marriage. Adams had hardly known his sons Charles and Thomas Boylston when he returned home in 1788, and he had not grown especially close to either in the intervening years. Charles, who was twenty-six in 1796, had studied law with Hamilton and was in practice in Manhattan. He was flourishing, but recently he had begun to display symptoms of alcoholism, a plague in Abigail's family background. Tommy, who at twenty-four was also a lawyer, had not yet begun his practice; instead, he was serving as the secretary to his eldest brother, John Quincy, named by President Washington to be the minister to Holland.[45]

When his annual vacations in Quincy ended, Adams made the difficult trip back to Philadelphia, where he quickly fell back into his familiar schedule of "tedious days and lonesome nights."[46] He rose early (a lifelong habit instilled while growing up on a farm), ate breakfast, read the morning papers, and walked—he could not ride, as he left his horse in Quincy in order to save money—before the Senate convened. Late in the afternoon, when the daily session ended, he took his second and final meal of the day, often in the company of friends from various New England delegations or acquaintances in Philadelphia. These long, convivial repasts were capped with wine and cigars, which Adams had smoked since early adolescence. In the evening he returned to "Bachelor Hall," as he christened his austere quarters, to tend his correspondence and to read.[47] It was a lonely existence, yet one that he endured in the hope of someday succeeding Washington. On the other hand, his job was stress-free, and he enjoyed good health all these years, save for the onset of pyorrhea, which robbed him of several teeth.[48]

After the damage caused him by his *Defence of the Constitutions of Government of the United States* and Davila essays, Adams published nothing for the duration of his vice presidency. He was even circumspect in his private correspondence, for during his early days in Congress several of his letters containing barbed references about colleagues had been captured and gleefully published by Tories.[49] However, enough of his outlook can be divined to see that he shared the Federalists' zeal for a powerful national government. Adams quietly supported Hamilton's economic initiatives, characterizing the Treasury secretary as extraordinarily able, industrious, and intelligent, although flawed by "too much disposition to intrigue."[50] He applauded Washington's handling of the Whiskey Rebellion, which he too judged a malicious inspiration, and shared the president's enmity toward the Democratic-Republican Societies. Like Washington, Adams anxiously prayed for peace during the Anglo-American crisis that erupted in 1794. It was better to suffer some depredations at Britain's hands than to fly into a ruinous war, he said, but there were limits to his tolerance. Hostilities, he said, were preferable to national disgrace. The Jay Treaty prevented both war and the humiliation of the infant nation, and, like Washington, he thought it best to accept the treaty despite its blemishes.[51]

Finally, as was true of most Federalists, Adams was alarmed by signs that the United States was democratizing. Before political parties existed in the 1790s, Adams had published warnings of how partisan electioneering—what he called the "Cankerworm" that had brought down every previous republic—would corrupt the American political system. When caught between powerful rival interests, democratic politicians inevitably would be driven to deceit, he had predicted. Virtue and integrity would vanish. Revenge and malice would prevail. Voters would be duped and the press misled, pushing the system toward an unsavory end: a democratic tyranny in which the majority plundered the minority. For Adams, the notion that government could realize the will of the people was disingenuous. Society was divided into so many competing interests that a single popular will seldom existed. Furthermore, while humankind was all one species, Adams insisted that "Man differs by Nature from Man, almost as much as Man from Beast." It was impossible that all could have their way or be fulfilled. Instead, Adams favored a system in which the brightest and most virtuous men could be drawn into public life but then be insulated from the necessity to pander to the popular thirst. If somehow the independence of good men could be preserved so that they could govern prudently and judiciously, the result would be good government for the greatest number.[52]

Adams believed that the repugnant excesses of the French Revolution—"when will [those] Savages be satisfied with Blood," he exclaimed after the September Massacres—confirmed his grim warnings about unbridled popular participation in the political process.[53] He additionally feared that the factionalism that thrived in America after 1792 would bring the infant United States to a similar end. For this, he laid much of the blame at the feet of Jefferson. While he credited Jefferson for his abilities and "general good disposition," Adams judged him harshly. He concluded that Jefferson was "poisoned with Ambition," and thought his outlook—his Anglophobia in particular—had been nourished by his indebtedness to British creditors. As the election of 1796 approached, Adams declared privately that should Jefferson be elected to succeed Washington, he would seek election to the House of Representatives in order to battle the Republican "Demons."[54]

Jefferson's view of Adams was more benign. Although aware of the wide gulf that separated their outlooks, Jefferson yet admired Adams' honesty and integrity, and never for a moment believed him to be a hated "Angloman."[55] Jefferson drew hope from Adams' greatest virtue, his stubborn and tenacious independence. If anyone could withstand the zealots in the Federalist Party, it was Adams. Indeed, Jefferson believed he would be less malleable than Washington, and in the spring of 1796 he almost appeared to suggest that Adams might be a better chief executive.

Above all, one thing was clear to Jefferson: whatever had been intended by the Constitutional Convention, the president exerted greater influence with the people than did Congress. This meant that the outcome of the pending election of 1796, the nation's first contested presidential election, would be of crucial importance.

6

"A Narrow Squeak"

The First Contested
Presidential Election, 1796

UNTIL EARLY IN 1796, when he signaled to Madison that he might after all be willing to seek the presidency, Jefferson had insisted that he would never return to public life. Madison was unlikely to have been surprised by Jefferson's about-face. He knew Jefferson's horror of being seen as lusting after office, but he also knew his friend had changed his mind before about coming out of retirement. Furthermore, since the Jay Treaty, Jefferson's correspondence had evinced a rekindling of his old partisan fervor. But until Washington officially announced his intention to retire, Jefferson said nothing about the presidency, even though in the spring the congressional Republicans had already agreed to "push" him and Burr, while the Federalists in Congress caucused and endorsed Adams and Thomas Pinckney.[1]

Adams was just as careful not to reveal an interest in the presidency, and for a time he struck a posture of indecision even while writing to Abigail. His family had claims on him, but so did the nation, he anguished. He found the prospect of becoming "the Butt of Party Malevolence" to be "bitter nauseous and unwholesome."[2] Yet he must consider his character. His reputation would be destroyed if it was thought he had turned his back on the presidency at this critical juncture. Could he meet the physical challenges of the job? His health was better than it had been at any time during the past fifteen years, and he felt strong and energetic. He was weary of public life, but he wrote, "I don't know how I could live out of it." He would feel better about himself if he became a candidate. "I believe I have firmness of Mind enough to bear [the presidency] like a Man, a Hero and a Philosopher."[3] Finally, on February 15 all pretense vanished: "I feel no ill forebodings or faint Misgivings" about the prospect of becoming president. Would it be best to serve only a single term, he wondered, or should he consider staying on for eight years?[4]

Adams' decision was never in doubt, and he abandoned his burlesque entirely when several influential Federalists, who had mostly ignored him for the past seven years, cozied up to him the instant they learned of Washington's decision. They called on him, deferred to him, and toasted him at dinners. Adams interpreted their blandishments as a sign that they wished for him to succeed Washington, and in the gloom of winter he began to prepare himself for the presidency. He allowed that he would have to work on his weaknesses, chiefly his volcanically irascible nature and his propensity for speaking before thinking. Despite those failings, he went on, his public career had been "Sweet and happy," and he expected that to be the case with his presidency as well. Suddenly Adams seemed downright giddy. "Hi! Ho! Oh Dear," he greeted his wife in a missive that said volumes about his joy at the prospect of becoming the president of the United States.[5]

Adams' only immediate worry was that Washington would be persuaded by those around him to stay on for a third term. During the gray days of January and February he watched the president and First Lady closely for telltale signs of their intentions, and when he detected Martha Washington acting "as gay as a girl," he breathed a sigh of relief, assuming the Washingtons were indeed bent on going home.[6] Furthermore, the president, who had largely neglected Adams since 1789, repeatedly invited him to tea or dinner during the first months of 1796, probably to slyly tutor the man who might be his successor. Adams gushed that they had discussed numerous issues and that Washington "never [had been] more frank and open." What is more, Adams was amazed to learn that Washington's "opinions and sentiments are more exactly like mine than I ever knew before."[7]

While Adams dissembled, Jefferson's correspondence bore little evidence of the looming presidential contest. Business and pleasure preoccupied him. He investigated a newly invented threshing machine, marketed his crops, anguished over damaging floods during the January thaw and a drought in April, frantically sought food for his slaves when his corn harvest suffered, attempted to sell a portion of his land, bred dogs, and of course supervised the daily construction at Monticello.[8] In the nine months prior to the election, Jefferson wrote only a couple of letters in which he mentioned public affairs, but from these it is clear that the sense of urgency he had felt during the fight over the Jay Treaty had slowly eroded. He now believed that the Federalist Party's moment had come and gone. It had won on the treaty, but at a heavy cost. Jefferson was also convinced that the Federalists had overreached after suppressing the Whiskey Rebellion. He expected their fortunes to plummet further when "the colossus" Washington, upon whom they had piggybacked throughout the decade, finally retired. If Adams succeeded to the presidency, Jefferson said, he would be unable to do much harm: he would be "overborne by the republican sense" of the general public, which wanted nothing to do with Great Britain or monarchy, and he would not have a majority in Congress.[9] Convinced that the throbbing crisis of the early years of the decade was gone, Jefferson once again was reluctant to reenter public life, but at the same moment he was unwilling to prevent his name from being put forward.

The election of 1796 began when Washington, in his Farewell Address in September 1796, at last publicly announced his decision to retire. His revelation acted "as a signal, like dropping a hat, for the party racers to start," the congressman Fisher Ames noted.[10] Even so, the principal candidates did not join the fray. Neither Adams nor Jefferson left their farms that autumn, and neither issued public statements or wrote so much as a single letter in an effort to round up support. Pinckney followed suit. These three held to the notion that the voters should come to them, rather than that they should go to the voters. This conformed to the political traditions of early America. Candidates in the colonial era had often provided the electorate with food and liquor, but they had not courted voters by traveling about speechifying, and they appear to have avoided the temptation to adopt a false persona in order to deceive their constituents.[11] With the exception of Burr, the candidates in 1796 adhered to those customs, as would presidential candidates—at least with regard to stump appearances—throughout the century that followed. Burr, however, did campaign, spending six weeks in New England cultivating members of the electoral college and local Republicans, a trip that only aroused suspicions among some southern Republicans, who feared that his real object was to eclipse Jefferson.[12]

If Adams, Jefferson, and Pinckney remained in the shadows, other party politicians were active. The outcome of the election hinged on the choice of 136 presidential electors in the sixteen states. In nine states the electors were selected by state legislatures. Elsewhere they were popularly elected. Before the American Revolution, voting had been limited to property-owning adult white males, disfranchising many. A recent study of prerevolutionary Virginia, for instance, concluded that only 12 percent of adult white men in that colony could vote.[13] The consensus among today's historians is that the percentage that qualified to vote before 1776 was lower in the South than in New England, and that the national average was in the neighborhood of 60 percent. After 1776 pressure for suffrage reform produced widely varying changes. By 1796 six states (Pennsylvania, New Hampshire, Vermont, North Carolina, Kentucky, and Tennessee) opened the vote to all white male taxpayers. The other states maintained property qualifications, but many had lowered the bar since independence.[14] Women and blacks remained disfranchised, and Catholics, Jews, and Indians were often denied suffrage. Nevertheless, not only was a greater percentage of the white male population eligible to vote than before the war, but many offices that had been appointive were made elective. Yet voting rights were often a confusing jumble of laws and customs. For example, some states set higher qualifications for voting for the upper house of the assembly than for the lower chamber, and still higher stipulations for voting for governor. There were no national laws regarding voting, save for the constitutional provision that those eligible to vote for members of the "most numerous Branch of the state legislature" were also eligible to vote for members of the lower house of Congress. Thus the states were free to determine who was eligible to vote in presidential elections.[15]

Exercising the right to vote often was a troublesome proposition in a rural, sparsely settled country where voters frequently lived far from polling places. In the 1790s in New Jersey, which was not untypical, an average of only four polling places existed per county, and in South Carolina there was often only a single place to vote in each parish. Moreover, for voters who had a farm to manage and multiple day-by-day chores to perform, including looking after livestock that required considerable attention, voting often was a low-priority matter. For many, it was a challenge to get to the polls and back home on the same day. Even if one got to the polls, voting could be a daunting experience. Not every state utilized the secret ballot, and many citizens were intimidated by voting orally. In addition, few states used printed ballots at this time. Voters were often simply given a blank sheet of paper and told to write their choice of candidates. Furthermore, electoral impropriety sometimes rendered the exercise meaningless. Election officials were at times accused of letting illegal voters into the polling place, opening or closing the polls when it suited them, and losing—that is to say, destroying—ballots. Yet despite the difficulties that faced voters, participation increased in the 1790s as the parties grew more disciplined and skilled in the art of electioneering.[16]

But in 1796 the Federalists and Republicans were still so loosely constituted that party discipline was nonexistent. Loyalty to the national ticket was often subsumed by regional and local issues, long-standing friendships, enduring hatreds, and personal ambitions. Neither party had a central committee to orchestrate campaign tactics, with the result that information about national affairs was often sketchy and unreliable, further contributing to the fragility of the partisan networks.[17] However, it would be a mistake to underestimate the role of the parties. Some degree of party organization, however primitive, existed in almost every state. What is more, each party was identified with a core set of ideas. Those who followed politics knew what the parties stood for, understood the stakes in this election, and—as has largely been true throughout America's political history—believed that the election of a candidate who was affiliated with a party afforded a general expectation of how that candidate could be expected to act once in office. Many political activists worked diligently to elect a philosophical comrade, but almost as often the most compelling reason to hustle for a set of candidates was to keep the other side out of power. As one Federalist in 1796 declared, this was a contest about keeping "the Virginia Philosopher from the chair." Many Republicans were no less obsessive about denying office to "Anglomen" and "monocrats."

The election was overshadowed by the Constitutional Convention's ill-conceived notion that electors were to "vote by Ballot for two Persons" for the presidency. The electoral college system was a calamity waiting to happen.[18] It already had provoked machinations in the contest to choose a vice president in 1788, and in 1796 it threatened for the first time to intrude on the selection of the chief executive. During this campaign, allegations were plentiful that Burr conspired to whittle Jefferson's vote total and that Hamilton, who like his fellow New Yorker seems always to have been suspected of chicanery by contemporaries, was busy plotting to deny victory to Adams.

Hamilton was suspect because almost everyone agreed that his interests would be better served by the election of Pinckney. He and Adams had enjoyed a cordial relationship during Washington's presidency, but they were not close, and given the generational chasm that separated them—Adams was twenty-two years older—as well as their strikingly dissimilar temperaments, little chance existed that they would ever grow close. Moreover, not only was Adams famously independent, but he was accustomed to unilaterally making difficult decisions, having been compelled to do so repeatedly throughout his long years abroad as a diplomat. No one, least of all Hamilton, imagined that Adams would be malleable. Pinckney was altogether different. More nearly Hamilton's age—seven years separated them—Pinckney had served as governor of South Carolina and as Washington's minister to London and special envoy to Madrid. He was affable, a bit impressionable, not especially accustomed to the hardball of politics, totally devoid of partisan experience at the national level, and not well known outside South Carolina.[19] If Pinckney was to come to believe that he owed his presidency to Hamilton—something that never would have occurred to Adams—or if the South Carolinian concluded that Hamilton, the experienced insider, would be a valuable asset (also a thought that was unlikely to cross Adams' mind), Hamilton might be the power behind the throne during the next four years.

The gossip about Hamilton's machinations in 1796 stemmed from the nearly universal belief that Adams would win one of the votes cast by every Federalist elector in New England and that Pinckney would receive one of the votes cast by every southern Federalist elector. It was the second vote that every elector would cast that constituted the wild card in this contest, and this factor caused many to surmise that Hamilton was scheming. The logic of those who suspected skullduggery was this: if the Federalist electors from New England cast their second vote for Pinckney, as the Federalist caucus had urged, but if one or two Federalist electors from other sections withheld their second vote from Adams, Pinckney's total would surpass that of Adams. If Pinckney's total also eclipsed that of Jefferson, he would be the second president of the United States. The temptations, and the stakes, were enormous, and for many it was too much not to presume that Hamilton was pulling strings to persuade South Carolina's electors not to vote for Adams. The belief that hanky-panky was being practiced was so widespread that when a Boston newspaper ran an article on the eve of the election alleging that the election in Vermont would be declared invalid due to irregularities (an action that would cost Adams the three votes from that state, and the election), it was widely assumed that Hamilton had planted the story in order to frighten New England's electors into balloting for Pinckney, their one remaining hope for keeping Jefferson out of the presidency.[20]

Madison and Jefferson excitedly speculated on Hamilton's alleged intrigue, as did Adams' supporters in New England.[21] For the longest time, Adams was the one person who discounted the rumors of Hamilton's betrayal. Not only had Hamilton worked for his reelection in 1792, but Adams preferred to believe that the former Treasury secretary would not risk trickery that might open the door for Jefferson to win. However, by December so many Federalists had apprised him of Hamilton's purported scheming—including Abigail, who censured Hamilton as a "subtle intriguer" along the lines of Julius Caesar—that Adams became convinced of the New Yorker's treachery.[22] His anger combusting, Adams sardonically charged—always in private—that Hamilton was as "great an Hypocrite as any in the U.S." He proclaimed him "a proud Spirited, conceited, aspiring Mortal always pretending to Morality, with as debauched Morals as old Franklin." For a time Adams feared that Hamilton would succeed in having Pinckney elected, an outcome that was tantamount to the election of Hamilton himself, he charged, as the South Carolinian would be no better than his toady.[23]

Jefferson, meanwhile, was tormented with a problem of a different sort. Federalists in Virginia revived the long-forgotten charges of his ineptitude, if not malfeasance, during his wartime service as governor. Accusations that he had lacked "firmness" in the face of Arnold's invasion of Virginia were hurled about in newspapers, broadsides, and handbills, and so too was the old allegation that he had left the state in the lurch when he fled to avoid capture by the enemy raiding party that appeared at Monticello in June 1781. Jefferson did not respond, but several of his supporters published depositions defending his conduct and touting his bravery.[24] Their efforts failed to elevate his spirits. As Election Day neared, Jefferson told Madison that he hoped Adams was victorious, and for once he meant precisely what he said.[25]

The hot battle in Virginia portended savage campaigns elsewhere, as electioneering in the press and at public gatherings revolved about the characters of Adams and Jefferson, while the other candidates were largely relegated to the sidelines. Portraying Jefferson as experienced, courageous, and trustworthy, Republican partisans painted a dismal picture should the Federalists remain in power. They depicted the election as a contest between those who embraced the rights of humankind and royalist Anglophiles who sought to preserve a society with limited opportunities for commoners. The Republicans retrieved Adams' *Defence of the Constitutions of Government of the United States* from the dustbin and exhibited it as evidence of his monarchical beliefs. In Pennsylvania

they distributed handbills that read: "Thomas Jefferson is a firm RE-
PUBLICAN—John Adams is an avowed MONARCHIST." A crowd at a
Philadelphia rally chanted "Jefferson and no king." The Republicans also
satirized Adams. Reviving memory of the presidential titles battle, they
labeled him the "Duke of Braintree" and "His Rotundity." He was accused of nepotism as well because two of his sons were on the federal
payroll.[26] Ludicrously, some alleged that the Federalists were plotting to
have the Adams family become America's royalty, with John Quincy
waiting in the wings to succeed his father to the throne. Nor was that all.
Adams' foes limned him as feckless, unwilling to listen to advice, disinterested, unreasonably slow to make decisions, and likely to be dilatory
in executing congressional legislation.

The Federalists gave as good as they got. They defended Adams as a
hero of the American Revolution who deserved to be president and could
be expected to follow in Washington's giant footsteps. In contrast, they
depicted Jefferson as "a weak, wavering, indecisive character."[27] He was a
philosopher, not a statesman, they charged, and they told the public that
"of all beings, a philosopher makes the worst politician." Jefferson, they
said, lived in an ivory tower and devoted his time to concocting imprac-
tical visions. According to a leading Federalist in South Carolina, Jefferson
was probably suited to be a college president, but he most certainly lacked
the temperament to become president of the United States. Some Federalists turned upside down Jefferson's commitment to religious liberty,
asserting that he was irreligious and hoped for the liberty not to worship. Furthermore, many Federalist bloggers suggested that Jefferson's
admiration of the French Revolution was proof that he was an "infidel"
and hence a danger to Christianity in America.[28]

By early autumn keen observers knew how the majority of electors
would cast their first ballot, but for the most part their second vote remained a mystery, and that injected an air of expectancy into the contest.
Seventy votes were needed to win in the electoral college. Adams was generally conceded to have forty-nine votes locked up—all of New England's
votes and the ten from Delaware and New Jersey. It was taken as a given,
meanwhile, that Jefferson was assured of forty-two votes, the eleven from
Tennessee, Kentucky, and Georgia, and all but two of the thirty-three from
North Carolina and Virginia. Otherwise, uncertainty prevailed.

As Election Day approached, Adams sank into despair, certain that
Pinckney would be "smuggled in" to the presidency by Hamilton's intrigues. He additionally thought that Jefferson would place second.[29]

Madison, on the other hand, gloomily predicted that Adams would be pushed over the top in the South, where he would harvest three or four crucial votes.[30] Jefferson said nothing.

Once the electors voted, the outcome could not be kept secret. Before Christmas, the results were known.

	Adams	Jefferson	Pinckney	Burr	Others
New Hampshire	6	—	—	—	6
Vermont	4	—	4	—	—
Massachusetts	16	—	13	—	3
Rhode Island	4	—	—	—	4
Connecticut	9	—	4	—	5
New York	12	—	12	—	—
New Jersey	7	—	7	—	—
Pennsylvania	1	14	2	13	—
Delaware	3	—	3	—	—
Maryland	7	4	4	3	2
Virginia	1	20	1	1	19
North Carolina	1	11	1	6	5
South Carolina	—	8	8	—	—
Georgia	—	4	—	—	4
Kentucky	—	4	—	4	—
Tennessee	—	3	—	3	—
TOTAL	71	68	59	30	48

The lack of party discipline was evident. Nearly 40 percent of the electors cast a ballot for someone not nominated by their party's congressional caucus.[31] Sixteen New England electors, fearing the likelihood of Hamilton's intrigue, refused to vote for Pinckney, dooming his chances. Had Pinckney captured those New England votes, he would have won the election. Yet it was party machinery—and a crucial Federalist blunder—that led Jefferson to nearly sweep Pennsylvania's electoral vote. Pennsylvania's Federalists, confident that they remained the majority party, pushed a measure through the state legislature in 1796 that changed the electoral procedure. The system of electing an elector from each congressional district was abandoned. It was replaced by the general ticket, or winner-take-all, system. Voters were to be presented with two general tickets, one containing a list of Federalist electors, the other the names of the Republican candidates for the electoral college. Fearing certain defeat, the Republicans organized and nominated a slate of electors consisting of men who were known through the state. Prior to the election they also issued fifty thousand ballots that listed the names of their candidates for

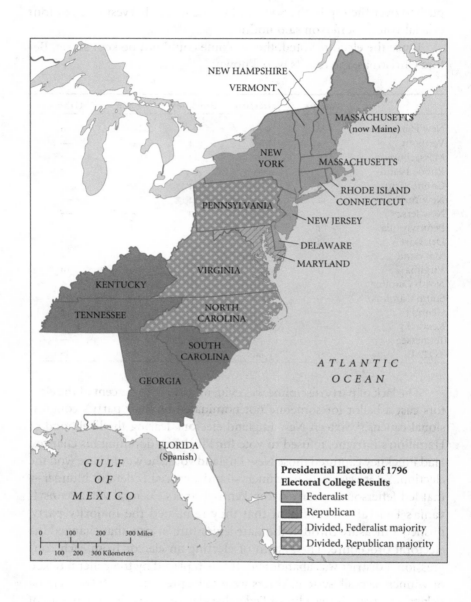

NEW HAMPSHIRE

VERMONT

MASSACHUSETTS
(now Maine)

NEW
YORK

MASSACHUSETTS

RHODE ISLAND
CONNECTICUT

PENNSYLVANIA

NEW JERSEY

DELAWARE

MARYLAND

VIRGINIA

KENTUCKY

NORTH
CAROLINA

TENNESSEE

SOUTH
CAROLINA

GEORGIA

ATLANTIC
OCEAN

FLORIDA
(Spanish)

GULF
OF
MEXICO

0   100   200   300 Miles

0   100   200   300 Kilometers

Presidential Election of 1796
Electoral College Results

Federalist

Republican

Divided, Federalist majority

Divided, Republican majority

the electoral college. Voters found it a helpful device. The Republican leadership presciently saw it as a clever ploy through which to secure votes. In addition, Pierre Adet, the French minister to the United States, almost certainly acting in collusion with leading Philadelphia Republicans, published a diplomatic note on the eve of the election that hinted that Paris saw the Federalist administration as pro-British. He additionally stated that henceforth France would treat American commerce with Great Britain as London treated American trade with French ports. A crystal ball was not required to see that this presaged Franco-American difficulties not unlike those that occurred between the United States and London after 1794. Philadelphia's Quakers were alarmed that war would ensue, and even some merchants were heard to say that perhaps Jefferson, who was known and respected in Paris, would have the best chance of reaching a peaceful accommodation with France. The result of these cunning tactics was that Republicans won Philadelphia for the first time and Adams was nearly shut out. Jefferson won fourteen of Pennsylvania's fifteen votes and would have won the other had it not been for a technicality in a backcountry district.[32]

Otherwise, as Madison had correctly calculated, the contest was determined in the South. Adams won seven votes from Maryland's ten electors, as well as one vote each from Virginia and North Carolina. Adams' Virginia vote came from a district with long-standing anti-planter proclivities, and as such it was a vote against Jefferson rather than for him.[33] His North Carolina vote was from a coastal district drawn to Federalist mercantile policies. In a sense, it was these two southern votes that gave Adams his narrow majority, for had Jefferson won both votes, he would have become the second president.

The election outcome laid bare once more the new nation's sectional divisions. Adams won the vote of every northern elector outside Pennsylvania, but only two below the Potomac. Aside from Pennsylvania, Jefferson did not win a single electoral vote in the North. Surprisingly, the contest did not especially rouse the populace, at least if Pennsylvania—where voting returns are extant—can be taken as a benchmark. Only 25 percent of those who qualified to vote in that state actually went to the polls, a smaller percentage than had troubled to vote in Pennsylvania's two previous gubernatorial elections.[34] The contest additionally demonstrated that, contrary to Jefferson's predictions that the Federalists had crested, considerable life was left in that party. It won both the presidency and control of the House of Representatives, capturing fifty-eight seats to forty-eight for their opponents. The canvass further revealed how misguided Hamilton's scheming had been. When several New England electors abandoned Pinckney to protect Adams, no one knew better than Hamilton what he had wrought. The election, he gloomily confessed, "proves me to be a very bad politician."[35]

Contemporaries divided over the meaning of the outcome. Madison attributed Adams' victory to the boost given the Federalist Party by the popularity of the Jay Treaty in the North.[36] Jefferson thought the Federalists had benefited from their ties to Washington, but he also assumed that many had fastened on Adams as deserving the presidency after years of service to the new nation.[37] It seems true too, as the historian Joanne Freeman has observed, that personal, regional, and political loyalties also influenced the final decision in a contest in which ambitious individuals and unstructured, undisciplined political parties competed for the big prize.[38]

Late in December Madison told Jefferson that he had finished in second place and would "be summoned to the place Mr. Adams now fills."[39] Jefferson appeared unperturbed. If anything, he seemed to be the individual least upset by the election outcome. While the issue was yet in doubt, he had remarked that he hoped to finish in second place and would not mind terribly if he ran third. Once the outcome was known, he put out the transparent fiction that he had never expected to win, as the North had more electoral votes and, what is more, northerners were better schooled in politics than their southern counterparts. He was comfortable taking a backseat to Adams, he added. "I am his junior in life, was his junior in Congress, his junior in the diplomatic line, his junior lately in our civil government."[40] Adams, meanwhile, rejoiced over his "narrow Squeak." He had feared that he might finish second, and had privately threatened to resign rather than spend another term as vice president. "I have been Daddy-Vice long enough," he quipped.[41] He had especially dreaded defeat and at times during the campaign sank into a purple melancholy. Knowing that at age sixty-one he would never resume his legal practice, he expected that defeat meant retirement, and retirement meant that he and Abigail would have to retrench to make ends meet. Above all, however, he trembled at what he imagined would be the dishonor of having been spurned by the electorate, and feared that an electoral loss would cause him to be viewed as an object of loathing. But he had won, and immediately thereafter he took steps to purchase a handsome new carriage suitable for one in his new station.[42]

Adams had two months to wait until Inauguration Day. He was ecstatic but at the same time mellow. He allowed that he "never felt easier in my

Life," as if his victory had lifted a terrible burden, yet he worried over his finances. His annual salary would quintuple to $25,000, but from that he would have to pay an annual rent of $2,700 on the President's House and furnish the residence as well. His plight induced him to abandon his earlier plan of purchasing a luxurious new carriage. Instead, he arranged to have his modest phaeton brought from Quincy, but not before he instructed Abigail to remove the coat of arms emblazoned on the door. Its presence would only invite "vulgar Insolence," he said.[43]

Presidencies are ordinarily shaped by crucial decisions made after Inauguration Day, but three choices were made before Adams took office that were to have an impact on his tenure. Once the outcome of the election was certain, Jefferson wrote a placatory letter to the president-elect. As Adams, a Federalist, would have to serve with a Republican vice president, Jefferson wished to assure him that he would not stir the waters. He also longed for an accommodation with his old friend, and in addition sincerely wished to see Adams succeed, as his success was "the only sure barrier against Hamilton getting in."[44] In his letter, Jefferson reflected on their earlier friendship and in expressive language confessed his "respect and affectionate attachment" for Adams. To these sugar-glazed chords Jefferson added two notes of advice. The looming French crisis, brought to center stage by Adet's pronouncement, would confront the nation with its greatest crisis since the end of the War of Independence. He urged Adams to pursue peace, telling him that if he avoided an unnecessary war, the "glory will be all your own." Finally, he warned Adams that his greatest threat would come not from his Republican foes but from "spies and sycophants" within his administration, an unmistakable reference to Hamilton and his acolytes.[45]

However, instead of mailing the letter, Jefferson first asked Madison to peruse it. Madison was aghast at what he read, fearing that the missive, with its suppliant air, would consign Jefferson to silence during the ensuing four years and probably undermine any thought of his candidacy for the presidency in 1800. Madison's counsel was that the letter not be sent, and Jefferson acquiesced. Astute from his party's perspective, the decision nevertheless had toxic consequences. Acting in the spirit of Washington's Farewell Address, Jefferson had sought to reduce the partisan strife that had embittered the preceding years. In addition, he and Adams once had forged such an extremely close friendship that neither shrank from offering the other advice or criticism. Jefferson's instinct had been to reach out to renew that bond, a step that might have resulted in candid discussions between himself and Adams over the next four years, avoiding countless misunderstandings and much ill-tempered dissidence. Madison's course obliterated Jefferson's gracious gesture and ensured that the fires of partisanship would continue to burn brightly.

Jefferson did not write again to Adams, and the two did not see each other until two days before Inauguration Day, when the incoming vice president visited the president-elect. Adams reciprocated the following day. Pleasantries dominated both conversations, but at some point in these meetings Adams made a startling proposal. He asked Jefferson to sail to Paris as an envoy extraordinary, the role that Jay had played in journeying to London three years before. Jefferson immediately declined. He was "sick of residing in Europe," he remarked, and besides, he thought it improper for the vice president to be away for a protracted period. Adams accepted his reasoning, and then broached the idea of naming Madison for the embassy.[46] The idea had merit. The choice of Madison would have been a magnanimous, nonpartisan beginning to Adams' presidency, and, given the Virginian's republican credentials, his embassy might have placated the leaders in Paris. Adams's hopes were dashed, however, when Madison, who earlier had confessed to Jefferson that he would never be up to making an ocean crossing due to "a singular disease of my constitution," refused to consider such an undertaking.[47] Once again, Madison had made a critical decision that would dramatically shape Adams' presidency.

Adams alone was responsible for the third choice. He retained Washington's cabinet, although none of its members had ever been close to him. Nor did Adams have a positive sense of their views or characters. He subsequently accounted for his decision—what he would always think of as his folly—by saying that he was previously "unpracticed in intrigues for power." Such an explanation was unconvincing coming from one who had spent three years in Congress and a decade in the venomous corridors of European diplomacy. He might better have said that he lacked executive experience. In addition, Adams knew that Washington lately had found it difficult to recruit talented cabinet officials, and he may have wished to avoid the annoyance of repeatedly soliciting men to serve him. He may even have despaired at finding better officials than those whom Washington had finally managed to recruit. Finally, Adams later claimed that his presidency would have been wrecked before it began had he dismissed Washington's cabinet.[48] He no doubt was under intense pressure to retain Washington's secretaries, but he failed to appreciate the powers he would possess as chief executive, and especially the opportunity at his fingertips to utilize patronage to build a loyal following. Jefferson, in contrast, immediately understood that Adams had blundered. The new president had surrounded himself with Hamilton's lackeys, he noted, and they "are only a little less hostile to him [Adams] than to me."[49]

Philadelphia lay in the grip of late winter on the day of the inauguration, March 4, 1797, although the dawn's soft gray pall soon gave way to a cloudless blue sky. The ceremonies began in midmorning with Jefferson's swearing in before the Senate. Neither Washington nor Adams attended. Two hours later, just before noon, the outgoing chief executive and the president-elect traveled separately to Congress Hall, a two-story redbrick structure crowned with a stately cupola that stood near Independence Hall. Washington, who walked from the President's House, arrived first. Adams, riding alone in his modest carriage drawn by only two horses, followed shortly. Simplicity was the order of the day. Adams was unescorted by militia or constables, unattended by bands or banners.

Washington entered the House chamber first. Attired in a black suit, he strode briskly to the dais amid a heartfelt ovation from the officials and lucky spectators who packed the small room. Moments later Jefferson, wearing a long blue frock coat, entered to polite applause. He and the audience had barely taken their seats before the doors were opened and Adams, dressed in a light gray suit with a sword strapped to his waist, strode into the hall. Like the other two, Adams' backswept hair was well powdered, but his suit was noticeably devoid of expensive buttons and knee buckles.[50]

Positioned between Washington and Jefferson, who stood six feet four inches and six feet two inches, respectively, and often struck others as statuesque, Adams' short, plump form was accentuated. He had barely slept the night before, and later remarked that this was the most anxious day of his life.[51] The format was for Adams first to deliver his inaugural address, then be sworn in. A hush fell over the chamber as he stepped forward to read his brief remarks. What he said sounded like countless subsequent inaugural addresses: the Union was strong, the Constitution was a blessing, and America's greatest danger came from abroad. Adams did hint that he wished to be what he once had called the "Father and Protector," the president of all the people, not the advocate of one section or a small faction.[52] When he finished, a patter of respectful applause filled the hall, but while he took the oath of office from Chief Justice Oliver Ellsworth, another New Englander, many in the room wept openly, not because of Adams' accession to the office but from a sense of loss, as all presumed this was to be Washington's final day of public service, and all nervously wondered whether the Union could endure without the glue that Washington had provided.

Washington alone did not appear to be unhappy. His countenance was serene as he prepared to return home forever, leaving public service and this post, which Jefferson soon would call an office of "splendid misery."[53] Adams believed that Washington's joy betrayed the notion that he was the true winner and Adams the loser on this day. "Methinks," Adams concluded, "I heard him think Ay. I am fairly out and you fairly in! See which of us will be happiest."[54]

7

"To Recover Self-Government"

The Partisan Inferno, 1797–1798

THE UNITED STATES AND FRANCE, allies since 1778, verged on a collision as Adams' inauguration approached. Caught in a desperate war and convinced that the Jay Treaty signified a rapprochement with Great Britain, France announced in 1796 that it would not tolerate trade between the United States and Great Britain. Washington responded to the challenge by sending Charles Cotesworth Pinckney to Paris to seek an accommodation.[1] Three days after he took office, President Adams learned not only that the Directory, the French government, had refused to accept Pinckney but that French depredations against American commerce were occurring on the high seas.[2] President Adams had a full-blown crisis on his hands.

He quickly summoned his cabinet to discuss the appropriate response. All the secretaries, except Attorney General Charles Lee of Virginia, were Federalist firebrands with close ties to Alexander Hamilton. Oliver Wolcott, at the Treasury, was the grandson of a colonial governor of Connecticut and son of a signer of the Declaration of Independence. He had studied and then practiced law during the War of Independence, and eventually entered public life at the state level. Courteous, outgoing, and respected for his punctiliousness, honesty, and industry, Wolcott had caught Hamilton's eye while serving as the comptroller in Connecticut, and was brought to the national capital in 1789 as the auditor in the new Treasury Department. From that point forward, he was devoted to Hamilton,

Oliver Wolcott by G. L. Nelson after John Trumbull. Wolcott,
Treasury secretary under Washington and Adams, proved to be
more loyal to Alexander Hamilton than to President Adams.

who steadily elevated him within the department. He succeeded Hamilton
in 1795. Wolcott's family had supported Adams in every national election,
although Wolcott himself had covertly backed Pinckney in 1796.[3]

James McHenry of Maryland had been named secretary of war by
Washington in 1795 after his four previous choices declined invitations
to serve. Born in Ireland, McHenry had immigrated in 1772 at age nineteen. He was a physician by the time the war broke out three years later,
and he immediately entered the Continental Army as a surgeon. In 1778
he joined Washington's staff, where he won friends easily and grew especially close to Hamilton, his fellow aide. After the war McHenry sat in
the Maryland legislature, the Constitutional Convention, and the Senate but shone in none.[4] Some thought he was barely competent, an assessment that Hamilton shared. When Washington searched for someone

James McHenry by James Sharples, Sr., about 1796–1800. McHenry served as secretary of war under Washington and Adams. He was Hamilton's sycophant and his snitch in Adams' cabinet. President Adams dismissed him in 1800.

to head the War Department, Hamilton advised that McHenry would "give no strength to the administration." Subsequently both spoke of McHenry's "unfitness" for high office.[5]

Wolcott and McHenry were likeable, but no one ever said that of Timothy Pickering, the secretary of state. Dour, querulous, and acerbic, Pickering had risen despite his inimical manner and in the face of scant achievement. Born into an old New England family, Pickering briefly pursued a legal career following graduation from Harvard. He quit to soldier during the war, joining Washington's staff in 1777, where he too fell under Hamilton's spell. Soon enough, Washington soured on Pickering, finding him to be a shoddy administrator, and he moved him from pillar to post in search of an assignment he might be able to handle. Pickering's last stop was running the quartermaster corps. Although honest, he bollixed that appointment as well, and Washington more or less told him so. But Washington brought him back into public life and in 1794, despite Hamilton's counsel that Pickering was

Timothy Pickering. Engraving by T. B. Welch from a drawing by Longacre after Gilbert Stuart. Pickering joined Washington's cabinet as war secretary but later served as secretary of state under both the first president and John Adams. He exemplified the Ultra-Federalists. Adams fired him in 1800.

prone to ill-considered judgments, reluctantly asked him to head the War Department after three others had turned down the job. A year later, after six others had refused the president's offer to become secretary of state, Washington in desperation once again turned to Pickering, who by then had begun to think of himself as indispensable.[6]

Adams and his cabinet clashed immediately. Hoping the French crisis could be resolved peacefully and honorably, the president proposed sending a bipartisan diplomatic commission to Paris. Wolcott, McHenry, and Pickering purpled with rage at the thought of sending a Republican to Paris, and they demanded that France accept Pinckney and negotiate solely with him. Furthermore, they insisted that the United States not make concessions to Paris. Adams backed off. He agreed to summon Congress to a special session in sixty days, although what he would tell the legislators was not determined. Wolcott, McHenry, and Pickering immediately, and covertly, divulged to Hamilton what had transpired, and requested their marching orders.[7] It began a pattern of false-hearted conduct that continued unabated for the next three years.

What they heard from Hamilton must have rocked the cabinet officers on their heels. He endorsed Adams' plan for a multimember commission, even welcoming a Republican among its members, but he stressed that America must convince France that it was not supine. Hamilton urged an upgrade of the navy, cavalry, and artillery, and the creation of a twenty-five-thousand-man provisional army. Incredibly, the three trucklers in the cabinet switched course and passed along Hamilton's recommendations as their own.[8]

That was largely the course that Adams took. In mid-May he welcomed Congress to its special session with a militant speech in which he urged everything that Hamilton had proposed, save a provisional army. In addition, he ultimately sent to Paris a bipartisan diplomatic team that included Pinckney, John Marshall—a Virginia Federalist—and Elbridge Gerry, who had been an Anti-Federalist and now was a Republican.[9]

The Republicans, who had demanded a bellicose policy in the face of London's commercial depredations in 1794, now excoriated Adams for his pugnacity. After listening in stunned silence, Jefferson privately carped that Adams' "inflammatory" remarks would create a spirit that would inevitably drive the nation toward war. Adams learned of Jefferson's criticism, and, hurt by what he believed was fresh proof of hypocrisy on the part of his supposed friend, roared privately that Jefferson's comments were "evidence of a mind, soured, yet seeking for popularity, and eaten to a honeycomb with ambition, yet weak, confused, uninformed, and ignorant."[10]

The Republican press swiftly turned on Adams. This was an about-face, as most of its editors, including Benjamin Franklin Bache, who published the Philadelphia *Aurora*, had treated Adams gently since his victory. Anticipating the exclusion of Hamilton and his acolytes from the inner circle of power within the executive branch, the *Aurora* had portrayed the incoming president as more republican than his predecessor—"ADAMS is an Aristocrat only in theory, but . . . WASHINGTON is one in practice"—and limned Adams as "incorruptible" and too independent ever to be "the tool of any man or set of men."[11] But the kid-glove treatment ended abruptly following Adams' speech.[12] The *Aurora* laid down a barrage against the president that would not cease during his term. It disparaged the commission that he was sending to Paris as consisting largely of Francophobes. It alternately portrayed Adams as an Anglophile and as a toady of the war hawks Pickering and Wolcott, who in turn were delineated as the minions of Hamilton, the real leader of the Federalist Party. Bache even urged Adams to resign before his masters used him to drag the nation into a ruinous war.[13] Other Republican scribes sneered that Adams, elected by only three votes, lacked a national mandate for pursuing such a combative policy, and many contended that his "mad projects" would have the United States and France at war before Christmas.[14]

With Madison recently married and retired to Montpelier, Jefferson took charge of organizing the opposition to the Federalists in Congress. Jefferson cultivated an image of detachment, and many of his foes were led to think of him as a dreamy, insular utopian. In reality, while he served as secretary of state, and now during his vice presidency, Jefferson was a meticulous, hands-on politician. His coterie of myrmidons (he characterized similar men in Hamilton's orbit as flatterers) gathered and brought him information and gossip. He devoured newspapers, listened to the Senate oratory, and grew masterful at the art of eliciting dinner-table scuttlebutt. He entertained regularly, bringing carefully selected guests to his table, where he pumped them in such an adroit manner that few realized what was occurring. Through these means he was unsurpassed in his knowledge of the habits and inclinations of numerous members of Congress. In addition, he was peerless at circulating rumor and innuendo and at fleshing out the Republican Party position. Jefferson also provided assistance—financial and otherwise—to Republican editors and penmen, including Bache and James Thomson Callender, a recent immigrant from Scotland who contributed hard-hitting essays to the *Aurora*.[15] And in the summer of 1797 these skills were partially responsible for the Republicans' success in blocking, or modifying, much of the Federalist military-preparedness program. The bill for a provisional army died quietly, and the naval buildup was scaled back to nothing more than putting previously funded construction projects on the fast track. Otherwise, Congress gave Adams what he had requested, including enhanced coastal defenses and authority to summon up to eighty thousand militiamen.[16]

Meanwhile, Jefferson's zealous commitment to the French Revolution cooled. Driven by the conviction that peace was crucial to the preservation of the republican gains secured by the American Revolution, Jefferson now counseled that true neutrality was the only prudent course for the United States.[17] As recently as the previous summer he had rejoiced unabashedly at French victories, and in May he had been ready to proclaim his willingness "to join my [French] brethren in European wars."[18] However, in mid-1797 he saw that anything short of a stance of absolute American independence of Europe would someday lead to undesired hostilities. Now his mantra was that "if we engage in a war during our present passions and our present weakness, our union runs the greatest risk of not coming out of that war in the shape in which it enters it."[19]

What did not change was Jefferson's cogent understanding of the linkage of foreign policy and domestic objectives. He saw clearly that the merchant class, through its economic leverage and ability to dominate the media (they "possess our printing presses," he allowed), had become the "most influential characters in and out of office" in all the northern states. Their loyalty, he went on, was solely to their economic well-being, which was best served through the United States' close ties to Great Britain. By "placing our public finances under their controul," he charged, the Hamiltonian revolution had vested a small class lodged in the eastern seaports with undue influence in every branch of the national government. "[O]ur merchants," he added, held in their hands the power to "bend the interests of this country entirely to the will of another." This imperiled American independence and foreshadowed the "bondage" of the citizenry. Against this tyranny, he believed, stood the Republican Party. Its mission, he now knew, was "to recover self-government" in order to "resist submission" to Britain. Obliquely, Jefferson spoke for the first time of a second revolutionary struggle. Independence had come in 1776, but now, two decades removed, American autonomy was again threatened, and by the identical forces that had earlier menaced colonial freedoms: America's Tory merchants, who controlled the Federalist Party, and Great Britain.[20]

To Jefferson, Hamilton remained the malevolent sorcerer who threatened what the American Revolution was meant to be. Even while out of
power, Hamilton's long reach extended to the epicenter of the executive
branch. Jefferson had come to believe that Hamilton had beguiled, perhaps even controlled, Washington. Now, he believed, those in Adams'
cabinet whom he labeled Hamilton's "Rogues" were manipulating the
new president. Jefferson was more certain than ever that the end sought
by Hamilton and his confederates was to have "none but tories hereafter
into any departments of [the federal] government" and to use the power
of that government to bury the states.[21]

Jefferson was hardly a dispassionate observer, and the conclusions he
had reached about Hamilton by 1797 were filled with half-truths. He was
correct in deducing that Hamilton wished to expand the power and boundaries of the United States, and in fact in his published writings since 1774
the New Yorker had often spoken wistfully of the day when an independent America would possess the strength to defend itself, secure its interests, and pursue its "grandeur and glory."[22] What Jefferson did not know
was that Hamilton had actually restrained his satraps in Adams' cabinet.
Hamilton fretted that the American public was not as outraged by French
depredations as it had been when Britain had violated American commerce. He wished to arouse his countrymen's anger at this abuse of national integrity and to prepare the country for what might be an
unavoidable war, but for the time being he hoped to avoid hostilities. He
feared that France, with help from the Indians in the Southwest, and possibly from some southerners, would be a potent adversary, and that if prod-
ded into war it might take New Orleans and Florida from its European
adversary Spain, confronting the United States with a worse predicament.[23]

Given the lag in communications, the Quasi-War Crisis, as scholars now
call the Franco-American troubles, simmered quietly out of sight for
months. As Gerry and Marshall did not sail until the summer of 1797
was half gone, Adams went home in July and did not return to Philadelphia until deep into the autumn, when that year's siege of yellow fever—
it had struck every year for five years running—finally lifted. Jefferson
stayed away even longer, and when he finally returned he was cautiously
optimistic. Perhaps the silence of the envoys meant that all had gone
well, though he worried that the Ultra-Federalists, the Hamiltonian extremists, were "panting to come to blows" and might invent a crisis.[24]

Jefferson thought Philadelphia a dreary place that winter, and not just
because of the damp cold. Partisanship had decimated the "pleasures of

society," he lamented, as invitations to galas hosted by those in high society had dried up for Republicans. The "high political passions" had usurped old friendships and ruined the possibility of amicable ties with those who differed politically. Previously, adversaries spoke to one another cordially, but now men "who have been intimate all their lives, cross the streets to avoid meeting, and turn their heads another way, lest they should be obliged to touch their hats." He envied those outside public life, who not only enjoyed "the society of their friendly neighbors" but—unlike the members of Congress—tended to "something every day which looks usefully to futurity." The party divisions that inhibited conviviality away from Congress Hall also encouraged rancorous battles, and even violence, on the House floor. In January, in the course of a tempestuous debate, Congressman Roger Griswold, a patrician Connecticut Federalist, insulted Matthew Lyon, an Irish-born Vermont Republican who in his youth had been an indentured servant (he once was sold by a master for a couple of head of livestock). Lyon retaliated by spitting in Griswold's face, and Griswold in turn thrashed the Vermonter with a cane. Lyon fought back with fire tongs. The brawl ended only when colleagues separated the gladiators, who by then were punching and kicking each other as they rolled about the chamber floor.[25]

Just days later, on March 4, the first anniversary of his having assumed the presidency, Adams learned that the French foreign minister, Charles-Maurice de Talleyrand-Périgord, had refused to receive the American envoys. Instead, they had been met by secret agents who demanded bribes and an apology from Adams—for his truculent speech to Congress—before the envoys would be permitted to see Talleyrand.

Adams was indignant. He raged that he would ask Congress for a declaration of war. By the next morning, however, the president had gotten a grip on himself. He released only one dispatch from the commissioners, a letter dated two months earlier that merely said that the mission had failed because no hope existed of being officially received by the French government.[26] Then he met with the cabinet to decide on the proper response. Throughout the winter, Adams and his cabinet had deliberated on the proper course to follow should their diplomacy fail. McHenry and Wolcott—after dutifully eliciting Hamilton's thoughts—had steadfastly recommended against a declaration of war. Pickering had concurred but proposed an alliance with Great Britain and a military campaign to seize Louisiana from Spain, on the pretext that otherwise France soon would take it from Madrid.[27] Each also favored expanding the existing army and creating a large provisional army, to be paid for

"Congressional Pugilists." This cartoon satirizes the brawl between Roger Griswold and Matthew Lyon on the floor of the House of Representatives in 1798. After Lyon spat in his face, Griswold (as the illustration depicts) came after him with a cane. Lyon retaliated, as shown, with fireplace tongs.

with a tax increase. The burden of responsibility fell on Adams. Though often accused by his enemies of acting impulsively while in the grip of passion, Adams wrestled with his choices for more than two weeks before reaching a decision. In the end, he decided against asking for war. Nor did he release the dispatches sent by the envoys, fearing that he would be compelled to go to war by the public outcry that was certain to follow. The message that he finally sent to Congress reiterated his plea for defensive preparations, including strengthening the navy and the enactment of new taxes. However, he did not request the creation of a provisional army or the expansion of the existing force.[28]

Hamilton was "delighted" with Adams' performance, save for his failure to urge the creation of a provisional army. To secure that end, he rushed into print a series of anonymous essays that vilified the Republicans as trucklers to the French and beat the drums for the creation of "a respectable army . . . led by a skillful and daring Chief!" Hamilton's glee was matched by Jefferson's despair. The vice president privately characterized Adams' message as "insane" and insisted that the president was Hamilton's "stalking horse" for bringing on war. Watching with what he called "gloomy apprehensions," Jefferson concluded that war now was as unavoidable as it was unnecessary. Madison concurred, questioning only his friend's belief that Adams was being manipulated by Hamilton. The president, he asserted, was a hothead bent on war, a "perfect Quixote as a Statesman."[29]

Many Republicans suspected that Adams had misrepresented the dispatches sent home by the American envoys, seeking to stampede Congress into an unprovoked war. Others believed it a manufactured crisis designed to aid the Federalists in state elections that spring. In this frame of mind, the Republican press and several congressmen launched a campaign to force Adams to divulge the contents of the dispatches.[30] If ever a political ploy backfired, this was it. Adams immediately complied with their wishes. He censored only the names of the French agents who had demanded bribes, identifying them as Agents X, Y, and Z. Instantly,

A New Display of the United States by Amos Doolittle, 1799.
This engraving, done after the rupture in the Federalist Party over Adams' policies toward France during the Quasi-War Crisis, nevertheless shows popular approval of the president.

Jefferson saw that his party had blundered egregiously. He said that the revelation of the XYZ Affair, as it became known, threw the "public mind . . . in[to] a state of astonishment" that removed all impediments to the enactment of "the war measures so furiously pushed by the other party."[31]

The crisis suddenly took on a momentum that left Adams feeling as though he was losing control. Soon he feared that not only would he be unable to resist extreme or intemperate measures that might inevitably bring on hostilities, but he might have to lead a deeply divided public into war. Losing weight and growing pale under the relentless pressure, he set out that spring to rally opinion. He took to appearing in public in a military uniform with a sword strapped to his side. Repeatedly he is-sued addresses that resonated with combativeness, expatiating on the similarities between the plight faced by the generation of 1798 and that of their forebears, who had met threats posed by hostile Indians in the colonial era and by Great Britain in 1776. The stakes, he declared, were extraordinary: the survival of American independence, republicanism, and the Union. Nevertheless, he made it clear that he would ask for war only as a last resort, and he frequently inserted a passage in his messages stipulating that his goal was peace on honorable terms.[32]

Adams soon discovered not only that a consensus was building be-hind his position but that for the first time in his long public career his popularity was zooming into the stratosphere. Federalists gushed at his "manly fortitude" and the "noble part" he was playing in "get[ting] rid of every tie which bound us to . . . seductive & perfidious" France.[33] The populace, inflamed by France's overt insult, rallied behind the president. He was received with gusto when he ventured forth, and on one occasion thousands of young men sporting black cockades paraded through Philadelphia's steamy, restless streets to the President's House, where they cheered themselves hoarse until Adams appeared. Large, respectful crowds greeted him when he traveled home to Quincy in midsummer, and some observers believed that the reception given him in New York City in July exceeded the tumultuous welcomes that the city had bestowed on Wash-ington. Some Federalists even privately said that they believed Adams' popularity now equaled that of Washington, and one exclaimed that he "will go down to posterity with greater lustre" than his predecessor.[34]

Patriotism soared, moving the wife of Britain's minister to remark that "this country breathes war."[35] In this atmosphere the Federalists pushed through their program. By July Congress had created the Department of the Navy, authorized the construction or refitting of thirty-seven warships, armed merchant vessels, and upgraded coastal fortifications. It was all to be paid for with revenue raised through new taxes on land, houses, and slaves. Adams had urged these measures. Congress also took steps Adams had not asked for. It more than tripled the existing army—to ten thousand men—and created a provisional army of another ten thousand as well, embargoed all trade with France, and abrogated the Franco-American treaties that the joyous public had welcomed twenty years before.[36]

Congress failed only to declare war, a step that many Ultra-Federalists had sought. War, said one, was the best way to silence forever the "factious, cutthroat, frog-eating, treaty-breaking, grace fallen God-defying devils" in Paris.[37] On July 1 the radicals secured a party caucus to consider declaring war, but the votes were not there. Rebuffed, the war faction settled for congressional authorization to seize any French vessel that imperiled American commerce, a step that was tantamount to an undeclared war. The Federalist-dominated Congress had gone further than Adams wished. On the other hand, it had done everything that Hamilton had covertly asked of it.[38]

Throughout that spring and summer the Republican press blasted its opponents, painting a lurid tableau of what lay ahead. The war that surely loomed would cost a king's ransom, it was said, and would culminate in an Anglo-American alliance that once again would leave British soldiers quartered in American homes. Adams was portrayed as the puppet of a cabinet that "fed him upon pepperpot . . . to bring his nerves to a proper anti-gallic tone."[39] Mostly, however, the Republicans were on the defensive, having been "taken by surprise" by the XYZ revelations. Even Jefferson acknowledged that his party comrades were "seeking on every side some hole to get out at, like an animal first put into a cage."[40]

Jefferson fell to agonized brooding, but he also held to the hope that the Federalists, who now could "carry what they please," would overreach and suffer a fatal self-inflicted wound. He did not have long to wait. Amid open talk of suppressing the *Aurora* and silencing Callender (by deportation, if necessary), Ultra-Federalist congressmen struck swiftly and harshly in high summer, pushing into law measures that curtailed civil liberties— the Alien and Sedition Acts. The Sedition Act, a naked step toward silencing the opposition press, was the most oppressive of the four measures. It provided for fines up to $5,000 and jail terms of up to five years for those who uttered or published "any false, scandalous, and malicious" statement against the United States government or its officials.[41] The other acts vested the president with the authority to deport aliens and increased the period that immigrants must wait to become citizens—and perhaps voters—from five to fourteen years.

Adams had not requested this legislation. Nor had Hamilton, who intervened with little success to palliate its severity. "Let us not be cruel or violent," he pleaded with party members, warning that "there are limits which must not be passed." "Let us not establish a tyranny." Hamilton feared a backlash. If the government "breathe[s] an irregular or violent spirit," its conduct "will do harm . . . to the cause." And with uncommon prescience, he said that he feared the zealots in his party would "push things to an extreme" and once again "give to faction [the Republican Party] *body* & solidarity."[42]

This time, however, Hamilton could not control the Ultras. Some, such as Senator Theodore Sedgwick of Massachusetts, who after 1776 had opposed the draconian legislation levied against the loyalists, ardently fought for the Alien and Sedition Acts. He and others candidly acknowledged that the French crisis afforded the Federalists "a glorious opportunity to destroy [the Republican] faction."[43] From the moment that the XYZ dispatches were made public, many Federalist newspapers had demanded that "traitors must be silent." Fenno's *Gazette of the United States* came up with a slogan: "*He that is not for us, is against us.*"[44] Fenno additionally decreed: "It is patriotism to write in favor of government— it is sedition to write against it."[45] This was the hour of retribution—the opportunity, under the cloak of national security, to settle old scores and to lay low a political opponent that had grown steadily more powerful over the past half dozen years. During the public discussion that took place while the sedition bill was under consideration, many Federalists took aim at the vice president, portraying him as the "Chief Juggler," manager, and moneybags behind the most important Republican newspapers. One denounced him as "the grandest of all Villains . . . that infernal Scoundrel Jefferson," a "traitor to his country."[46] Adams signed the bills into law, a step that would subsequently be seen as the greatest blot on his presidency. He did not defend his action at the time, and later he never offered a convincing defense for having accepted these repressive measures. It was a step that was consistent with his philosophy of governance, which was largely to acquiesce to Congress on domestic matters while jealously guarding the president's prerogative in the area of foreign policy. What is more, faced with what at the time appeared to be a virtually certain war, Adams must have been desperate to hold his party together, even at the cost of accepting what was demanded by the extremists within its ranks. However, the simplest explanation for his behavior is that he was comfortable with draconian measures against those whom he perceived to be dangerous to national security.

Jefferson, meanwhile, watched in horror. He gloomily remarked that the Federalists were emulating the radical French revolutionaries. Like the Jacobins, their plan was to foment and maintain a crisis atmosphere, for the people were more manipulable in the supercharged air of heightened tension. He also despaired that the Federalists, whom he had fought to a standstill between 1792 and 1797, had regained the whip hand. They controlled the presidency and Congress. They had ground the Bill of Rights under their heel and were certain to keep "warring against" the "real principles" on which the new nation stood. He shuddered that there was "no length" to which they would not go, and "no event, therefore, however atrocious, which may not be expected." Yet through it all, Jefferson remained optimistic. Time and events ultimately would "bring round an order of things" synonymous with the spirit of 1776. It had to occur, he said, because most Americans yet cherished the true meaning of the American Revolution.[47]

8

"Our Bonaparte"

Summer 1798 to Autumn 1799

HAMILTON BELIEVED that the military-preparedness steps taken by Congress had almost put the nation "where we ought now to be." Although he publicly characterized these as defensive measures, Hamilton quietly, and only among his closest confidants, spoke of more aggressive designs. Florida and Louisiana were the "key of the Western Country," he declared, and their possession was "essential to the permanency of the Union." It was his view that the "whole land force" of the United States should be used to seize Spain's dominions from St. Augustine to New Orleans. When military operations began, he added, the "command . . . would very naturally fall upon me."[1] This was because during the summer of 1798 Washington had accepted Adams' offer to serve as commander of the Provisional Army, but on two conditions: that he be permitted to remain at Mount Vernon until a French invasion was imminent, and that Hamilton be named inspector general, the second in command. Adams abhorred the prospect of Hamilton being in charge while the titular commander languished at home, but he dared not challenge Washington.[2]

Hamilton was not ready to share his grandiose plans with the public, but for some observers the frenetic push by the Ultra-Federalists to create the army, then to get it into Hamilton's hands, was akin to watching the pieces of a puzzle come together. However, not everyone interpreted the emerging picture in the same manner. Some believed that the Federalists simply sought to put General Hamilton in a position to ladle out posts in the burgeoning officer corps, a proven way to build a political faction. Others feared that Hamilton and his allies plotted a more sinister course, including using the army to enforce the Alien and Sedition Acts, much as the British ministry in the 1760s had planned to use its regulars to implement parliamentary taxation.[3] There were also those who surmised that Hamilton, impulsive for glory, was a military adventurer. They saw him as a dashing and dangerous figure with unsettling similarities to Napoleon, who just now was beginning to cut a swath across Europe. The First Lady, for instance, called Hamilton "a second Buonaparty." Jefferson thought him "our Buonaparte."[4] Abigail Adams had never trusted Hamilton. Two years before, she had warned her husband that she "read his heart in his wicked eyes" and found that the "very devil is in there."[5] Jefferson had distrusted Hamilton since 1791, when at a dinner party he had heard him proclaim that Julius Caesar was the greatest man who ever lived.[6]

The events of that summer were something of an epiphany for Adams. He had never been comfortable with Hamilton, in whom he saw an unslakable "delirium of Ambition," and since the election of 1796 the president had believed that Hamilton "hated every man young or old who Stood in his Way" in his never-ending quest after "the highest Station in America. " Even so, no dustups between the two men had occurred during the initial eighteen months of Adams' presidency.[7] However, once Adams became aware of how hard Washington had worked to secure the inspector general post for Hamilton, he believed that he saw matters with greater clarity. He now came to suspect that Hamilton not only had been manipulating some of his cabinet secretaries but had exploited President Washington as well. "Washington . . . was only a viceroy under Hamilton, and Hamilton was viceroy under the tories," Adams concluded. The president was veering toward Jefferson's outlook. He too was beginning to believe that Hamilton harbored adventurous designs, and like the vice president, Adams took to referring privately to Hamilton as "Caesar."[8]

While Adams wrestled with these troubling thoughts, Jefferson watched in despair, for the first time suspecting that his foes might be invincible. How, he wondered, could the Federalists be contested should a free press be destroyed? In his darkest moments Jefferson even feared that Hamilton, in a desperate effort to extinguish the last vestiges of dissent, would invade

Virginia with his Provisional Army, much as he had led an armed force into western Pennsylvania to suppress the Whiskey Rebellion.[9] Less than a quarter century after the Declaration of Independence, Jefferson concluded that Hamilton held the hammer over the American anvil.

Faced with a national government that had become a "foreign jurisdiction . . . pregnant of abuse," the vice president decided during that pivotal summer to undertake an astounding act.[10] Jefferson was a revolutionary who had risked life and limb for American independence. He had also hazarded his public career to conspire with republican radicals in Paris in 1789. He remained a risk taker, and in 1798 he settled on a desperate, high-stakes ploy. Confident that most Americans had never desired a national government of the scope and strength that the Federalists were now seeking, Jefferson readied a profound challenge.

Jefferson took to his desk at Monticello in the last hot days of summer and wrote that the framers at the Constitutional Convention—delegates who represented twelve separate states, not the nation—had formed a "compact" to vest the national government with certain explicit powers but leave the "residuary mass" of the people's "rights to their own self-government" within the states. Yet, Jefferson asked, who now was to determine if the national government overstepped the bounds assigned it in the Constitution? No "common judge" existed, and it would be ludicrous for federal authorities to be the "final judge of the extent of powers delegated to itself." Each state would have to decide. Each state, he insisted, must have the authority to declare improper steps taken by the national government to be "void, and of no force" within its jurisdiction.[11] The vice president had drafted a doctrine of state nullification. What Jefferson had proposed was nothing less than the overthrow of the constitutional settlement of 1787–88, for nullification would have emasculated the national government and restored the states to the predominant position they had occupied under the Articles of Confederation. This was a dangerous enterprise, and Jefferson cloaked his authorship under a mantle of secrecy, then had an acquaintance shepherd his anonymous statement through the Kentucky legislature, while Madison's friends pushed a nearly similar resolution through the Virginia assembly early in 1799. However, by the time the Virginia and Kentucky Resolutions had been enacted, President Adams had taken steps that dramatically altered the nature of things.[12]

Adams, together with virtually every member of Congress, fled Philadelphia in July, hoping to escape before the yellow fever resurfaced. Abigail

fell ill during the trip home, but not from the fever. Her husband described her symptoms as "almost a diabetes." Nabby said it was a "Bil-
ious disorder." A biographer has concluded that Abigail experienced a
physical collapse brought on by the strain of her—and her husband's—
public responsibilities and from worry over her children.[13]

This was to have been an especially joyous vacation. Without telling
her husband of her plans, Abigail had decided to expand Peacefield. Work
had begun the previous autumn, as soon as the president and First Lady
departed for Philadelphia, and was managed in her absence by a cousin
who lived nearby. A wing consisting of a downstairs parlor for Abigail
and a second-floor library for John was added to the house, and the

Abigail Adams by Gilbert Stuart, 1800/1815. Stuart began this portrait in
1800, when the First Lady was fifty-six and the presidential election was
under way. The painting was not completed for several years.

existing dwelling received a fresh coat of paint and other cosmetic improvements. It was to have been a surprise for Adams, but a Quincy neighbor accidentally let the cat out of the bag during a visit with the president in Philadelphia in June. Adams was not angry. In fact, he was delighted and had relished this trip home more than most. Instead, this vacation turned into the dreariest he had ever experienced, for Adams feared that Abigail might be dying. Indeed, it was only when the first signs of autumn were apparent, about three months after she first fell ill, that she at last showed signs of improvement, and even then for some time she remained too weak to read or write.[14]

Distraught throughout the summer over Abigail's illness, and enervated by summer temperatures that seemed to be stuck in the nineties and on several occasions topped a hundred degrees, Adams did little work before October. At times he refused even to receive visitors who came on political business. But as Abigail improved, he began to regularly correspond with the members of his cabinet and to pore over diplomatic communiqués. As his thoughts returned to the French crisis during his final days at home, Adams made only one decision: he would not ask Congress to declare war. With Hamilton in command of the army, Adams was more anxious than ever to avoid war, and more convinced than ever that the army was not needed. That autumn he told McHenry that "there is no more prospect of seeing a french Army here, than there is in Heaven," a sign that a sea change had occurred in the president's thinking since the onset of the XYZ crisis.[15]

Adams delayed his departure for the capital until mid-November, when Abigail finally was well enough to come downstairs. The journey that followed was perhaps the worst of the near score of trips that he made over the years between Massachusetts and Philadelphia. The First Lady, of course, was unable to accompany him, and Adams left knowing that he would not see her again for five months or more. He was so concerned and lonely that he sat apart from the others when the presidential party stopped from time to time to water the horses, devoting his time to drafting missives to Abigail. He wrote still more in the evenings. His journey was made all the worse when first he suffered a recurrence of pyorrhea, which caused his face to swell painfully, and later when the weather turned blustery and cold, with early-season snow showers. The only good news was that this was perhaps the fastest of all his trips between New England and the Delaware Valley. He alighted at the President's House just thirteen days after the journey began.[16]

Jefferson summered at home as well, leaving the capital before Congress adjourned in order to escape what he called the Federalists' "follies." One of Virginia's senators promised to keep him informed of happenings in Philadelphia—"if I am not Guilotined" by the Federalists, he waggishly added.[17] Like Adams, Jefferson remained at home longer than he had intended—for five months—mostly to superintend the never-ending construction of Monticello, as he had reached the dismaying conclusion that progress was possible only when he could keep an eye on the workers.[18] Jefferson finally departed for Philadelphia in mid-December, and on his return he noted that the crowds were smaller than they had been on his homebound journey in the spring. He immediately concluded that the new taxes, a standing army, and the Alien and Sedition Acts had acted as "powerful sedatives" against the hot temper of the earlier times, causing the citizenry to reexamine "the XYZ dish cooked up" by the Federalists.[19] When he reached the capital, Jefferson read Adams' State of the Union address, delivered three weeks earlier, and to his surprise discovered that the president had been "so unlike himself in point of moderation."[20]

Jefferson was intuitive. The Adams who returned to Philadelphia in November differed in striking ways from the man who had left it in July. He came back determined to control his administration and to break free of those in the cabinet who had controlled him. While at home he had brooded over the meaning of Hamilton's appointment as the real commander of the Provisional Army and over his own powerlessness in the episode. Before leaving Quincy, Adams resolved that henceforth if "I shall ultimately be the dupe of [intrigue], I am much mistaken in myself."[21]

If he was clear on that score, Adams' views on how to respond to France were still jelling when he returned to the capital, but he was coming to believe that the French government was ready for an accommodation. Shortly before leaving Quincy, he had been visited by Gerry, who had stayed on in Paris for months after Pinckney and Marshall came home. Gerry had met often with officials, high and low, and was convinced that France desired peace with the United States and would welcome the dispatch of another American envoy.[22] On Adams' first day back in Philadelphia, he met with Dr. George Logan, a Philadelphia Quaker who had traveled privately to Paris in mid-1798, where he had been received by Talleyrand. He also told Adams that France was ready to receive an American minister.[23] Washington passed along similar tidings from his acquaintances in Paris, as did William Vans Murray, minister to the Hague, and John Quincy, now minister to Prussia. Unofficial letters from Talleyrand also reached Adams' desk that promised respectful treatment for any American diplomat who might be sent to Paris.[24]

Two other factors shaped the president's thoughts. During his journey to the capital, Adams—like Jefferson—had noted that the crowds that greeted him were smaller and less demonstrative than they had been in July. He too concluded that the war fever had abated. That autumn, moreover, eastern Pennsylvania was rocked by protests against the new taxes. While the president denounced those who broke the law, he privately welcomed the less bellicose mood, knowing that it would give him a freer hand to pursue peace. In fact, just as he had ratcheted up public opinion over the summer, Adams now sought to defuse the hysteria, taking pains in his State of the Union message to emphasize his adherence to a "humane and pacific" policy. He added that while "we do not fear . . . war, we shall give no room to infer that we abandon the desire of peace. . . . It is peace that we have uniformly and perseveringly cultivated."[25]

Adams' views had taken shape slowly since the summer. He had gradually come to believe that the French crisis could be peacefully, and honorably, resolved through another diplomatic mission, but initially he planned to take no steps until he received Paris' official assurance that America's diplomats would be received. In the end, however, Adams acted without waiting for further word from Talleyrand. He was stirred to act by the receipt of troubling new information about Hamilton. For weeks rumors had swirled about the capital that Hamilton was plotting to use his army against the Spanish in Florida and the southwestern country, and even to unleash it on Virginia. Adams had given the tattle little credence until mid-February, when a Federalist insider showed him copies of private letters written recently by Hamilton. The general had bloviated about "taking possession of those countries [Spanish Florida and Louisiana] for ourselves" before France got its hands on them. He had also waxed on about the Virginia and Kentucky Resolutions, and the radical dissenters in Virginia who wished "to break down [the United States] constitution" and destroy the Union. "[W]ith a view to the possibility of internal disorders" below the Potomac or in the western region, Hamilton added, he would need a sizeable force to suppress this "regular conspiracy to overturn the government." To this he added: "When a clever force has been collected let them be drawn towards Virginia for which there is an obvious pretext & put Virginia to the Test of resistance."[26]

To Adams' thinking, this was proof of Hamilton's treachery, the veritable smoking gun that explained the behavior of the Ultra-Federalists

since his first day on the job. In the high-voltage atmosphere that prevailed within the President's House that winter, Hamilton's letters made
an extraordinary impression on Adams, much as had the purloined
Hutchinson letters in 1773. Hutchinson's secret correspondence led Adams
to the conclusion that a grand trans-Atlantic conspiracy existed to eradi-
cate colonial liberties. Hamilton's machinations, seemingly laid bare in
these missives, appeared to aim at the prevention of a peaceful settlement with France. War, Adams concluded, would ensure Hamilton the
opportunity to employ the army for his personal advancement and the
enhancement of the Ultra-Federalists who backed him. From that day
forward Adams believed Hamilton was "the most restless, impatient,
artful, indefatigable and unprincipled Intriguer" in the land, a charlatan
who had treacherously conspired "to close the avenues to peace, and to
ensure a war with France."[27]

A decade earlier in the *Defence*, Adams had written of the imperative need for the United States to have a powerful chief executive who
could act as "father and protector" of the people and the nation. That
official—the only official in the United States who was elected to represent people throughout the nation—was to be the caretaker of national
security and the guardian of both the citizenry and republicanism against
rapacious private interests and evildoers. In 1799 Adams believed that he
had no choice but to act as the father and protector to save republicanism and the infant nation from sinister forces within his own political
party. He decided to send an envoy to Paris immediately and to announce
his decision without first having consulted his cabinet, a step that he
had never before taken on a substantive matter. He believed he had no
other choice. If forewarned, several of his cabinet secretaries might resign in protest, destroying his peace initiative before it began. He knew
that springing this surprise would be risky business. To blindside his
party was to hazard tearing irreparable fissures in its structure, damage
that would jeopardize his chances both of being nominated in 1800 and
of winning reelection. Yet if his decision was politically ill-advised, it
was an act of supreme statesmanship. He risked the loss of his office and
his reputation to pursue what he saw as essential for the survival of the
nation and the American Revolution. Adams struck on February 18. He
sent a message to Congress announcing that he was dispatching William
Vans Murray to France as a minister plenipotentiary. He was acting, he
said, on the "plausible appearance or probability of restoring tranquility." Jefferson realized immediately what this meant: Adams' bold act
"renders desperate every further effort towards war."[28]

Republican scribes were ecstatic (they were "slovering Adams with their praise," Pickering raged), while a firestorm raged within the Federalists' ranks.[29] Many fumed with "Surprise, indignation, grief & disgust," according to a New England party stalwart. "[A]lmost universal disgust" and incredulity was aroused by the president's sudden announcement, proclaimed another Ultra.[30] Some Federalists found Adams' action inexplicable, unless of course he was out of his mind. One hinted darkly that Adams was an "evil" to the party and nation, and another even prayed that on his next trip to Quincy he might suffer a fatal carriage accident. Several despaired that he had wrecked everything they sought, including the hoped-for destruction of the revolutionaries in France.[31] The one thing the Ultra-Federalists agreed on was that Adams would "never recover from the wound he gave himself." In the face of his act, a congressman declared, "a total loss of confidence" now existed "in the wisdom and prudence" of the president. Virtually without exception, the radical members of the Federalist Party shook with an inextinguishable *deep rooted disgust* toward Adams, more than one said.[32] Within hours of Adams' dramatic step, at least one meeting was arranged between the president, his cabinet, and high-ranking Federalists in Congress. No record of what transpired has survived, save that Adams hinted that the session was stormy and that he made two concessions. Rather than sending a lone plenipotentiary, he agreed to send three envoys—ultimately he named Chief Justice Oliver Ellsworth and William Davie, the governor of North Carolina, to join Murray—and he consented to postpone their departure until further assurance was received from Paris.[33] Two weeks after his daring act, Congress adjourned without expanding the army, once a cherished aim of the Ultras. Thereafter, Adams, weary and disheartened, departed for Quincy, where he remained for seven months, prompting many Ultra-Federalists to grumble venomously that he had virtually abdicated the presidency. Actually, Adams had few peers when it came to industry, and he appears to have kept to his job while at Peacefield. The post rider arrived at his door daily with correspondence and reports from officials, including his department heads. The diplomatic pouch, bulging with materials from abroad, came regularly as well.[34] Adams read everything, and on average he wrote a letter to one or another member of his cabinet every third day. He believed this was adequate, as Congress was not in session and there was little to be done with regard to the French crisis until definitive word arrived from Europe. Yet his protracted absence from Philadelphia isolated him from the public and especially from those within his party who wished for an approachable and visible leader.

Adams left Peacefield only four times in the course of his long stay. He attended the graduation ceremony at Harvard, participated in Boston's July 4 parade, launched a warship in nearby Boston Harbor, and reviewed the Boston Artillery Company (donning full military garb for the occasion). Otherwise, throughout the summer Adams betrayed signs that his burdens were getting the best of him. Evincing a melancholy born of the belief that his presidency was ruined, his appetite disappeared and he lost weight. His fretful wife was driven to purchase nine barrels of apple cider in the hope that its restorative powers might help. Adams' temper steadily soured as well, resulting in numerous unpleasant incidents. When General Knox called at Peacefield, Adams treated him with a contemptuous incivility, and when a group of naval officers and Harvard students came unannounced for a visit, he irascibly scolded them for appearing without an invitation. At one point his mood grew so black that the First Lady tried to keep state papers out of his hands, fearing he might take some action that he would later regret.[35]

However, Adams' dark mood did not extend to the enforcement of the Alien and Sedition Acts. Pickering, who was the chief enforcement officer, repeatedly beseeched the president to sign orders for the deportation of aliens. Adams considered numerous cases but signed orders banishing only three aliens, all Frenchmen who, as it turned out, had already fled the country. He additionally—and mischievously—considered employing either the Alien Friends Act or the Sedition Act against William Cobbett, a British citizen who edited the Federalist *Porcupine Gazette*, an inflammatory journal that heaped vitriol upon the president for having opted to pursue negotiations with France. If he was serious about Cobbett, Adams shrank from acting. Nevertheless, his administration strenuously enforced the Sedition Act. At least seventeen indictments were handed down, two of which Adams vigorously defended in private.[36]

Meanwhile, Adams closely followed the news from Europe, and by midsummer 1799 he concluded that the time had come to order Ellsworth and Davie to sail. He had learned that a majority of the Directory had been ousted in a coup d'état in June. In addition, Murray sent him several optimistic reports. The clincher, however, came on August 6, when at last he received assurances from Talleyrand. That same day Adams directed Pickering to ready the instructions for his envoys' immediate departure and indicated that he expected they would sail by the end of the month. He pointedly told his secretary of state: "I expect the cooperation of the heads of departments."[37]

Pickering, however, did not cooperate. While Adams enjoyed the last warm days of summer in New England, the secretary of state quietly stalled, hoping to prevent any action until Adams came to the capital, probably late in November—a ploy designed to keep the French crisis percolating through the election of 1800. But Adams learned of Pickering's latest treachery from Benjamin Stoddert, his secretary of the navy, an official whom the president had chosen after the department was created in 1798. Stoddert, never part of Hamilton's clique, warned Adams against those "artful, designing men" in the cabinet who were plotting to destroy the peace initiative and, perhaps, Adams' hopes for reelection. He urged Adams to come to the capital at once.[38] Adams might have immediately dismissed Pickering for insubordination, but more than ever he feared to do so. The Federalist Party was hanging together by the slenderest of threads, and an open break between Adams and Pickering—men who represented the two poles of the frangible party—could prove fatal to the president's chances of renomination or his reelection in 1800. However, Adams did cut short his vacation and on September 30 departed for Trenton, where the governmental heads had fled to escape Philadelphia's latest bout with yellow fever.

His nerves already frayed, Adams learned while passing through New York that Charles, his second son, who now was twenty-nine, had been ruined by alcoholism. That malady had left Charles' legal practice in an irreparable shambles and imposed an uncertain future on his family; what is more, it threatened his life. A year earlier Adams had confessed to Abigail that he envied Washington for having no children. His own offspring caused him more grief, he said, than his worst political enemies. Now, tired and nearly at the end of his tether emotionally, Adams reproached his son as a "Rake" and a "Beast," and declared: "I renounce him." Adams did not attempt to visit his afflicted son, never again wrote to him, and never again saw him.[39]

From New York, Adams hurried to Trenton. Plagued by a severe cold by the time of his arrival, he rested in his lodging for a couple of days, the home of two maiden sisters who nursed their special guest with hearty meals and doses of rhubarb and calomel. Finally well enough to work, Adams at last summoned his balky cabinet. As he must have anticipated, Hamilton's trio of satellites, obstinate and unruffled, sought to persuade him to further delay sending the envoys. When that approach failed, Pickering procrastinated by objecting to the instructions, which had been prepared in the spring. Adams listened with stolid "coolness and candor," or so he later said, and for the sake of harmony even consented to rework the instructions, a task that was achieved through irksome daily meetings that consumed nearly a week. When those sessions were nearly finished, Hamilton arrived, "altogether unforeseen unrequested and undesired by me," the president remarked.[40]

Hamilton, who must have been tipped off by his toadies to their lack of success, had made a long, hard ride on horseback from Newark. He met with Adams twice, perhaps three times, to discuss army issues. Then he requested a final meeting. Adams alone left a description of the session that followed, and there can be little doubt that Hamilton would have described differently what occurred. Adams remembered sitting in reproachful silence, dabbling fitfully with his cigar, as Hamilton condescendingly addressed him in the manner that a pedantic professor might lecture a class of freshmen. Hamilton was accustomed to having his way, usually by playing his audiences with virtuosity. It was a unique talent, and he had used it to regularly carry Washington's cabinet, manipulate Adams' closest advisors, sway Washington himself, and exert considerable influence with hordes of congressmen. This, however, was his first go at changing Adams' mind. The tack that Hamilton chose was a wide-ranging lecture, in this instance on European affairs. It was the sort of prolix performance that so often had worked so well. In this instance, his objective was to demonstrate that conditions in Europe were not propitious for the dispatch of the envoys. As his presentation spun on, Adams recollected, Hamilton flailed with agitation and his voice became steadily louder. Portraying him as an "[over]wrought . . . little man," Adams subsequently alleged that Hamilton betrayed a fatal misunderstanding of the realities of the European situation. He had "talked like an impertinent ignoramus," Adams added. Hamilton's discourse and his rhetorical flourishes were unavailing. If Adams' account is to be believed, the meeting terminated when he finally, curtly and decisively, dismissed his bitter rival. Hamilton was beaten. Finally on November 3—eight months later than he had originally intended—Adams' envoys at last embarked for Paris.[41]

Adams arrived in Philadelphia later that month and soon was joined by the First Lady, who was anxious to see old friends one last time before the capital was transferred to Washington in about six months.[42] They had been in town only a few days when word arrived that Washington had died unexpectedly on December 14 at Mount Vernon. He was sixty-seven and had enjoyed thirty months at home after leaving the presidency, a happy, busy, and healthy period until the very end, when he was afflicted with what is now thought to have been acute epiglottitis.[43] Adams proclaimed

December 26 as the official day of mourning, and on that cold winter day he, Jefferson, and Hamilton—in his military uniform—processed on foot from Congress Hall to the German Lutheran Church at Fourth and Cherry for the service, which lasted nearly five hours, much of it consumed with eulogies.[44]

Once this sad day was past, Adams returned to presidential business. Little could be done with regard to France until definitive word was received from the commissioners, and that in all likelihood would not be before the fall of 1800.[45] In the meantime, Adams took pains to do nothing provocative. His State of the Union message once again was quite moderate in tone, and—at least according to the First Lady—Congress greeted it with "more applause & approbation" than any previous speech her husband had given.[46]

Otherwise, Adams waited, watched, and—like many others in Philadelphia—turned his attention increasingly to the election of 1800, now only a year away.

The President's House in Philadelphia by W. Breton. This was the residence of Washington and Adams throughout most of their presidencies. Located on High Street, near Independence Hall, it previously was the home of Robert Morris, and was considered to be the grandest house in the city. Washington also resided there during the Constitutional Convention as the guest of the Morris family.

9

"We Beat You by Superior Management"

Winter and Spring, 1800

MANY OF THE ACTIONS taken by President Adams in the first months of 1800 bear the stamp of a man seeking to rehabilitate himself on the eve of an uphill election battle. Attuned to the apparent changes in popular sentiment, Adams asked Congress to reduce expenditures while he suspended further enlistments in the Provisional Army and stopped signing commissions for prospective officers. In the spring, in the wake of his actions, moderates of all shades combined to pass congressional legislation that discharged those in the service. The Provisional Army was history. Meanwhile, Adams took steps to shore up his base in the South. He tried, but failed, to dilute the authority of the Treasury Department, and made clear his displeasure with the Bank of the United States, at least as it had been constituted in 1791.[1]

Adams stayed his hand on what he most wished to do: purge his cabinet of its renegade elements. He was waiting for the right moment to act, knowing that it was too risky to strike before the Federalists nominated their candidates for president in 1800.[2] Meanwhile, Jefferson rejoiced in the belief that the Federalist Party had at last crested and now was ebbing. A "wonderful & rapid change is taking place," especially in the middle Atlantic states, where the "tide is now turning," he exulted. Jefferson attributed the woes of his opponents to a growing realization that "it is *impossible* the French should invade us," and to a mounting conviction that the Federalists had distorted the intent of the Constitution's framers. The people, he remarked, ardently wished to "get back to the true principles of that instrument." But Jefferson was certain that nothing had turned heads more than the Federalists' heavy taxes. The United States had "got to the plenum of taxation in 10 short years of peace," he charged. Above all else, Jefferson remained certain that change was coming because the spirit of 1776 "is not dead. It has only been slumbering. The body of the American people is substantially republican. . . . [T]hey have been the dupes of artful manoeuvres & made for the moment to be . . . instruments . . . of seducers [who] have wished war." No more. The people had awakened, he believed.[3]

Jefferson was prescient. In scattered elections in 1799, the Republicans won control of the New Jersey legislature and captured the governor's chair in Pennsylvania. In New England, previously a Federalist bastion, three districts returned Republicans, including Matthew Lyon, the pugilistic congressman, who was elected while serving jail time after being convicted under the Sedition Act.[4] But for Adams the most crushing blow came in the spring elections in New York. Every observer understood the importance of New York, a large state and one in which Adams had won all twelve of the electoral votes en route to his three-vote victory over Jefferson four years earlier. Adams was stunned, therefore, when he learned early in May that the Republicans had carried the day in the state assembly elections. He knew that the presidential electors in New York were chosen by the legislature. No one had to explain to him what that would mean in the election of 1800: all twelve of New York's electoral votes would be cast for the Republican presidential candidates.

Carrying New York City had been the key to the Republicans' statewide victory. The party had swept the canvass in Manhattan, winning every seat that was contested, a huge win that provided the Republicans with the margin needed to control the legislature. Many immediately concluded that the Federalists were doomed nationally in 1800 as a result of the disaster in New York. Abigail Adams laconically remarked that it "is generally supposed that N York would be the balance" in 1800. John Dawson, a Republican congressman from Virginia, was more expressive. "The Republic is safe. . . The [Federalist] party are in rage & despair."[5] The Election of 1800 was not over, but the outcome of the spring election in New York had definitely cast the Federalist Party into the role of underdog.

It was paradoxical that the election in New York City might determine the contest nationally, for few Americans—and few New Yorkers, for that matter—were urbanites. Ninety percent of the state's population lived in rural areas, not strikingly different from the national pattern. At first blush, it was odd that the Republicans had carried New York City, a stronghold of Nationalist, then Federalist, strength. Since the end of the war, most residents of Manhattan, including its workers, had concluded that their well-being hinged on the existence of a strong central government capable of establishing and maintaining a thriving commerce. However, beginning in 1796 fissures in the Federalist Party's base became apparent. Hamilton acknowledged during that year's canvass that the city's workers had come to see every election as "a question between the Rich & the Poor." He was correct. In the municipal elections of 1796, two-thirds of the voters who were too poor to own property abandoned the Federalist Party for Republican candidates.[6]

What was happening in New York City was beginning to occur elsewhere. To growing numbers of workers, including skilled artisans, the Federalist Party appeared to be the home of the gentry, the party of comfortable gentlemen who did not work with their hands and whose world consisted of property ownership and financial speculation. To one observer who earned a living by the sweat of his brow, and who doubtless spoke for many of his cohorts, the Federalists seemed increasingly to represent those who did not really earn a living, but lived instead off inheritances and "money at interest, rents . . . and fees that were fixed on the nominal value of money." Moreover, he added, Federalists waged a remorseless battle against every inflationary tendency, keeping a tight rein on the supply of money, to the displeasure of cash-hungry workers but to the "advantage of the Few."[7]

Many were coming to see the Federalists as Jefferson long had seen them: as monocrats and Anglophiles, royalists who hoped not only to conserve the scorned hierarchical and deferential practices of the Anglo-American colonial past but to frustrate the shining promise of the American Revolution. The Federalist mantra was that a stable society was essential to the well-being of a republican government. Furthermore, many Federalists wore their gentility on their sleeve, such as Fisher Ames, who was in the habit of referring to the party as the "wise, the rich, and the good," or others who at times spoke of it as "the wise, the rich, and the well-born."[8]

To many dock jockeys, sailors, and unskilled laborers who struggled to keep their heads above water, as well as to skilled tradesmen and small-business owners who aspired to greater social and economic opportunities, the Federalists had taken on the appearance of nabobs and grandees who preferred to keep their distance from their social inferiors. Many from the middling and lower social orders were convinced that the Federalists believed that only those who exhibited the stamp of gentility were qualified to hold important public offices. It was presumed too that many among the elite looked down their noses at newly minted self-made men, disparaging those who had recently acquired wealth as "mushroom gentlemen," a tart expression suggesting that the arrivistes had emerged suddenly from the dung heap. Like their conservative counterparts in England, Federalists seemed comfortable with stuffy levees in their genteel mansions, soirees in posh clubs, and a rigid, hierarchical social structure. To many, they appeared to want to keep the lower sort in their place and to make them all too aware of that place. Many were convinced that the average Federalist wished an America modeled on a British society that featured a genteel tradition and a citizenry reduced to demeaning displays of deference. Many had overheard Federalists proclaim that the "people are without virtue" or that they were a "herd" that walked on "their hind legs." Many knew of Federalists who had opposed expanding suffrage and who had suggested that a broader electorate would ensure that the "mediocrity would gain possession of all power." Many bristled at the pomposity of Federalists who preferred not to shake hands with those beneath them. It struck some as revealing that while Republican writers used pseudonyms such as "Equality," "Democraticus," or "Reformatist," Federalist essayists disdained pen names that might be associated with the spirit of 1776. Others noted that as soon as the Federalists gained control of the mint—when Jefferson left the State Department in 1793—all symbols of liberty, such as the Liberty Tree or the Liberty Cap, were removed from the federal currency. Furthermore, Federalists not only scoffed at popular participatory politics, upholding social traditionalism, they were committed inflexibly to an elite-directed economy.[9] The opposition press had hammered away at the hidden agenda of the Federalists since at least 1791, yet for some it was the reaction of the most conservative Americans to the French Revolution and the Jay Treaty that first lent credence to Republican polemics. For others, it was the Alien and Sedition Acts, new federal taxes, the Provisional Army, and the seeming lust for war with France that brought the political issues of the day into clearer focus. Five months before the crucial spring election of 1800 in New York, Jefferson had been among the first to see that the "eyes of the people [on Manhattan had been] opened." He predicted "the best possible prospect" for his party.[10]

Nevertheless, despite the apparent bitterness of many workers, the Federalist defeat in the 1800 election in New York City was not foreordained. Throughout the 1790s the Federalists had been resilient, daring, and masterly in the techniques of appealing to popular opinion. The party had elected a president in 1796 and built an impressive congressional majority in 1798. That they failed in 1800 in Gotham owed much to the shrewd and prescient vision of Aaron Burr, who guided the Republican opposition, capably mobilizing and orchestrating the growing disenchantment that Jefferson and others had discerned. Burr constructed a political web that flowed down and out from a central committee to small councils at the ward level. He threw open his house to party workers during the two months prior to the election, providing meals, refreshments, and even sleeping quarters to those who worked around the clock for the party. He spoke at street rallies, an almost unheard-of practice in that day for one of his stature. He arranged regular party meetings at Martling's Tavern—the "wigwam" to Republicans, the "pig sty" to their foes—at which the party message was disseminated and the organizational nuts and bolts were put together. The Republicans also carefully selected a slate of celebrity legislative candidates, men with name recognition, including a former governor, a Revolutionary War general, and the postmaster of the United States. Finally, on Election Day Burr sent party workers into the wards to rally the voters and assist them, if need be, in getting to the polls. Each had a list containing the names of residents in the block to whom he was assigned, and each literally campaigned door-to-door. Burr even arranged for German-speaking party operatives to get out the vote in neighborhoods inhabited by recent German immigrants. What is more, Burr personally spent ten hours on Election Day at a polling place where Federalist chicanery was thought likely.[11]

Burr understood the realities, and possibilities, of the democratic politics that were just taking shape in urban America, but his party also benefited from the poor leadership of the Federalists. Hamilton was away from the city during some of the contest, and even while in town he was so distracted by his army duties that he dabbled fitfully with preparations for the pending canvass. While Burr micromanaged his party's preparations for the election, Hamilton recruited chaplains, procured supplies, deployed troops, drafted a military code for Congress to consider, searched endlessly for credible junior officers, perused the needs of the navy (which did not fall within his jurisdiction), and helped the secretary of war write a proposal for the creation of academies for the

training of army and navy officers. Hamilton appeared to be overconfi-
dent. His party had won handily in recent municipal elections, and as
this contest approached he announced that the voters' "dispositions are
not bad." His approach was business as usual. The Federalists presented
the voters with a slate of unknown candidates, including bankers and
attorneys from elite law firms, men described by one Republican as
haughty sorts in "kid gloves [who] cannot shake hands with an honest
man who is poor."[12]

The Federalists' insensitivity toward the workers cost them dearly.
Although the Federalists carried three of the seven wards in Gotham,
and lost two others by the narrowest of margins, the Republicans scored
lopsided wins in the Sixth and Seventh Wards, newly settled neighborhoods on the Upper East Side and Upper West Side, respectively. Each
contained the city's heaviest concentrations of the poor. In the Seventh
Ward, often called the "cartmen's ward" by contemporaries, the propertyless totaled approximately 65 percent of the population; 85 percent of
the residents of the Sixth Ward were propertyless. The Federalists captured 52 percent of the vote in the First through Fifth Wards, but the
Republicans took over 65 percent of the votes in the Sixth and Seventh
Wards combined, and that was sufficient to sweep them to victory, as
they captured all thirteen assembly seats at stake in Manhattan as well as
seven of the nine seats in the upper house of the legislature.[13] "We have
beat you by superior *Management*," Burr crowed.[14] The First Lady reached
the same conclusion. New York's Republicans "laid their plans with more
skill than their opponents," Abigail Adams noted.[15]

Jarred by the specter of defeat in the autumn, Hamilton importuned
Governor John Jay to call a special session of the Federalist-dominated
New York legislature so that it might act before the newly elected assem-
blymen took their seats. Hamilton's plan was for the outgoing assembly
to enact legislation providing for the popular election—in districts—of
the state's presidential electors, a ploy virtually guaranteed to ensure that
the Federalists would capture nine or ten of the twelve electoral college
slots. Jay refused to be a party to such an underhanded scheme.[16]
Thwarted at that turn, Hamilton fired off directives to his friends among
the Ultras. In the coming congressional caucus, he proposed, the party
must nominate Adams and Charles Cotesworth Pinckney as its candidates, then unite behind them. This now was a matter of "urgency." If
Adams was dumped, the Federalists could not count on New England,
the very heart of the party's strength and a region that possessed one-
fourth of the total electoral votes. It was essential that the party remain

intact, Hamilton wrote, for that alone "can possibly save us from the fangs of *Jefferson*."[17]

The Federalists had already caucused when Hamilton's missive arrived. Some Ultras, including Pickering and Wolcott, had conspired to dump Adams, replacing him with Chief Justice Ellsworth, another New Englander, but there was little mood for overthrowing the chief executive. Thus the caucus nominated Adams and C. C. Pinckney, as Hamilton had hoped, and it urged the party's electors to cast their two presidential votes for those candidates. Jefferson labeled Pinckney's selection a case of "hocus-pocus manoeuvres."[18] In fact, the Federalists had acted as pragmatists. The Federalists, who had to do well in the South now that they were certain of losing New York, hoped that Pinckney would siphon away some of the second votes of Republican electors from the South. If their strategy succeeded, Pinckney's combined vote totals in the South and the North might be sufficient to win the contest.

A few days after the Federalists made their decision, the Republican congressmen caucused and nominated Jefferson and Burr. Unlike their foes, the Republicans stipulated a choice for president. Their electors were told that Jefferson was the party's first choice.

Philadelphia was immediately awash with tattle about Federalist intentions. As its caucus had not designated Adams as the clear-cut choice for president, many saw the makings of yet more Hamiltonian wile.[19] The president, his spirit soured by events and repeated signs of perfidy among the Ultras (some of which he learned about through the communiqués of an anonymous correspondent who signed his letters "Yr. Friend"), was one who bought into the notion of a Hamiltonian plot against him. Adams was certain that Hamilton, in league with Pickering and McHenry, and perhaps Wolcott, had schemed to prevent his nomination.[20]

Two days after the Federalist caucus, on May 5, 1800, Adams at last felt free to fire McHenry and Pickering. Most contemporaries saw his act as premeditated, and many believed he was driven by vengefulness, both of which were true. Some also believed that the dismissals of the two hard-liners was designed as a "peace offering" to France, but that was untrue. Had this act been part of his peace initiative, Adams would have taken the step much earlier. More than anything, Adams acted with an eye on the coming presidential election. Not only did he wait until he was safely nominated, but he shrank from removing Wolcott, which would have risked his solid support in Connecticut. Furthermore, around Christmas, Adams told Wolcott that his reelection hinged on appealing to moderate elements in both parties. By purging Pickering and McHenry, he was boldly underscoring for moderates his fabled independence and steady commitment to achieving an honorable peace. In addition, with the loss of New York, Adams knew that he must have support in the South to win in December. Soon after Pickering's removal, the president named Virginia's John Marshall as his successor to head the State Department.[21]

Though Adams acted with forethought, he may not have intended to take the step precisely when he did. In all likelihood, he had planned to wait another couple of weeks until Congress had adjourned and he was on the cusp of departing Philadelphia. Instead, on May 7, a routine meeting with McHenry turned suddenly hostile when the war secretary made a niggling objection over a trivial matter. Adams' pent-up fury boiled over. The president unloosed a torrent of invective, charging McHenry with treachery, labeling him "arrogant," and accusing him of ineptitude and inefficiency as an administrator. As Adams worked himself into a lather, his virulent dislike of Hamilton also burst forth. He blamed him for the party's debacle in New York City and added that Hamilton was an inveterate conniver, "a man devoid of every moral principle—a Bastard." As if he could think of nothing worse to say to one of the satellites of the inspector general, Adams told McHenry that "Jefferson is an infinitely better man; a wiser one, I am sure." If he lost the election, Adams threatened, he would return to Quincy and draft for posterity an account revealing both Hamilton's venality and the perfidy of his minions in the cabinet. When at last he ran out of steam, Adams curtly concluded: "You cannot, Sir, remain longer in office."[22] The following morning McHenry submitted his resignation, whereupon Adams baldly informed Pickering that he too was through. Ever after, Adams swore that Pickering had to go not just because of his insubordination but because he had repeatedly neglected his duties.[23]

While the Republican press cheered the president's action, the Federalists were stunned. Some of the more moderate party members sought to persuade their brethren in the Ultra wing to refrain from seeking revenge on Adams, lest they "crumble the federal party to atoms." Not everyone listened. Theodore Sedgwick, the Federalist Speaker of the House, declared that Adams' latest act was fresh proof that he was "a very *unfit* and *incapable* character," and added that if "we must have an *enemy* at the head of the Government," he preferred that it be Jefferson, who could be opposed "& for whom we are not responsible."[24]

None was so shaken as Hamilton. In the course of a year his dreams had been shattered, first by the president's peace initiative, then by the demise of the Provisional Army, and finally by the ramifications of the electoral debacle in New York. Jefferson's election was a real possibility, and it was not impossible that Adams might be reelected. In either circumstance, an inveterate foe would occupy the presidency for the next four years. Not only would he be without influence, but Hamilton churned with anxiety at the prospect that under either Jefferson or Adams a national "loss of reputation" would ensue. Each would dismantle the army, and perhaps the navy as well. He feared too that Jefferson would seek to drastically alter the Constitution, incorporating radical ideas hatched by the likes of Paine or the revolutionaries in France. In May 1800 Hamilton predicted that the United States was on the eve of "Revolution and a new order of things." He forecast that a "new and more dangerous *Era* has commenced."[25]

10

"The Boisterous Sea of Liberty"

The Campaign of 1800

CAMPAIGNING IN 1796 had not begun until Washington announced his intention to retire, about a hundred days before election day. Things were different in the election of 1800. "Electioneering is already begun" in the capital, Abigail Adams noted in November 1799, thirteen months before election day.[1] Indeed, around this time Pennsylvania's senator James Ross introduced legislation to create a "Grand Committee"—it was to consist of the chief justice of the United States and five members of Congress—to adjudicate any disputes in the election of the president. As the chief justice was a staunch Federalist, and as that party controlled both houses of Congress, Ross' bill seemed to many to be an attempt by the Federalists to steal the election. The bill went nowhere, but its introduction and the Republican response to it—one who was close to Jefferson labeled it a "deadly blow . . . aimed at us"—was a signal that the presidential contest was under way.[2]

So too was the publication a few weeks later of James Callender's *The Prospect Before Us*. A Scotsman with a poison pen, Callender had been forced to flee to Ireland, then in 1793 to Philadelphia, to avoid arrest for his writings. The pamphlet that got him in trouble in the old country—an assault on the British constitution—had been read with delight by Jefferson while he was secretary of state. Jefferson also savored Callender's subsequent work, especially when he not only lashed

out at Hamiltonianism but broke the story in 1797 that while Treasury
secretary, Hamilton had been involved in an extramarital affair with a
married woman and supposedly—it was never proven—provided her
husband with public monies and insider information to purchase his
silence. Thereafter, Jefferson visited Callender in his lodging and agreed
to underwrite additional malicious squibs. Soon other Republicans with
deep pockets came forward, likely at the behest of Jefferson, to bankroll
the journalist. Calumny dripped from Callender's pen in several essays
that he wrote during the next year. He unsparingly flayed Washington as
a liar who longed to be a dictator. He called Hamilton "the *Judas Iscariot*
of our country" and charged that he was a monarchist willing to sell out
the United States to Great Britain. Callender depicted Adams as a war-
monger and a "poor old man" who was "in his dotage." The Federalist
Party, he said repeatedly, was the foe of the rights of man.[3]

Callender's hatchet jobs soon landed him in trouble. On two occasions thugs visited his apartment, terrorizing his family and curtailing
his literary productivity. The Sedition Act stopped it altogether. Broke
and frightened—and a widower as well, as during his idleness his wife
had died (in slovenly conditions, it was rumored)—he fled Philadelphia
for Virginia. He was so poor that he was compelled to walk from Pennsylvania to below the Potomac. One object that he had in mind in coming south, he said, was to find a new wife, a "hearty Virginia female" who
could "fatten pigs, and boil hominy, and hold her tongue." But his principal aim was to find work, and in that he succeeded, landing a position
with the Richmond *Examiner*.[4] A year later, in 1799, he sent Jefferson the
page sheets for *The Prospect Before Us*, a philippic against Hamilton,
Adams, and their party. Jefferson was pleased. Telling Callender that the
book "cannot fail to produce the best effect," the vice president once
again provided funds to assist in the completion of the campaign tract.
Soon after the pamphlet appeared, Callender discovered that he was not
safe even in the South. He was arrested under the Sedition Act and in-
carcerated in Richmond.[5]

Callender wrote *The Prospect Before Us* in his customarily toxic style.
His object, he said, was to "exhibit the multiple corruptions of the Federal Government, and more especially the misconduct of . . . Mr. Adams."
He alleged that the Quasi-War crisis would never have occurred had it
not been for the "intemperance" of the president's rhetoric, his steadfast
antipathy toward France and the French Revolution, and the anti-French
vitriol that had poured from the Federalist press over the past decade.
Warming up, he charged that Adams should not even be the president;

he owed his victory in 1796 to trickery and the Federalists' refusal to permit qualified voters to choose the presidential electors in many states. For the past four years, he went on, the nation had groaned under Federalists who, like the Tories before 1776, "love English supremacy and hate American independence." Since the end of the war their secret agenda had been "yoking us into an alliance with the British tyrant," an end they now sought to accomplish by manufacturing a war with France. He urged his readers to see to Jefferson's election in 1800 and to defeat Adams, "the father of the alien and sedition acts," and Pinckney, who was "synonymous with insignificance."[6]

While Callender sat in his dark cell in Richmond, John and Abigail Adams left Philadelphia for the last time as president and First Lady. Abigail was the first to depart, leaving in mid-May for Peacefield, but not before she plied her husband with ample medicinal advice: take hot baths daily but be sure the water was not too hot, as that would "drive the Blood to the Head" with adverse effects.[7] Eight days later the president set off too, but his carriage rolled south, not northward. His destination was the new federal city, which had been under planning and construction since Jefferson and Madison had cut the deal with Hamilton on the Assumption Bill almost ten years earlier. Adams was due to arrive a few days before the federal government. He had signed an order directing all department heads to commence operations in the new capital on June 15, and moving began as soon as Congress adjourned. The government was so small that the combined archives of the State, Treasury, War, Navy, and Justice Departments fit into seven packing cases.[8]

The president took a circuitous route to the Chesapeake. First he headed west to Lancaster and York, then southeast through Frederick and Baltimore, and finally down to the Potomac. His peripatetic journey suggests that he was on the campaign trail, desperately looking for support in Pennsylvania and Maryland. Just hours before departing Philadelphia, in fact, Adams had pardoned three men condemned to death for their roles in eastern Pennsylvania's rebellion against the Federalist taxes. The timing of his gesture hints that it too was politically motivated, as support was strong in the backcountry for the rebels who languished on death row. Adams' roundabout journey created a great pother in numerous dusty villages along the way. His arrival invariably drew a large and friendly crowd that came to hear him deliver a brief speech. His theme varied little from one town to the next: he emphasized that his goal was national independence and that he opposed an alliance with either France or Great Britain; he accentuated his role in the American Revolution; and he reminded listeners of his blood ties to Samuel Adams.[9]

Adams reached Washington early in June, just as the region's customary sultry summer set in. He remained for ten days, lodging in a hotel near the Capitol. He stayed busy throughout his visit. One day he rode out to Mount Vernon to visit Martha Washington. On two occasions he crossed over to Alexandria, once to tour the town and participate in a brief ceremony in his honor, and once to dine at the elegant home of his loyal attorney general, Charles Lee. He attended dinners and teas, and inspected government buildings, finding that the home of the Treasury Department, an unadorned two-story brick structure a mile west of the Capitol, was the only one completed and ready for occupancy. The Capitol was still under construction, but the north wing (the Senate's chamber) was to be ready by November.[10] While most visitors disparaged Washington as an ugly mass of construction in the uncivil

Georgetown and Federal City, 1801 by T. Cartwright. When Abigail Adams saw Washington for the first time in 1800, she thought it a wilderness. She wished that the capital had remained in Philadelphia.

outlands, Adams claimed to "like the seat of government very well," and especially the President's House, where he longed to "Sleep, or lie awake," during the ensuing four years.[11]

Adams found that work was far from complete on the President's House, but he was assured that it would be habitable, though not finished, by the time he returned in November. He had alternatives to chose from. A District commissioner offered the president temporary occupancy in his choice of three completed dwellings, while a resident of Washington volunteered to lease his home to Adams, boasting that it featured the "best kitchen in America," a huge oval room on the ground floor that would be grand for receptions, and a cellar with "a passage to the outhouse." Adams declined. He wished to live where all his successors would live.[12]

Eager to get to Quincy, Adams set out for home in the half-light of dawn on June 14. The trip that he faced was about 125 miles longer than that from Philadelphia, so the customary sixteen-day journey stretched into nineteen hot, dusty days of weary travel. He paused briefly in Baltimore, probably to mend fences in a state that he had narrowly carried in 1796. His passage through New Jersey was especially disappointing. The Federalist Party in that state ignored him entirely. There were no receptions, no crowds, and no speeches. Philadelphia's *Aurora* reported that when Adams stopped for the evening, he walked the streets alone, dressed in "the free and uninterrupted garb of a private citizen," occasionally meeting friendly Republicans with whom he enjoyed a convivial drink and discoursed on "things ordinary and local."[13] Once he left New Jersey, he did not linger anywhere, including New York, which he breezed past, heartlessly adhering to his pledge to avoid his son Charles.

Jefferson had gotten home in May, following a roundabout trip that included a visit with Maria, his younger daughter, in Chesterfield County. Throughout that summer and fall, Jefferson radiated an unwonted optimism with regard to public affairs. Knowing that Adams' envoys would be received in Paris, he anticipated a negotiated settlement to the Quasi-War. He reveled in the belief that the Ultra-Federalists were waning, and he was overjoyed that his foes had "not been able to carry a single strong measure" in Congress that spring. What is more, when the Republicans won control of the New York legislature, Jefferson exclaimed that "New York determines the election" of 1800. From the moment that he arrived on his hilltop in Virginia, Jefferson was confident that the "tide of . . . public opinion sets strong against the federal . . . party."[14]

Although early in the year Jefferson confessed that those "who know me, know that my private gratification would be most indulged" should public affairs "leave me most at home," he appeared more eager in 1800 to hold high office than at any time since the eve of independence. The Federalists had frightened him badly during recent years, most especially by their Sedition Act, and that summer he watched helplessly as Callender was convicted and sentenced to nine months in jail and a fine of $200 in a trial that Jefferson saw as a political action and judicial mockery.[15]

Jefferson, like Adams, acted like a candidate. From Monticello, he urged friendly scribes to write polemics on his behalf, helped with the expenses incurred in publishing and distributing these writings, and purchased some tracts in bulk and saw to it that they got into the hands of influential officeholders who would put them to good use. His itinerary upon leaving Philadelphia in the spring of 1800 also suggests campaign motives. He had paused in Richmond, which he usually avoided altogether, perhaps to shore up the Republican base in the face of recent Federalist successes. In addition, alone among the candidates, Jefferson wrote numerous letters in which he spelled out his convictions, producing a party platform of sorts. "I am for preserving to the States the powers not yielded by them to the Union," and for preventing the further encroachment of the executive branch on the rightful powers of Congress, he wrote. "I am for a government rigorously frugal and simple," and for retiring the national debt, eliminating a standing army and relying on the militia to safeguard internal security, and keeping the navy small, lest it drag the nation into "eternal wars." He continued: "I am for free commerce with all nations; political connections with none," adding that he wished to remain out of the warfare that had ravaged Europe for most of the past decade. "I am for freedom of religion, and . . . for freedom of the press, and against all violations of the constitution to silence . . . our citizens."[16]

By early summer all signs pointed toward his electoral success in December.[17] Mostly cheerful tidings reached Monticello, including further evidence of the implosion of the Federalist Party. In October Alexander Hamilton published a savage attack on Adams that for scurrility equaled the worst assaults by the most noxious Republican scribes, including some who now languished in jail. The *Letter from Alexander Hamilton, Concerning the Public Conduct and Character of John Adams*, fifty-four pages of unremitting vilification, was called by the *Aurora* "the most gross and libelous charges against Mr. Adams that have ever yet to be published or heard of." Indeed, even though Hamilton's publisher had taken the extraordinary step for that day of having issued the pamphlet under a copyright, the *Aurora* immediately reprinted its juiciest parts, claiming shamelessly that the purpose of the copyright law was the dissemination of knowledge.[18]

Hamilton wasted little time in informing his readers that "there are great and intrinsic defects in his character, which unfit" Adams for any high office. He built a case for Adams' steadfastly wrongheaded behavior as a congressman and diplomat, but the bulk of the essay focused on the "serious errors" of his presidency. Hamilton acknowledged that Adams was bright and well educated, but those attributes were vitiated by his vanity, "distempered jealousy," "extreme egotism," and such an "ungovernable temper" that he frequently behaved outrageously toward those who served him. Legions in the capital "have been humiliated by the effects of these gusts of passion," he charged. In addition, Adams was prone to spurn the "prudent" advice of his cabinet and to act impetuously. Unlike Washington, who "consulted much, produced much, resolved slowly, resolved surely," Adams was given to hasty and "premature" decisions, the result of "either instability of views, or want of sufficient consideration beforehand." Adams, Hamilton concluded, "has certain fixed points of character which tend naturally to the detriment of any cause of which he is the chief, of any Administration of which he is the head." His "ill humors and jealousies" had divided his party, assisted unfriendly foreign powers, alienated potential friends, and torn down much that President Washington had achieved, and they might have set in motion events that could bring the Union to the brink of doom.[19]

Many in both parties thought Hamilton's spray of venom was the product of a fevered mind, and the editors of the modern edition of his papers concluded that it "revealed that he had become an inept politician."[20] Those historians who instead have portrayed the *Letter* as a cagey, deliberate move have generally maintained that Hamilton wrote the tract to ensure Jefferson's election. The Federalists might then regroup as an opposition party—as the Nationalists had done after the War of Independence—and reemerge stronger than ever in 1804. Hamilton himself lent credence to that theory, for immediately after the electoral disaster in New York he exclaimed that he preferred Jefferson's election to that of Adams. "If we must have an *enemy* at the head of the Government, let it be one whom we can oppose & for whom we are not responsible, who will not involve our party in the disgrace of his foolish and bad measures."[21] However, as Hamilton shortly thereafter repudiated that sentiment, it is likely that the *Letter* was written with an altogether different end in mind.

Hamilton hated to lose, and his actions customarily resulted from carefully calculated strategic planning. He knew that he would have no influence in an administration headed by Adams, Jefferson, or Burr. However, Hamilton could presume that if Pinckney triumphed, he might again be politically prominent. Pinckney was not exactly a long shot. Knowledgeable observers believed that Adams and Pinckney would capture most of the votes from New England, Delaware, and New Jersey, while Jefferson and Burr would sweep Virginia, New York, Kentucky, Tennessee, and Georgia. The election, therefore, would be decided in the five remaining states—Pennsylvania, Maryland, North Carolina, South Carolina, and Rhode Island, the one New England state seen as a toss-up. In 1796 Jefferson had won thirty-three votes from those five crucial states, followed by Burr with nineteen, Thomas Pinckney with eleven, and Adams with only six. To win in 1800, C. C. Pinckney clearly had to harvest more votes than his brother had won four years before. There were those who believed that Pinckney would win the election if he received the vote of every elector in North and South Carolina.[22] Hamilton may have agreed, but given the myriad of uncertainties in those five unpredictable states—not to mention his oppressive doubt that all New England electors would indeed cast their second ballot for Pinckney—he more likely suspected that Pinckney's best chance of victory would come if no one gained a majority of the votes. In that event, the House of Representatives would select the next president from the five highest finishers.

Seen in this light, Hamilton's authorship of the *Letter*, while risky, was hardly irrational. Indeed, throughout the campaign he pursued a well-conceived three-pronged strategy. First, he sought to ensure that Adams would not win in the electoral college, and his pamphlet aimed at sowing sufficient doubts about the president's character in the minds of electors that one or two would turn away from him. Second, Hamilton sought electoral votes for Pinckney. In 1796 eighteen New England electors who voted for Adams had withheld their second vote from Thomas Pinckney. In May 1800, Hamilton had exhorted the Federalist nominating caucus to recommend that the party's presidential electors cast their two ballots for Adams and Pinckney, and he steadfastly held to that design, reiterating the directive in his *Letter*. Hamilton came to New England in the summer of 1800, ostensibly to disband the Provisional Army brigade cantoned in Oxford, Massachusetts, but most, including Abigail Adams, believed that the real design of the "intriguer" was to "create Heart burnings against the president."[23] In fact, Hamilton's mission was not to steal votes from the president—which he knew was most unlikely in New England—but to ensure that the Yankee electors cast their second votes for Pinckney. If Hamilton achieved his goal in New England and all the region's electors cast their two votes for Adams and Pinckney, and if in addition South Carolina's electors gave their two votes to Jefferson and Pinckney, it was quite likely that Pinckney would win the election. However, if New England went for Adams and Pinckney, and if all the electors in South Carolina balloted for Pinckney and Adams, the odds were good that the two Federalists would best Jefferson and Burr but finish in a tie. This was where the third leg of Hamilton's strategy came into play. His *Letter* especially targeted the members of the House who would decide the election in the event of a deadlock between Adams and Pinckney. Written after the fashion of a legal brief, Hamilton's *Letter* cataloged Adams' unworthiness while it dilated on Pinckney's strengths. Pinckney, Hamilton wrote, was "distinguished . . . for the mildness and amiableness of his manners, the rectitude and purity of his words, and the soundness and correctness of his understanding, accompanied by a habitual discretion and self-command, which has often occasioned a parallel to be drawn between him and the venerated WASHINGTON."[24]

Pinckney meanwhile walked a fine line, and never more so than after the appearance of Hamilton's *Letter*. Whatever chances his brother might have had in 1796 had been doomed when New England's Federalist electors deserted him in order to protect Adams. C.C. knew that his hopes would be dashed as well if he too was abandoned by the president's supporters. While in private he, like Hamilton, said that Adams was unfit to be president, Pinckney publicly forbade those electors who were committed to him to forsake Adams. He also dispatched letters to New England Federalists in which he stressed the instructions he had given to his supporters. Pinckney's only hope—slim, to be sure—was to have every Federalist elector cast his two votes for the two Federalist nominees.[25]

Hamilton's *Letter* was published nine days into Adams' return trip from Peacefield to Washington, and the president knew nothing of it until he reached the new capital. Even so, the canvass was in high gear by then, and Adams was all too aware of what to expect from the press. Decreeing that the "engine is the press," Jefferson believed that the print media was the best vehicle for toppling the Federalists. The Republicans indeed assailed their adversaries with gusto in newspapers, pamphlets (tracts that typically ran from about fifteen to fifty pages), and single-page circulars and broadsides, that generation's equivalent of today's sound bites. So many Republican newspapers now existed that some Federalists exclaimed that the Jeffersonians had set up printing presses in every town and country throughout the land.[26] The Federalists could be excused for having exaggerated. The number of Republican newspapers had dramatically increased. In 1795 only eighteen Republican newspapers had existed, about 14 percent of the nation's total of newspapers. Three years later Republican organs constituted approximately 28 percent of the nation's press. They exploded following the enactment of the Sedition Act—further testimony to the imprudence of the measure—so that by the campaign of 1800 Republican newspapers amounted to about 40 percent of the partisan press in the United States. Often the expense of founding these newspapers was borne by the Republican gentry, especially in the South, where advertising revenue was difficult to procure, but in one instance a corporation, whose object was to found a Republican newspaper, was established and sold stock to find the start-up capital. On the whole, however, these newspapers were the creation of a new breed of printers who were driven by ideology and partisanship and who saw themselves, in the words of historian Jeffrey Pasley, as "vigilant watchmen to alert the virtuous to the encroachments of power before it was too late."[27]

The Republicans also established committees of correspondence, societies, and clubs to help with the distribution of its literature. In Virginia a General Standing Committee of five directed ninety committees of correspondence throughout the state, while in New Jersey similar committees were in place in most townships and in every county to communicate "useful information to the people relative to the election" and to distribute rejoinders to Federalist recriminations. Probably only Pennsylvania's Republicans came close to matching this organizational machinery. For example, they divided Philadelphia County into forty-six districts, each with an election committee, while Lancaster, to the west, was broken down into twenty-one parcels, each with the goal—in the words of a party functionary—to "condense the rays of political light and reflect them strongly on all around."[28] New Jersey's Republicans, received considerable assistance from party activists in Philadelphia, but largely on their own initiative they succeeded in cobbling together what one scholar concluded was a "sophisticated and enthusiastic" electoral apparatus throughout the state. Committees of correspondence and various other sorts of organizational machinery sprouted with the end in mind of distributing literature and, according to their foes, employing "electioneering ruses" to sway voters.[29] Although the Republican superstructure in New England was more rudimentary, the party had assembled a sprightly organization in Boston, if Congressman Ames can be believed. He claimed that "the Jacobins" in the New England hub were better "trained, officered, regimented, and formed to subordination" than the militia; everywhere one went, including even funerals, he despaired, the "whisperers against government" were out and about.[30] Some Federalists fancifully convinced themselves that Jefferson pulled all the levers in this adroit campaign, cobbling together the organizational network and determining the party line to be taken. They were persuaded that Jefferson and the "Knot of Jacobins" who resided with him in the Francis Hotel in Philadelphia functioned as a national committee that planned and managed the campaign.[31] They considerably overstated matters. While both parties were better organized and more disciplined than in 1796, what little central direction existed in 1800 was confined almost solely to the state and municipal levels.

If it was any consolation to Adams, the Republican press was gentler to him than Hamilton had been. After the calamity in New York, many Republican editors thought Adams' candidacy was doomed, and so they concentrated their heaviest fire elsewhere. The paramount charges made against Adams were that he had abandoned his Revolutionary commitment to liberty and that he was a monarchist. One scribe said that he was "a most stupendous fabric of human invention," an apostate who merely pretended to be a true friend of revolutionary republicanism.[32] Tench Coxe, once a Federalist and an undersecretary in Hamilton's Treasury Department, dashed off a pamphlet in the midst of the campaign in which he claimed to have heard Adams say that he favored a hereditary presidency for the United States. Readers were reminded that Adams shared responsibility for the Alien and Sedition Acts (though subsequently Jefferson confessed that his party never believed that he was

John Adams by C. B. J. Fevret de Saint-Mémin. President Adams was approximately sixty-five, in the midst of his battle for reelection, when he sat for this portrait drawing in 1800–1801. It was made possible through a "physionotrace," a device that traced the profile of the subject.

"the author of . . . the measures") and were cautioned that if he had another four years in the presidency, those repressive laws might become permanent. Some newspapers contrasted Adams' pre-1776 writings with the *Defence*, written a dozen years later, to allege that after the American Revolution he had transformed himself into an "Angloman" who supposedly longed to model America's social and political system on the one that existed in Great Britain. More than a few Republican editors were only too happy to make certain that their readers were aware of the charges that Hamilton had levied against the president.[33]

Convinced that Charles Cotesworth Pinckney was likely to run ahead of the president, some Republicans focused their attacks on him. Pinckney was limned as a mediocrity, a soldier who had never really shone and a statesman who had not especially distinguished himself. One Republican journal insisted that he was a man of "limited talents" whose "temper [was] illy suited to the exalted station" of the presidency.[34] It was said that even the Federalists thought him a lightweight but chose him anyway because his youthful residence in England had rendered him an Anglophile. His "politics are much higher toned than those of Adams," it was said, and he was profiled as a nabob cut from the same cloth as the English aristocracy.[35] What is more, he was allegedly under Hamilton's thumb, making him the best vehicle for the restoration of the Ultras.[36] One Republican characterized Pinckney as the stalking horse that would "permit Caesar [Hamilton] to govern."[37]

However, the Republican press focused less on Adams and Pinckney than on what the Federalist Party presumably stood for. One party activist asked why the Republican Party was "so zealously attempting a change of men," then answered his own question: so as to never again "have such acts as the alien and sedition laws . . . or . . . too intimate a connexion with any foreign power" imposed on the nation; so that "dangerous and expensive armaments" financed by heavy taxation did not continue; and in order that "peace may be established and wars avoided."[38] The Republicans indicted their adversaries as Anglophiles who wished not only to save or to reestablish the society and customs of the colonial past, but to build the nation's economy and political system on the British template. Charging that there was little to distinguish the Federalists from the Tories of 1776, Republicans excoriated the Federalists for seldom mentioning the War of Independence or recalling the wartime destruction sown by Britain's redcoat armies. In addition, it was said, the Federalists had developed amnesia over London's hiring of German mercenaries and were blind to Britain's postwar commercial discrimination and the Royal Navy's depredations against American shipping and sailors. The Federalists were limned as political apostates who mouthed republican ideas while they sought "to sap the very foundation of public liberty." In the ideal world of the Federalists, it was said, the new nation's central government would not be responsible to the people, and most Americans, like most Englishmen, would become vassals to their princely rulers. This was a contest, said one Republican newspaper, to determine "whether we shall have at the head of our executive a steadfast friend of the Rights of the People, or an advocate for hereditary power and distinctions." What is more, like the British people, they too would groan under a ruling class of corrupt stockjobbers who saw peace as their greatest enemy.[39] Although the financiers and securities speculators amounted to only one six-hundredth of the British population, according to one screed, they ruled with an iron hand, remorselessly seeking war for profits and the destruction of every vestige of republicanism. Like vultures, they plundered the inhabitants of that forlorn island, leaving them "in rags, hunger and wretchedness."[40]

Hamilton took much of the heat. The Republican press went on at length about the remarkable speech "the ambitious, amorous little Hamilton" had given at the Constitutional Convention. Lest anyone had forgotten, readers were reminded that behind the closed doors of that gathering he had endorsed monarchy and urged "the establishment of a permanent executive, and . . . the total suppression of the states." If he had his way, it was said, the American citizenry soon would bow before "the throne of a powerful and almost absolute monarch."[41] His policies as Treasury secretary were savaged as well. He had shackled the new Republic with a national debt akin to that in Britain. In two hundred years the British budget had grown thirtyfold, with most of the spending plowed into the maintenance of the army and the obligations imposed by the debt. Despite a decade of peace, Hamilton and the two Federalist administrations had run up a national debt in excess of $20 million, roughly one-third as much as had been accumulated in the entire War of Independence.[42] One scribbler called Hamilton's funding plan the "most memorable piece of imbecility and impudence that was ever imposed on a nation," and numerous Republican writers assailed the debt that had arisen from the recent Federalist military preparations, steps that they characterized as unnecessary.[43]

The Republicans insisted that much that the Federalists had done mirrored the very missteps for which Great Britain had been censured in the Declaration of Independence: cutting off trade with parts of the

world, imposing a swarm of officers on the Republic, creating a standing army, seeking to make the military independent of civil authority,
and wishing to thwart the will of the people. Others insisted that their
foes—whom they alternately labeled the "monarchic, aristocratic, tory
faction" and the "Anglo-federal party"—were bent on rolling back many
of the political and social achievements won in the American Revolution. They might as well have set about to "burn the Parchment" of that
treasured document, one screed insisted.[44] The Federalists were portrayed
as caring only for merchants and financiers. It was a party whose members were obsessed with financial gain, a faction "roaring and bellowing
. . . to obtain pelf." Their "system of speculation has been deeply inter-
woven with their views," so that the ultimate end of every Federalist policy,
like that of their high-rolling counterparts who were milking dry the
British people, was the "pecuniary and personal aggrandizement" of the
commercial elite.[45]

One Republican paper neatly listed for its readers the supposed differences between the two parties. In summary form, the highlights were:

Federalist	Republican
1. Condemned the principles of 1776	1. Longed to restore the principles of the Revolutionary patriots
2. Monarchist	2. Foes of monarchy
3. Bent on war with France	3. Wished peace with the world
4. Hatred of the people	4. Appealed through reason to the people
5. Had made victims of new immigrants	5. Prefer equal laws for all citizens and would-be citizens
6. Inaugurated an economic bonanza for the affluent	6. Would call to account those who plunder the public
7. Supporters of established churches	7. Would separate church and state
8. Increased the public debate and taxes	8. Favored a reduction of both taxes and the public debt
9. Wished to meddle in Europe to preserve the balance of power	9. With Washington, prefers not to meddle in Europe's affairs
10. Used the Sedition Act to destroy a free press	10. Favored freedom of the press
11. Favored an established church and powerful priesthood	11. Favored religious freedom [46]

The Republican message consisted largely of a full-bore attack on
the Federalists, but the party scribes also defended Jefferson. Little was
said about Burr. Jefferson was offered up as a friend of farmers and
American commerce, and by late summer Republican newspapers were

publishing the campaign autobiography that he had written upon returning to Monticello in the spring. Readers were also frequently reminded that he had authored the Declaration of Independence, "the most
sublime production of genius which either the ancient or modern world
has exhibited." They were told too that Jefferson had never profited financially from his many years of public service. Quite the contrary, he
had served at great personal sacrifice.[47] Essayists reiterated that Jefferson
favored reducing taxes and terminating the standing army and that he
was opposed to those who sought to impose their religious beliefs on
others. Republicans insisted that the election of Jefferson would usher
in a new era, a second birth of freedom akin to that of 1776.[48] Becoming
free of war was a component of the freedom they envisioned, and while
branding the Federalists a war party, they declared that "[w]ith *Jefferson*
we shall have peace."[49] Another blogger said that Jefferson's motto was
"peace on earth and good will to men."[50] Presenting Jefferson as "mild,
amiable, and philanthropic," Republicans asked what it said of those
detractors who questioned such a man with such beliefs.[51]

Southern Republican scribes sometimes elaborated on the states' rights
creed of the Virginia and Kentucky Resolutions, but party activists in the
North ignored that vexed topic almost entirely.[52] Republicans everywhere
stressed their commitment to the Constitution and insisted that the battle
over approving the Constitution was ancient history. The "real character-
istic parties of the day are the *Republican* and *Anti-Republican*, the friends
of peace and . . . the partizans of war and foreign nations."[53] In this vein,
Republican journals portrayed the party as the home of "true republicans" who had made the American Revolution and remained faithful to
the "principles that predominated in '75, when the war erupted."[54] Characterizing the election of 1800 as a battle for the salvation of the dreams
that had driven the American Revolution, one writer declared: "If your
independence was worth achieving, it is worth preserving." The real meaning of the election, said another, was to determine if the people were actually self-governing and able to secure their interests.[55]

The Federalists did not equal the organizational successes of the Republicans. Too often, in fact, their efforts were more amateurish and consisted of an improvisational effort to respond to the charges of their foes.
Nevertheless, by late in the decade they had some party machinery in place,
though it may have functioned better in state contests than in the presidential election. In addition, not only were most of the nation's newspapers pro-Federalist, but the party drew on its adherents' economic resources
to publish a considerable number of pamphlets and broadsides, and they

tried to put in place the machinery needed to distribute these materials.[56] To be sure, the Federalists laid down a withering barrage against the opposition. Having held power for a decade, they were compelled to defend their record. Before May, when Adams dismissed McHenry and Pickering, and the party suffered its disastrous setback in New York, numerous Federalist writers lavished praise on the president. Thereafter few Federalist newspapers outside New England championed him. Nevertheless, the president had his supporters among influential Federalists, including John Marshall, John Jay, Congressman Harrison Gray Otis, and Noah Webster, the noted lexicographer and editor of two New York newspapers. The president's defenders portrayed him as a trenchant thinker who was known and could be trusted. Throughout the Quasi-War Crisis, they argued, Adams had avoided precipitate actions, and he had stoutly resisted the temptation to go war. Instead, he had labored painstakingly for an honorable peace. Dr. Benjamin Rush, a leading figure in Philadelphia, told the public that he had known Adams for a quarter century and had never heard him defend monarchical government or advocate an Anglo-American alliance. Others testified on behalf of Adams' affinity for the Constitution and his belief that it was a perfect fit for the infant Republic.[57] Some Federalists also linked Adams with Washington as selfless patriots. Soon after Washington's death, a New England newspaper carried a paean to the fallen hero—"Lost is the father, fall'n the Virtuous friend"—that closed with the sunny news that "yet a Fabius in our land survives, / And yet an Alfred in an Adams lives."[58] On occasion a Federalist journal published a stirring encomium to Adams. In October, for instance, the *Washington Federalist* endorsed the president on the grounds that "his principles are founded on the experience of ages [and that he was] Deeply versed in legal lore, profoundly skilled in political science; joined to the advantage of forty years' unceasing engagement in the turbulent and triumphant scenes, both at home and in Europe, which have marked our history, learned in the language and arts of diplomacy, more conversant with the views, jealousies, resources, and intrigues of Great Britain, France and Holland, than any other American; alike aloof to flattery and vulgar ambition, as above all undue control [he has as] ... his sole object ... to present freedom and independence of his country and its future glory."[59]

As the campaign developed, some Federalist writers openly insisted that Pinckney's chances of winning were better than those of Adams. They often portrayed Pinckney as a committed Federalist but not an extremist. His record was exemplary, they insisted. He had served with valor during the war, winning the esteem of General Washington, and afterward his record in civil office had been punctuated by statesmanship and virtue.[60] As was true of Washington, his defenders said, it was "impossible to fix any blot on the character of General Pinckney." Combining "the character of the citizen and the soldier," he, like Washington, would be dedicated to "the preservation of the peace and prosperity of our nation."[61]

Both parties engaged in what now would be termed negative campaigning, an assault on their adversary's program and leadership rather than an emphasis on their own platform. The Federalists, for instance, left no stone unturned in their attempts to link the Republicans with the bloody excesses of the French Revolution. Jefferson and his adherents, they charged, embraced the same "cant of jacobinical illiberality" as their radical friends in France; like their counterparts across the ocean, they were "artful and ambitious demagogues" who led "discontented hotheads," "democratic blockhead[s]," and "cold-hearted Jacobin[s]." Furthermore, like the revolutionaries who had shaped behavior in the mean streets of Paris, the Republican leaders espoused a "creed of atheism and revolution."[62] The Federalists condemned the French Revolution, insisting that it not only had failed to improve the lives of the French but had left the citizenry to face a "forlorn and desolate" future. Now, predictably, the revolutionary disorders had resulted in the elevation of a despot. Napoleon may have put "the *Guillotine* . . . behind the curtain," but his tyranny and endless wars would soak the soil of Europe with blood.[63] What is more, like Napoleon and his Jacobin predecessors, the Republican leaders in America longed for war with Great Britain. The objective of the Republicans was to finish off the British rulers and assist the French.[64] The Federalists shied away from defending Great Britain, but they painted a lurid tableau of what would happen if hostilities erupted with the British: the American economy would be wrecked, revenue would dry up, and the commercial fleet would be idled. Above all, the United States government under Republican leadership would be too weak to adequately wage war.[65]

Jefferson was subjected to ceaseless obloquy. As a young attorney he was said to have gulled his clients. His wartime conduct after 1776 had been deplorable. While others sacrificed, he had lived comfortably, "secure in his retreat . . . from the fangs of a blood-thirsty foe." Or so he had thought. When the enemy approached Monticello in 1781, he had run like a jackrabbit, abandoning his post as governor in the great emergency. He next "peeped out of his hermitage" only when "the storms of war had subsided," and solely for the purpose of "seeking fame." They fumed that Jefferson's war record was one of "pusillanimity" and "uninspiring patriotism,"

Thomas Jefferson by Rembrant Peale. Jefferson was fifty-seven when he sat for this painting early in 1800, shortly before leaving Philadelphia for the final time as vice president.

demonstrating unequivocally that his "nerves are too weak to bear anxiety and difficulties, and at the sight of danger they . . . will shrink."[66]

According to the Federalist line, Jefferson had been transformed into a dangerous radical during his sojourn in France. The "shades of [his] character grew darker and darker" as he embraced the "crimes" of the French Revolution, even urging "active malevolence." By 1792, when the Republican Party had begun to take shape, his head was filled with a "stock of visionary nonsense." To put Jefferson in charge, said a Federalist, would be akin to "scattering poison into the ailments of life," as it would be deadly to the American body politic. For one Federalist scribbler after another, Exhibit A of Jeffersonian wrongheadedness was the so-called Mazzei Letter.

In 1796 Jefferson had written a lengthy letter to Philip Mazzei, a former neighbor in Virginia who had moved to Italy. Much of the mis-

sive concerned his friend's business affairs in Virginia and news of mutual acquaintances, but in a single short paragraph Jefferson had candidly aired his thoughts on political matters, never imagining that his
confidentiality would be breached. However, Mazzei turned over the letter
to the Paris *Moniteur*, which published it in January 1797. Five months
later it was reprinted in Noah Webster's New York *Minerva*, and soon
thereafter Federalist newspapers throughout the United States splashed
the letter across their pages. Jefferson had charged that American liberty
and republicanism were endangered by "an Anglican, monarchical and
aristocratic party" that controlled the presidency, Senate, and federal
judiciary. Those Federalists were "all timid men who prefer the calm of
despotism to the boisterous sea of liberty." Driven by the hope of pecuniary rewards, they wished not only to tie the United States to Great
Britain but to thoroughly recast America on the "rotten as well as [the]
sound parts" of the British model. This was standard Republican fare,
but the letter's most inflammatory line followed: "It would give you a
fever were I to name to you the apostates who have gone over to those
heresies, men who were Samsons in the field and Solomons in the coun-
cil, but who have had their heads shorn by the harlot England."[67] The
"Samson" to whom Jefferson had referred was obviously President Washington. The "Solomons" included John Adams and virtually every Federalist who sat in Congress.

The Federalists had a field day with the Mazzei Letter during the
fevered campaign season in 1800. They sardonically rebuked Jefferson as
a "Solomon of Jacobinism," characterized him as a zealot who would
"loosen all the bonds of society"—a code for social leveling—and depicted him as consumed with "hatred of WASHINGTON" and the Constitution.[68] A Georgia Federalist called Jefferson the "head of the French
party in America" and labeled him the "greatest villain in existence."
Speaking at a banquet in Boston that summer, Hamilton proposed a
toast that American craftsmen might "never act as the *Journeymen* of
Jacobinism; nor as *Master-workmen* in the Mazzeian *Babel*."[69]

The Federalists also fixated on Jefferson's religious beliefs, malign-
ing him as an atheist. This was grounded on what Jefferson had written
in *Notes on the State of Virginia*, drafted in 1782 and first published in the
United States in 1788. Jefferson had lauded the Virginia Declaration of
Rights of 1776, which provided for religious toleration, but, wishing to
go further—he hoped for a law that would separate church and state—
Jefferson had dilated on the "rights of conscience," about which individuals were "answerable [only] to . . . our God" and never to the state.

He then added that "it does me no injury for my neighbor to say there are twenty gods, or no God. It neither picks my pocket nor breaks my leg."[70] Those two sentences were reprinted endlessly in Federalist newspapers as proof of Jefferson's impiety. In addition, Federalist scribes cautioned that Jefferson viewed the clergy as "curses in a country." Primarily, however, they depicted him as a "howling atheist" and "infidel." Filled with contempt for Christ, Jefferson supposedly embodied iniquities that would bring on the moral decline of the United States.[71] In New England people were told to hide their Bibles should Jefferson be elected, and the warning went out that his election would call down God's vengeance on the United States. Though more from the pulpit than the press, lurid tales were told of bizarre worship services at Monticello at which Jefferson supposedly prayed to the Goddess of Reason and offered up dogs on a sacrificial altar.[72] One Federalist newspaper advised its readers to vote for "GOD—AND A RELIGIOUS PRESIDENT or impiously declare for JEFFERSON—AND NO GOD."[73]

The final Federalist message was an appeal against rocking the boat. One writer even insisted, "Change is from the very nature of things an

THE PROVIDENTIAL DETECTION

"*The Providential Detection.*" Dating to the election of 1800, this Federalist cartoon depicts the federal eagle preventing Jefferson from burning the Constitution on the altar of French despotism.

evil. To change even from bad to good, is not at all times expedient or safe."[74] Few went that far. Most emphasized that the past decade had been a time of peace, stability, and prosperity, the result of the two Federalist administrations and of the Constitution—for which the Federalists claimed credit, while attempting to link the Republicans to the Anti-Federalists of 1787–88. All of history, one newspaper said, had been a struggle between those who wished "to overthrow and to preserve the established order . . . to produce and to prevent revolution." That writer, and numerous others, portrayed the Republicans as bent on drastic change that would take the American people into uncharted waters. Their unnecessary and dangerous steps, some Federalists warned, could result in the secession of the northern states, leaving two hostile nations divided at the Hudson, the Delaware, or the Potomac to face off as inveterate enemies.[75] Stay with the Federalist Party, their newspapers urged, as "events have uniformly proved them to be the best Judges of the true interests of their country."[76] This was a slant adopted by Adams. Eleven days before the election, in his annual message to Congress, Adams found "reason to rejoice at the prospect which presents itself" and declared that "we ought to fortify and cling to those institutions which have been the source of such felicity and resist with unabating perseverance . . . those dangerous innovations which may diminish their influence."[77]

Campaigning in this election was not confined to the print media. Festive political dinners were scheduled, such as the Republican affair in Lancaster, Pennsylvania, at which those present drank sixteen toasts— one for each state—to everything from Jefferson to the peace commission, before devouring half a ton of beef and pork. In Kensington, a working-class district in Philadelphia, Republican artisans toasted Jefferson, the "choice of the people." Both parties held picnics and barbeques, crowned inevitably by speeches and songs. Those at Federalist celebrations sometimes concluded the evening by belting out tunes that pledged resistance against their "rude foe[s]." Parades reached a wider audience. Federalist street shows were more likely to feature militia companies and pay homage to General Washington, whereas Republican parades often included a small float prepared by artisans and depicting some scene such as "Liberty Under Siege." A Republican parade in Williamsburg, Virginia, culminated in burning an effigy of Adams, while another in York, Pennsylvania, concluded with burying Federalist emblems, including black cockades.[78] Republicans also held rallies at which they planted liberty trees and liberty poles, symbols that had become popular during the struggle for independence. Some of the liberty poles contained inscriptions, as did one in Newburgh, New York: "1776. LIB-ERTY. JUSTICE. THE CONSTITUTION INVIOLATE. NO BRITISH ALLIANCE. NO SEDITION BILL." In Vassalborough, Maine, the liberty pole was christened by the burning of the Alien and Sedition Acts at its base. Sometimes the liberty poles were short-lived, as in Dedham, Massachusetts, where the "federal young men" of the town cut down this new symbol of the Republican Party.[79] Federalists additionally whispered the story that Jefferson cohabited with one of his female slaves at Monticello, an allegation that would not be published for another three years.[80]

The election of 1800 unfolded in stages. Electoral contests were scattered throughout the year, although most were slated for early autumn. The state legislatures, including those that were elected in 1800, possessed enormous power over that year's presidential canvass. For one thing, they chose the presidential electors in eleven of the sixteen states. In the five states of North Carolina, Kentucky, Maryland, Rhode Island, and Virginia the electors were chosen by popular vote. This was a decline from the seven states that had permitted the qualified voters to choose electors in 1796 (Georgia, Pennsylvania, and Massachusetts had rescinded popular voting, while Kentucky for the first time authorized it). Furthermore, where electors were popularly elected, it was left to state legislators to determine whether their province would employ the general ticket system—a winner-take-all arrangement in which voters balloted for a slate of electors representing one party or the other—or to permit presidential electors to be elected from designated districts. In 1800 three states (Kentucky, North Carolina, and Maryland) permitted the election of presidential electors by popular vote in districts; Rhode Island and Virginia opted for general tickets chosen by popular vote.

Utilization of general tickets enabled the majority party in the legislature to rig the contest to its benefit. In Virginia, for instance, where the Federalists had scored victories in eight of the nineteen congressional races in 1798, the Republican-dominated legislature in 1799 ditched the district plan that had been in place in the three previous presidential elections in favor of the general ticket format.[81] With justification, the Federalists howled that the system was designed "to exclude *one-third* at least of the citizens of Virginia from a vote for the President of the United States," as it guaranteed that the Federalist presidential candidates would be shut out in Virginia.[82] But the Federalists acted similarly. Federalist-dominated Massachusetts, which always before had chosen its electors by districts, responded by transferring the choice of electors in 1800 to

the state legislature, a step taken because some of the sixteen congressional districts were blossoming into Republican strongholds. In one
instance, legislative machinations of this sort backfired. In March 1800,
two months before the crucial assembly elections in New York, the Republicans had backed a bill in the New York legislature that provided for
district elections, hoping by this means to secure up to a third of the
electors. The Federalist defeated the measure, certain that they would
win control of both legislative houses and elect all the state's electors
under the general ticket arrangement. Their miscalculation would cost
them dearly, as the spring election tipped control of the legislature to
the Republicans.[83] Meanwhile, Connecticut's Federalist legislature sought
to ensure a favorable outcome through another ploy. It passed a "stand-
up" election law mandating that all votes be cast publicly and orally, an
intimidating procedure that ordinarily favored those in power.[84]

Since the state elections in New York, the prevailing wisdom had
been that Adams could not be reelected. Jefferson and Pinckney seemed
the better bets. The president, however, clung to the dubious hope that
he might somehow eke out a victory. Yankee friends had privately informed him that Hamilton's trip to New England, which many mistak-
enly believed had been undertaken for the purpose of backstabbing the
president, had backfired. There was "no rational ground for discourage-
ment," at least in Connecticut, one trusted acquaintance told Adams that
summer. Furthermore, by early autumn it seemed possible that Pennsylvania might not participate in the balloting in the electoral college.
Pennsylvania's Republicans wanted to retain the general ticket format
for choosing electors, the system that had served them well four years
earlier. Federalists wished to return to the district system, hoping to win
at least some electoral votes in the state. However, Pennsylvania's lower
house was lopsidedly Republican, while the upper chamber—half of
whose members had been elected in 1797—remained in the control of
the Federalists. Not surprisingly, the legislators promptly deadlocked,
and the issue remained unresolved as August's heavy heat gave way to
autumn's chilly nights.[85] In 1796, Jefferson had won fourteen of the fifteen votes cast by Pennsylvania, but if the legislature was unable to agree
on a method for choosing electors, it would not participate on election
day in 1800, and Jefferson would be the big loser. In fact, the votes that
he would lose in Pennsylvania would cancel out the twelve votes that he
was certain to win in New York. These factors were causing observers
everywhere to think that the election would hinge on how South Carolina voted. If that state's electors gave their votes to Jefferson and

Pinckney—as in 1796, when they had given an equal number of votes to Jefferson and Thomas Pinckney—either might win the election. Or if they gave their votes to Adams and Pinckney, either might be elected. If they gave their votes to Jefferson and Burr, everyone assumed that Jefferson would be the third president of the United States. Word from South Carolina early in October was that the Federalists likely would dominate the assembly and that C. C. Pinckney, from "good faith & . . . good policy," would instruct the Federalist electors to vote for Adams and himself.[86]

Adams' lingering hopes crashed in October and November. First, the ubiquitous Tench Coxe furnished the Philadelphia *Aurora* with an indiscreet letter that Adams had written to him eight years earlier. Adams had portrayed the Pinckneys not only as treacherous and deceitful but as Anglophiles who were not to be trusted to adequately defend the interests of the United States. The *Aurora* wasted no time publishing the letter, and by mid-autumn numerous newspapers across the land had rushed the damning missive into print. Hamilton referred to it as well in his *Letter*, pointing to the communiqué as an example of Adams' habitual jealousy of all others. His "suspicion . . . of a man so meritorious" as Pinckney proved once and for all, Hamilton had declared, that Adams was a poor judge of character. Pinckney did not respond, but his brother, in the interest of party harmony, dismissed the letter as a forgery designed to influence voters. Adams, knowing that he was likely gravely wounded in South Carolina, claimed unpersuasively that he had no recollection of having penned the missive, and he wrote a truckling note to Pinckney in a desperate effort to patch up their relationship.[87]

The final blow for Adams came when the South Carolina legislature was elected in mid-October. When the voters took to the polls, it was with the sense that their votes would decide two elections: one for control of the state legislature and the other for the presidency. That at least was what South Carolina's Charles Pinckney reported to Jefferson.[88] This Pinckney was the second cousin of Thomas and C.C. Only forty-three, he had already sat in Congress under the Articles of Confederation and in the Constitutional Convention, and he had served as governor; currently he was a member of the United States Senate. Unlike his more famous cousins, however, Senator Pinckney was a Republican, having defected after the Federalists spurned his bid for a coveted diplomatic position. Many South Carolina Federalists thereafter privately referred to him as "Blackguard Charlie" for his political apostasy, but in him they faced a tenacious foe who was committed to his new party and dedi-

cated to electing Jefferson—and in the process furthering his own political ambitions.

The contest in South Carolina was filled with surprises. It started
badly for the Republicans. The outcome in Charleston—where the Federalists captured fourteen of the fifteen contested seats—was known
before the results came in from the backcountry. The "Weight of Talent,
Wealth, and personal and family influence Brought against us" was too
much to overcome, Charles Pinckney ruefully confessed to Jefferson. He
neglected to mention that the Republicans had been outpoliticked as
well. Perhaps having learned from the party's defeat in Manhattan,
Charleston's Federalists courted the voters and got them to the election
booth. The Republicans subsequently admitted that their foes had seen
to it that "*the Lame, Crippled, diseased and blind were either led, lifted or
brought in Carriages to the Poll.*" They additionally charged that Federalist poll managers had permitted many to vote who were ineligible, some
after accepting bribes to mark for Federalist candidates.[89] But if the Republicans had been flattened by a steamroller in the city, the reverse soon
was true in the sun-seared backcountry and Piedmont. Jefferson had
been popular all along among the smaller farmers who inhabited those
regions, men who viscerally disliked the Bank of the United States, had
never cottoned to the notion of a strong national government, and were
outraged by what would come to be known simply as "'98," the year of
Federalist repression and heavy taxes.[90]

When the rural votes were counted, it was clear that the great majority in the new legislature (roughly 81 of 151) were partisans of Jefferson.
Actually, the assembly was to be about evenly divided between committed Federalists and Republicans, but up to sixteen other representatives
were unaffiliated with either party, although almost all were demonstra-
bly pro-Jefferson. On the face of it, this appeared to guarantee that
Jefferson would receive eight electoral votes from South Carolina. But
nothing about the election of 1800 was that simple. Many of the
Jeffersonians were also devoted to Charles Cotesworth Pinckney, the revered native son. Yet he continued to insist that any elector who voted
for him must cast his second vote for Adams. Would the legislature choose
electors who were committed to Jefferson and Burr, Jefferson and
Pinckney, or Pinckney and Adams?[91] Much arm-twisting remained before the electors were chosen on December 2, the day before election
day. In the meantime, the most likely guess—it was the one made by
virtually every observer—was that the South Carolina legislature would
give Jefferson eight votes and that Adams would get nothing. But would
the eight remaining votes go to Pinckney or to Burr?

Blackguard Charlie made certain that Jefferson was aware of all that he had done in the legislative election. Despite a painful injury suffered in a carriage accident that summer, he claimed to have "incessantly laboured to carry this Election." He had been disavowed by his kinsmen and threatened with censure for having remained in South Carolina to politick rather than going to Washington to tend his Senate responsibilities. The Federalists, he went on, said he was the "*sole cause*" for their undoing in South Carolina. And on the night that the legislature was elected, he sent word to Virginia boasting of "our very fair prospects."[92]

Word of the election in South Carolina moved northward slowly as November dawned. The reaction almost everywhere was the same: Adams was finished. James Gunn, a Federalist senator from Georgia, rejoiced that "Adams is no longer the *mar-plot*." Madison, at Montpelier, breathed a sigh of relief. A "good result will take place" in South Carolina, he exclaimed, as he was certain that Jefferson would get enough of that state's electoral votes to push him over the top. Abigail Adams was in Baltimore, en route to Washington, when she learned of the vote in South Carolina. Instantly she said the news meant that her husband would not be reelected. "The consequence to us personally," she remarked, "is that we retire from public life: for myself and family I have few regrets. . . . I shall be happier at Quincy. . . . I have little to mourn over."[93]

By coincidence, the First Lady learned of the tidings from South Carolina on the same day that word arrived in Baltimore of the Treaty of Mortefontaine, an accord signed forty-five days earlier outside Paris by the commissioners her husband had sent to France to negotiate an end to the Quasi-War. The envoys had not gotten all that the president wanted. France had refused to pay compensation for the spoliations or to accede to all of America's commercial demands. Yet, like the Jay Treaty, this pact—if ratified by the Senate—meant an honorable peace that would vindicate Adams' diplomacy.[94]

Jefferson was still at Monticello when the election results from South Carolina reached Virginia. He made no comment initially. He watched and waited for additional information from friends in Columbia, the state capital, but Jefferson had a good feel for how the electoral college voting would go. As election day approached, he calculated that he and Burr led Adams and Pinckney by fifty-eight votes to fifty-three. He knew that Adams would win some of the nineteen votes in Rhode Island and Pennsylvania, if the latter state participated, but Jefferson was confident that the president could not get enough votes in those two states to bring him up to the seventy needed for a majority. Nor did he believe the presi-

dent would receive a single vote from South Carolina. Adams would remain a viable candidate only if no one received a majority of the electoral vote, for in that situation the House would decide the election from
among the four candidates. Jefferson did not believe that was in the offing. The vice president reckoned that he had only to garner twelve of the
twenty-seven undetermined votes from Pennsylvania, Rhode Island, and
South Carolina in order to secure a majority of the electoral votes, while
Pinckney had to win seventeen of those twenty-seven votes for a majority. It was conceivable that Burr might equal Jefferson's vote total, but
the vice president did not think that would occur. He said privately that
he expected one elector, and possibly two, from Georgia to withhold
their votes from Burr.[95] On election eve, Jefferson saw Pinckney as his
most formidable rival. As for the contest between them, Jefferson added,
"the issue of the election hangs on S[outh] Carol[in]a."[96]

11

"The Intention of Our Fellow Citizens"

The Election of 1800

ON ELECTION DAY—December 3—the presidential electors, according to the Constitution, were to "meet in their respective States, and vote by Ballot for two Persons, of whom one at least shall not be an Inhabitant of the same State with themselves." While the electors traveled to their respective capitals at the beginning of December, politicians everywhere devoured rumors and crunched numbers. No one was better at this than Jefferson. Each day a combination of news and scuttlebutt reached the common table at Conrad and McMunn's, where Jefferson lived in Washington, and he gleaned further information in the Senate cloakroom on Capitol Hill. Jefferson was savvy enough to separate the legitimate reports from the bogus, and by early December he knew that he had been disappointed in Rhode Island, which would give him nothing in the electoral college. However, by then he also knew that Pennsylvania would participate. A last-minute compromise had been reached between the state's House and Senate that gave the Republicans eight electors and the Federalists seven. It was less than he had hoped for and less than he had won there in 1796, but more than he would have gotten had the deadlock persisted. As Election Day dawned, Jefferson was back where he had been a couple of months earlier: the outcome was too close to call, and South Carolina remained the key. Adams, meanwhile, believed that Pinckney would receive all eight votes from his home state, making him the winner, while Jefferson would be chosen for a second term as vice president.[1]

If Adams was discouraged by the course of politics when he awakened on Election Day, he received even worse news during that day, when word reached the President's House that thirty-year-old Charles Adams had succumbed four days earlier to the ravages of alcoholism. When the president had renounced his son more than a year earlier, neither he nor the First Lady had known that Charles was dying, though both knew that the disease could be fatal. True to his ignoble vow, the president had not seen Charles again, nor had he written him, and it was only when Abigail reached Washington about three weeks earlier that Adams had discovered that his son was on his deathbed. Abigail had visited her son as she passed through New York en route to the new capital, and it was readily apparent to her that Charles was near death. She sat with him, held his hand, and talked gently to him, though he often was delusional, partly from the illness, partly from painkillers. The president had two weeks to write a last letter, but he never took up his pen, and following Charles' death he coldly remarked that there was nothing to be said. Indeed, for a very long time he said nothing, though much later he acknowledged that this loss was the heaviest burden he had ever borne.[2] While Adams sat in despair on Election Day, the presidential electors voted.

The electoral college ballots, by law, were not to be opened and officially counted until February 11, but there was no chance that the outcome of the contest could be kept secret for ten weeks. In fact, within a day or two of Election Day the residents of the capital knew the vote totals for Virginia, Maryland, and nearby Delaware. In the days that followed, tantalizing rumors swirled through the capital about the outcome in distant states, until at last on December 12 the *National Intelligencer*, a Washington newspaper, broke the news that neither Adams nor Pinckney had received a single vote in South Carolina. Basing its story on credible reports from only thirteen of the sixteen states—the three states not yet heard from were Georgia, Tennessee, and Kentucky, all indisputably Republican strongholds—the journal declared that Jefferson and Burr had triumphed. In recognition of the Republican nominating caucus' decision that Jefferson was the party's first choice, the newspaper added: "Mr. Jefferson may, therefore, be considered our future President."[3] Jefferson likewise thought that was the case. Upon reading the *National Intelligencer*'s scoop, he confided to his son-in-law that he believed he had been elected straightaway, as he continued to think that one or two electoral votes had been withheld from Burr in Georgia. "I believe we may consider the election as now decided," he happily remarked.[4]

Jefferson was wrong. When Georgia was heard from, it was learned that each of its electors had cast his two ballots for Jefferson and Burr. Just before Christmas, several newspapers printed the final tally:

	Jefferson	Burr	Adams	Pinckney	Jay
New Hampshire	—	—	6	6	—
Vermont	—	—	4	4	—
Massachusetts	—	—	16	16	—
Rhode Island	—	—	4	3	1
Connecticut	—	—	9	9	—
New York	12	12	—	—	—
New Jersey	—	—	7	7	—
Pennsylvania	8	8	7	7	—
Delaware	—	—	3	3	—
Maryland	5	5	5	5	—
Virginia	21	21	—	—	—
North Carolina	8	8	4	4	—
South Carolina	8	8	—	—	—
Georgia	4	4	—	—	—
Kentucky	4	4	—	—	—
Tennessee	3	3	—	—	—
TOTAL	73	73	65	64	1

Jefferson and Burr had tied at seventy-three votes apiece. The predictions that the outcome hinged on South Carolina had been accurate, but it alone had not decided this election. Occurrences in several states, not least New York, had been crucial as well. Indeed, Abigail Adams' forecast in May that her husband could never recover from his party's calamitous defeat in Manhattan had been dead on target, as the president had been buried under the avalanche of New York's twelve electoral votes for Jefferson and Burr. Had the two Federalist candidates swept either New York or South Carolina, Adams would have been reelected and Pinckney would have become the vice president, for one Federalist elector in Rhode Island had withheld his vote from the South Carolinian, balloting instead for John Jay.

Some aspects of the canvass were evident. The rival parties remained divided along sectional lines. Eighty-six percent of the electoral votes won by Adams were cast by electors from northern states. Jefferson received nearly three-fourths of his votes from southern electors. It was also clear that party discipline was much improved over the previous

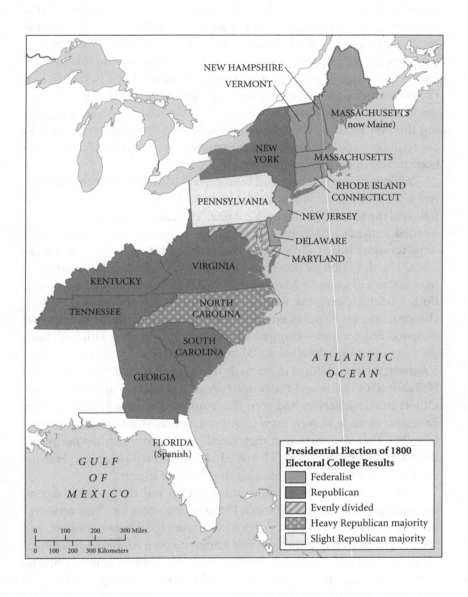

NEW HAMPSHIRE

VERMONT

MASSACHUSETTS
(now Maine)

NEW
YORK

MASSACHUSETTS

RHODE ISLAND
CONNECTICUT

PENNSYLVANIA

NEW JERSEY

DELAWARE

MARYLAND

KENTUCKY

VIRGINIA

TENNESSEE

NORTH
CAROLINA

SOUTH
CAROLINA

GEORGIA

ATLANTIC
OCEAN

FLORIDA
(Spanish)

GULF
OF
MEXICO

0   100   200   300 Miles

0   100   200   300 Kilometers

Presidential Election of 1800
Electoral College Results

Federalist

Republican

Evenly divided

Heavy Republican majority

Slight Republican majority

presidential canvass. Whereas roughly 40 percent of the electors had not adhered to the decisions of the party caucuses in 1796, only one elector of 138 broke ranks in 1800. It was apparent as well that the constitutional method of choosing the president had rapidly led to the emergence of party organizations, and that as the parties crystallized, the role that the Founders had envisioned for presidential electors ebbed into oblivion. For instance, Hamilton had argued in *Federalist* No. 68 that the electors would act with "discernment" in reaching "detached" decisions regarding the best possible choice for the presidency. Instead, by the second contested presidential election, the members of the electoral college had become the operatives of their national party.[5]

What is more, Jefferson had been correct to assume that the Federalists' high-water mark had occurred in 1798, in the milieu of outrage that followed the revelation of the XYZ Affair. Thereafter, the party's flood tide receded in the face of its new taxes and the repressive Alien and Sedition Acts. Yet more was at work than a backlash against those Federalist measures. The defection of those who worked with their hands, apparent in Manhattan's election in May, appears to have been replicated elsewhere. Both Elbridge Gerry, the Republican candidate for governor of Massachusetts, and the Republican congressional candidate in the district that included Boston won a majority of the city's vote in 1800, although both ultimately lost to Federalist candidates who carried the rural countryside. Similarly, the Republicans in Pennsylvania won all six assembly seats from Philadelphia County and the congressional seat allotted to Philadelphia.[6] Others beside Jefferson had seen this coming. Nearly a year before the Federalist debacle in New York City, for instance, Washington cautioned friends within the party that they faced political ruin if they permitted themselves to be popularly identified with arbitrary measures, Francophobia, and resistance to loosening the bonds of society.[7]

One of the strange twists to this election was that Adams' defeat, and Jefferson's victory, owed much to the voting behavior of urban workers, especially in New York. Adams had never lived ostentatiously, and for the past quarter century he had gotten by on a modest government salary and his investments. During roughly half of that time—while he served in Congress and during his eight years as vice president—he dwelled in extremely humble quarters. Furthermore, Adams not only was the son of a part-time tradesman but had lived most of his adult life in cities, practicing law in Boston and diplomacy in Paris, Amsterdam, and London, and occupying high national offices in New York and Philadelphia. He preferred the tranquility of bucolic Peacefield, but he was comfortable with urban ways. Jefferson, in contrast, had been born to the leisure class and lived virtually all his life in a material splendor that Adams could only imagine. In addition, his wealth was derived from inheritance and the labor of others, mostly bondsmen, and not from his own toil. And he was famous for his enmity toward cities, which he called great "sores" that sapped national virtues.[8]

The New York debacle notwithstanding, the Federalists would have elected one of their candidates had they carried rural South Carolina. But the "Wind having changed" there as well, as Blackguard Charlie Pinckney noted, the Federalists lost what had been their southern stronghold throughout the 1790s. In this instance the party was undone in the rural enclaves where the Federalist program, especially its embrace of the Bank of the United States and a strong central government, had never been popular. In this contest the Jeffersonians were organized as never before and able at last to overcome debilitating differences that had always previously undermined what one native of the state called the "Country Republican Interest."[9]

Not only could South Carolina have seen to the reelection of Adams, but it held it in its hands to make Pinckney the vice president. Had the state's electors given their two votes to Jefferson and their native son, as had occurred in 1796, Charles Cotesworth Pinckney would have finished a single vote behind the Virginia Republican. During the last two weeks before Election Day, South Carolina's assembly had wrestled with the selection of its presidential electors. The whip hand had been held by the uncommitted legislators. Incredible bargaining had taken place— Fisher Ames might have been thinking of South Carolina when he remarked that this election was "more complicated with underplot" than "an old Spanish play"—to win over the uncommitted. In the end, the uncommitted would not desert Jefferson, and Pinckney would not abandon Adams. The "trimmers," as the uncommitted were called by others in the legislature, finally threw in the towel in the face of the general's intransigence and reluctantly agreed to support Burr. Pinckney had remained honorably loyal to the instructions of his party's caucus, but his was a savvy performance. If he finished in a tie with Jefferson—which appeared to be the best he could hope for—Pinckney had to know that it was most unlikely that he could win in a House of Representatives in which the Republican Party would control a majority of the state delegations. If Pinckney was to have any chance of winning the presidency in 1804, he knew that he had to retain the support of New England's Federalists, which he might lose by forsaking Adams in 1800.[10]

Adams ever after blamed Hamilton for his electoral defeat. He was convinced not only that the *Letter* had cost him some support but that Hamilton was personally—perhaps deliberately—responsible for the Federalists' electoral disaster in New York. The president was wrong on both counts, but Hamilton had played at least some role in Adams' failed reelection bid. Hamilton and his gang of sycophants had conspired to prevent the sailing of America's envoys for three crucial months in the summer and fall of 1799, a sulky and treacherous obstruction that was calculated to forestall a diplomatic settlement until after the election. In the end they had their way, as word of Adams' crowning diplomatic achievement had not reached America until nearly mid-November, by which time virtually all the electors had been chosen. Had the envoys sailed when Adams first wished them to go (March 1799) or when he ordered their departure (August 1799), word of the accord with France likely would have reached the United States at least by midsummer 1800, and it might perhaps have turned the heads of enough electors to alter the outcome of the vote.

Adams was also the first presidential candidate to fall victim to the notorious three-fifths clause in the Constitution. Had slaves not been counted in the apportionment of state representation in the electoral college, Adams would have edged Jefferson by two votes, sixty-three to sixty-one.[11] Sage political maneuvering contributed to Adams' defeat as well. Virginia's switch to a general ticket format emasculated Adams and his party in that state, robbing the Federalists of perhaps as many as eight electoral votes. Had Adams received only five votes from Virginia, he would have edged Jefferson in the electoral college. Or had Governor Jay asked the New York assembly to legislate that electors be chosen by districts, as Hamilton had beseeched him to do, Adams would have carried the state, probably by a four-vote margin. In that event, the outcome of the election of 1800 would have been exactly reversed, as Adams would have won seventy-three electoral votes to Jefferson's sixty-five.[12]

But Adams was not the only candidate who was injured by vote-manipulating plans. Like Virginia, Massachusetts switched from the district to the general ticket format, and from choosing electors by popular vote to permitting the legislature to make the decision. That may have cost Jefferson one or two votes. He was undoubtedly hurt far more badly by what transpired in Pennsylvania. As the Republicans received nearly two-thirds of the votes cast in the state and congressional races, Jefferson might have captured anywhere from eleven to all fifteen of the state's electoral votes had either the general ticket or district elections been in play. Instead, as a result of the legislative compromise, Jefferson received only eight votes from Pennsylvania.[13]

When the electoral college vote was known, many Federalists—including Adams—attributed their defeat to ruinous fissures within the party.[14] That argument is unconvincing. The Federalists won largely where they had scored victories in 1796, and they lost where they had suffered defeats four years before. New York and South Carolina were the principal exceptions, and the Federalist defeats in those states were wholly unrelated to the dissonance between the rival wings of the party. Nor did Hamilton's open assault on Adams contribute to the president's failure to win reelection. No evidence exists that the sulfurous *Letter* caused any elector to withhold his vote from Adams. Then again, Hamilton's primary audience had been the members of the House, who he prayed would have to decide between Adams and Pinckney, and by an incredibly narrow margin he missed his opportunity to play the role of kingmaker. If anyone was injured by Hamilton's outrageous smearing of Adams, it was Hamilton himself. Mostly in private, but on occasion in public, some Federalists criticized him for having published his scurrilous charges, calling the pamphlet "an indiscreet ill-timed publication ... utterly inescapable of producing any good." Some even thought it succeeded only in revealing the Ultra-Federalists to be dangerously misguided warmongers.[15] Hamilton knew that for the foreseeable future he had no prospect of exercising power at the national level. Honeycombed with vindictiveness toward Adams, upon whom he heaped all the blame for the erosion of his political fortunes, Hamilton immediately turned his energies to blocking Adams' subsequent appointment of his son-in-law, Nabby's husband, to a post as surveyor of the port of New York. Hamilton won that petty battle.[16]

At first blush little evidence exists that a seismic shift in the strength of the parties had occurred since the presidential election of 1796. While the populace was gripped by the exciting contest—voter turnout appeared to be much greater than in 1796, approaching 70 percent in some places—surface indicators suggest a remarkable continuity in the outcome of this contest and its predecessor.[17] The electoral vote totals for Adams and Jefferson in 1800 remained precisely the same as in 1796 in eleven of the sixteen states. Take away New York and Jefferson won fewer electoral votes than he had four years before. Aside from New York, Adams' showing was poorer in only two states, Maryland and Virginia, where he lost merely three votes that he had won in 1796. Jefferson fared worse in two states, Pennsylvania and North Carolina, where he lost nine votes from his 1796 tally. A similar pattern is also discernable in the congressional elections in 1800. Seven House delegations remained intact, and in most states merely one or two seats changed hands, almost always involving Republicans who unseated Federalists. Substantive change occurred only in Virginia, where the Republicans gained six House seats (leaving the Federalists with only a single representative), and in Massachusetts, where the Federalist majority of twelve to two vanished and the two parties equally divided the congressional seats.

The surviving records, though fragmentary, suggest that the popular vote in the various state and national contests often was close, especially in many of the northeastern states. Adams' fate was sealed in New York, but even in Gotham the Republicans' margin of victory was hardly a landslide. The Federalists carried three of the seven wards in New York City and, overall, about 46 percent of the total vote.[18] The parties were similarly evenly balanced in several states. In New Jersey and Maryland the Republicans appear to have won 51 percent of the votes. In five states—North Carolina, South Carolina, Vermont, Rhode Island, and New York—the winning party garnered only 52 percent of the votes (yet in all save North Carolina every electoral vote went to the majority party). In Delaware and Massachusetts the winning Federalists may have garnered as much as 55 percent of the vote. Taken collectively, the scant surviving records suggest that the Republicans received about 52 percent of the votes cast in the various national and state races in 1800. These figures, however, do not include the votes in Kentucky, Tennessee, and Georgia, where the Republicans almost certainly scored landslide victories.[19]

Despite the continuity with the election of 1796 and the slim differences in the electoral vote totals in many states, signs of significant change abounded. The Republicans, who had won only about one-third of the votes cast in the two previous gubernatorial races in Massachusetts, captured almost 49 percent of the votes in the race for the statehouse. Pennsylvania had been shading toward the Jeffersonians in recent years, but in 1800 the Republicans won a lopsided 65 percent of the votes cast in the legislative elections and captured ten of the thirteen congressional contests and nearly three-fourths of the state assembly seats. Although the Federalists swept the electoral votes in New Jersey, the party's congressional vote totals dropped from a high of 65 percent in 1796 to just 49 percent in 1800. Furthermore, whereas the Federalist Party won two of New Jersey's five congressional seats in 1798, it failed to capture a single House district in 1800. Federalists had won seven of nineteen seats in Virginia's congressional delegation in 1798 but only one in 1800. In Maryland the two parties equally divided the state's electoral votes, but the Republicans won a majority of the contests for seats in the House of Representatives. Rhode Island gave all four of its electoral votes to Adams, but Republicans won the state's two congressional seats. Since 1798 the Federalists had held twelve of the sixteen congressional seats in North and South Carolina, but those posts were equally divided after the canvass of 1800.[20]

Indeed, control of Congress changed hands as a result of this election, underscoring the impressive triumph of the Republicans. The Federalists had controlled the House of Representatives since the off-year elections in 1794, consistently maintaining a ten- to twelve-seat majority through three election cycles. Not only had the Federalists always dominated the Senate throughout the decade, but the party had widened its control of the upper chamber in the elections of 1794 and 1796. However, as a result of the elections of 1800, the Republicans gained a lopsided majority in the House—they would control sixty-nine seats to the Federalists' thirty-six—and they took control of the Senate for the first time, with eighteen seats to the Federalists' thirteen.

If nothing else, these figures suggest that Adams, disconsolate at his alleged repudiation by the populace, could in fact have held his head high. He had run a considerably better race than that conducted by his Federalist Party.

The election of 1800 was a harbinger of looming troubles for the Federalists. Losing urban contests was politically unhealthy, especially as the nation's city populations were growing. Since 1790 the urban population in the United States had grown by about one-third. In the next twenty years it would more than double, as cities rose from containing about 5 percent of all American inhabitants to nearly 8 percent.[21] Perhaps more disconcerting to the Federalists was that both of the new trans-Appalachian states were solidly Republican. Not only had Jefferson and Burr captured all of the electoral votes of Tennessee and Kentucky, but all of the congressmen from those states were Republicans as well. Only one more eastern state (Maine) would enter the Union, whereas seven new western states would be created in the next quarter century.

The Founders had not planned for the people's voice to be heard in the selection of the president. However, in the nation's second contested presidential election, the popular vote was crucial to the outcome. Not only was what had occurred in New York City of paramount importance, but the Republicans had carried four of the five states in which electors were chosen by popular vote. Jefferson subsequently remarked

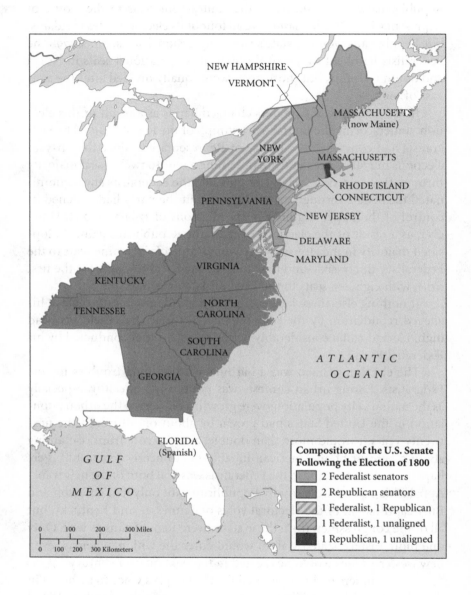

NEW HAMPSHIRE

VERMONT

MASSACHUSETTS
(now Maine)

NEW
YORK

MASSACHUSETTS

RHODE ISLAND
CONNECTICUT

NEW JERSEY

PENNSYLVANIA

DELAWARE

MARYLAND

VIRGINIA

KENTUCKY

TENNESSEE

NORTH
CAROLINA

SOUTH
CAROLINA

ATLANTIC
OCEAN

GEORGIA

FLORIDA
(Spanish)

GULF
OF
MEXICO

| 0 | 100 | 200 | 300 Miles |
| 0 | 100 | 200 | 300 Kilometers |

**Composition of the U.S. Senate
Following the Election of 1800**

2 Federalist senators

2 Republican senators

1 Federalist, 1 Republican

1 Federalist, 1 unaligned

1 Republican, 1 unaligned

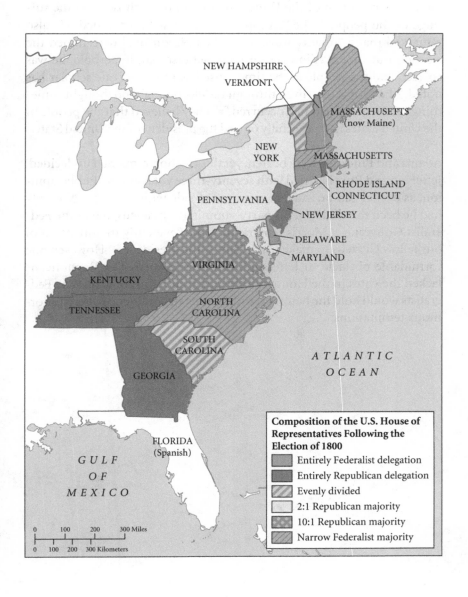

NEW HAMPSHIRE
VERMONT
MASSACHUSETTS
(now Maine)
NEW YORK
MASSACHUSETTS
RHODE ISLAND
CONNECTICUT
PENNSYLVANIA
NEW JERSEY
DELAWARE
MARYLAND
VIRGINIA
KENTUCKY
NORTH CAROLINA
TENNESSEE
SOUTH CAROLINA
GEORGIA

ATLANTIC OCEAN

FLORIDA
(Spanish)

GULF
OF
MEXICO

0   100   200   300 Miles
0   100   200   300 Kilometers

Composition of the U.S. House of Representatives Following the Election of 1800

  Entirely Federalist delegation
  Entirely Republican delegation
  Evenly divided
  2:1 Republican majority
  10:1 Republican majority
  Narrow Federalist majority

that something "new under the sun" had happened in the election of 1800—the president of the United States had been chosen by "the suffrage of the people." The "nation declared its will," he added. He also remarked that a "mighty wave of public opinion" had determined the election outcome.[22] Allowing for some Jeffersonian hyperbole, he was correct, and the people at the time sensed as much. As one scholar has noted, "the people who lived through the election of 1800 thought something momentous had just occurred."[23] They believed that the people of the United States had peacefully ousted the president of the United States.

Adams and Pinckney were beaten, yet this election remained undecided. Jefferson and Burr had tied with seventy-three votes apiece. Public opinion, as best as can be gauged, appeared to side with Jefferson. Not only had he been the choice of his party's nominating caucus, but as the Federalist Gouverneur Morris remarked, "it was evidently the Intention of our fellow Citizens to make Mr. Jefferson the President."[24] However, one formidable obstacle to Jefferson's election loomed. The Republicans lacked the votes in the House to elect either Jefferson or Burr. The Federalists would hold the hammer, and to some that influence offered enormous temptations.

12

"Give Them the Horrors"

The House Decides the Election

THE ELECTION OF 1800 had ended in a tie between the Republican nominees, a further sign that the Constitutional procedure for electing presidents was archaic. The problem arose because the framers, having failed to foresee the emergence of political parties, vested each presidential elector with two votes. Shortsighted in that respect, the Framers nonetheless had expected that it would be commonplace for no one to win in the electoral college. Thinking that two candidates would sometimes tie with more than a majority of the electoral votes, or more likely that no candidate would secure a majority, the Framers had anticipated that the electoral college would in fact often serve as a nominating panel that selected candidates from among whom the House of Representatives would choose the president.[1] For those occasions when the electoral college failed to produce a clear winner, the Constitution tersely outlined the procedure that would ensure for electing the chief executive:

> if there be more than one who have such Majority, and have an equal Number of Votes, then the House of Representatives shall immediately chuse by Ballot one of them for President; and if no Person have a Majority, then from the five highest on the List the said House shall in like Manner chuse the President. But in chusing the President, the Votes shall be taken by States, the Representation from each State having one Vote.

This passage, and existing federal law, brought several things about the election of 1800 into focus. The House was to decide between Jefferson and Burr. Its choice was limited to those two, as neither of the Federalists had equaled the vote of the Republican candidates. In addition, the states were to be equal in the House's balloting, each having one vote. A multimember delegation—which in 1800 meant any but tiny Delaware—would somehow have to reach a decision on what its vote would be. The Constitution and election law also stipulated that the votes of the electoral college were to be counted in the Senate on the second Wednesday in February and that the House was to act "immediately" to decide an unresolved election. Under these rules, the Senate would tally the electoral votes on February 11 and the House, presumably, would begin voting immediately thereafter. February 11 would not roll around until nearly seven weeks had passed since the results of the electoral college outcome were known.

Ordinarily the majority party in the House of Representatives holds the upper hand, but that was not to be true in electing the president in 1800. The Federalist Party had a sixty-four-to-forty-two majority in the House, but the Republican Party commanded the lion's share of delegations. Even so, the Republicans did not control a sufficient number of delegations to elect one of their nominees outright. In 1800 the Union was made up of sixteen states. If each state voted—that is, if none abstained—the votes of nine states would be needed to elect the president. The Republicans controlled eight delegations and the Federalists six, with two states deadlocked, as follows:

Republicans	Federalists	Deadlocked
New York	New Hampshire	Maryland
New Jersey	Massachusetts	Vermont
Pennsylvania	Rhode Island	
Virginia	Connecticut	
North Carolina	Delaware	
Georgia	South Carolina	
Kentucky		
Tennessee		

Actually, Maryland's eight congressmen consisted of five Federalists and three Republicans, but one of the Federalists announced his intention of voting for Jefferson, while his four party brethren—from long-standing antipathy toward the vice president—were committed to Burr. Vermont's

two-member delegation was also split, with its Federalist member committed to Burr and its Republican to Jefferson. Even though the Republicans, including Jefferson, loudly insisted even before Christmas that
each of the eight Republican-dominated delegations would adhere to
the wishes of the May party caucus and cast its vote for Jefferson, that
still left Jefferson one vote short of being elected.[2] This "produced great
dismay & gloom on the republican gentlemen here," Jefferson remarked,
"and equal exultation in the Federalists." To which, he added, "February
... will present us storms of a new character."[3]

Before Christmas there was talk of holding a second national election, but not only did the Constitution say nothing about such a procedure, the prevailing wisdom was that Federalists had little to gain from
another canvass. Nothing came of the idea.[4] At the beginning of January
Madison offered two commonsense solutions for resolving the deadlock. One was for the current House to adjourn sine die sometime in
February, after which President Adams could summon the just-elected
Seventh Congress into a special session to meet at noon on March 4,
Inauguration Day, the instant when his term and that of the Sixth Congress, elected in 1798, expired. The beauty of this solution, from Madison's
perspective, was that the Republicans would control a majority of the
state delegations in the new House of Representatives, ensuring Jefferson's
election. However, congressmen then were no more inclined than now
to relinquish power, and the Federalist-dominated Sixth Congress had
no wish to adjourn. Madison additionally proposed that the sitting House
take one vote to determine that it was hopelessly deadlocked, after which
at noon on March 4 Jefferson and Burr would jointly call the newly elected
Seventh Congress into a special session.[5] This seemed a patently uncon-
stitutional procedure, or at the very least a step that would have required
an exceedingly broad interpretation of that document. Jefferson ignored
Madison's brainstorm.

However, if a president was not selected by noon on March 4, when
Adams' term ended, the country would be without a chief executive for
nine months, until the recently elected Congress convened—as was pre-
scribed by the Constitution—near the end of the year. Republicans, of
course, were disturbed by such a prospect, especially as in the interim
the current Federalist-dominated Congress would be in total control.
Thus, even though Jefferson brushed aside Madison's nostrums, he approached Burr in the hope of finding a solution. In mid-December, as
the outcome in the electoral college could be seen with greater clarity,
but before the final tally was definitively known, Jefferson wrote Burr a

cryptic letter in which he appeared to suggest that if the New Yorker accepted the vice presidency, he would be given greater responsibilities than the previous vice presidents had been given. Burr responded quickly and reassuringly. He spoke of "your administration" and in veiled language seemed to ask what authority Jefferson was ready to grant him. Burr also appeared to propose that he be given a cabinet post in addition to the vice presidency. In his letter to Jefferson, as well as in others that he wrote before Christmas that were shared with Jefferson—or that were published and Jefferson read— Burr pledged his intention to "disclaim all competition" for the presidency, swore not to provoke "a disadvantageous schism" within the Republican Party, insisted that he would not be "instrumental in counteracting the wishes and expectations of the United States," and promised that he would "never think of diverting a single vote" from Jefferson.[6] All these letters were written before Christmas. Thereafter, Jefferson wrote Burr only once before the issue was resolved two months later, a missive in which he cautioned that the Federalists would attempt "to sow tares between us, that they may divide us and our friends."[7] While only that single letter was dispatched, it stretches credulity to presume that no discussions occurred between intermediaries.

Meanwhile, the Federalists were discussing their options. Several ideas took shape. Some advocated tying up the House proceedings to prevent the election of either Jefferson or Burr. With no one occupying the presidency, the rules of succession would kick in between March and December, leaving it to the Federalist president pro tempore of the Senate—if one could be elected by that deeply divided body—or to the Speaker of the House (Theodore Sedgwick, a Massachusetts Federalist) to wield executive authority for nearly the balance of the year.[8] That scheme had numerous adherents, and it worried Jefferson to the point that he apparently attended every Senate session in January and February so that he would be on hand, if necessary, to cast the tie-breaking vote that would prevent the body from electing a pro tempore.[9] A considerably smaller number of Federalists wished to utilize their House majority to invalidate several votes in the electoral college on technical grounds, a step that would make Adams the winner and eliminate the need for House action. Questions indeed existed about alleged voting irregularities in South Carolina and Georgia, but the evidence was thin. Besides, not only was the process of investigating abnormalities and disallowing votes likely to take months to play out, but because the Ross bill had failed in the spring, Congress was without an existing procedure to follow for deciding a disputed election. Furthermore, to abort the election of the Republican candidates was certain to bring on a crisis of alarming proportions that few congressmen were eager to face.[10]

Yet another element among the Federalists urged the party to throw its support to Burr. Speaker Sedgwick, who hardly saw Burr through rose-tinted glasses, was a leader of the faction that championed this course. Sedgwick regarded Burr as an "unworthy," "selfish," immoral megalomaniac. However, he also saw Burr, a native New Yorker, as experienced in the politics of a mercantile state and more receptive than Jefferson to the notion of a strong national government. Burr, he reasoned, not only would understand the needs of merchants but was a far better bet than Jefferson to "justly appreciate the benefits resulting from [the] commercial & other national systems" that had been put in place by Hamilton and Washington. Sedgwick was immeasurably harsh toward Jefferson, whom he saw as a French toady, a "sincere & enthusiastic democrat,"
and likely a devotee of the Virginia and Kentucky Resolutions (neither Sedgwick nor any other Federalist was aware that Jefferson had concocted the resolves). Burr, said Sedgwick, was the lesser of two evils, a scoundrel to be sure, but "a mere matter-of-fact man" who "holds to no pernicious theories" beyond gaining personal power, and who had no romantic ties to any foreign nation.[11]

Other Federalists, quite unlike Sedgwick, admired Burr. To "Courage he joins Generosity and cannot be branded with the Charge of Ingratitude," said one. But most were pragmatists who saw Burr furthering the interests that Federalists had long embraced. Congressman Robert Goodloe Harper of South Carolina, for instance, was impressed that "Burr's temper and disposition" provided "ample security for a conduct hostile to the

Theodore Sedgwick, about 1808, by Gilbert Stuart. A native of western Massachusetts, Sedgwick served as a U.S. senator and later as the Speaker of the House. In the latter post, he fought against Adams's nomination and reelection in 1800, and sought Burr's election during the House battle early in 1801.

democratic spirit." Still others saw that if Burr, with Federalist help, won the presidency, most southern Republicans would see him as a treacherous backstabber who had betrayed Jefferson. Under those circumstances President Burr, to forge a workable coalition, would have to find his allies from among Federalists in New England and the mid-Atlantic states. Finally, some Federalists backed Burr from the belief that should his presidency truly become "productive of evils," he would be easier to get rid of than Jefferson, who would have the whole weight of the "virginia party" behind him.[12]

A handful of Federalists who understood the growing democratization of American politics favored Jefferson because they thought it both honorable and prudent to surrender power to the clear-cut popular choice. Besides, by pursuing that course the party could not be sullied by subsequent charges of intrigue and deception, and when the populace wearied of the Republicans' "pernicious measures," the Federalists would "remain *free united* and without *stain*."[13]

Hamilton also preferred Jefferson, but he came at it from a different angle. He and those in his orbit who favored Jefferson did so because they found him to be less a curse than Burr. In October Hamilton had brutishly labeled Adams "unfit" to be president. In January he characterized Burr as "the most unfit man in the U.S. for the office of President." "As to *Burr* there is nothing in his favour." Burr was "without Scruple," a morally bankrupt and "unprincipled . . . voluptuary" who would plunder the country. He was dangerously ambitious, and when his enterprise was combined both with his daring and his "infinite art cunning and address," Burr had the potential to become a deadly menace. What Burr sought, Hamilton insisted, was "permanent power," and if he became president, he might destroy the Constitution and erect in its stead a "system . . . sufficient to serve his own turn." Put Burr in the President's House, Hamilton maintained, and the inevitable result would be "Disgrace abroad [and] ruin at home," for "if he had any theory 'tis that of simple *despotism*." Hamilton confessed that as much as he would relish the opportunity to "contribute to the disappointment and mortification of Mr. J[efferson]"—whose democratic "politics are tinctured with fanaticism" and whose character was shot through with hypocrisy—Burr was the one man he could not support. Jefferson was "*able*," Burr was "*dexterous*"; Jefferson was "*wise*," Burr was "*cunning*." Jefferson had tempered his Francophilia and, though misguided, was committed to the Constitution; Burr stood for nothing save personal aggrandizement. In short, Burr was the "most dangerous man of the Community."[14]

Some Federalists saw little to choose from between Burr and Jefferson but wished to string things out in the hope of inducing one of the Republican contenders to make a deal. Hamilton was one of the first to advance such a notion. No stranger to backroom bargaining, he urged the Federalists to seek the following assurances: "1. The support of the present fiscal system. 2. An adherence to the present neutral[ity] plan. 3. The preservation and gradual increase of the Navy. 4. The *keeping* in office all our Foederal Friends except" the cabinet secretaries. Such a strategy had two advantages, to Hamilton's way of thinking. "[T]hrow out a lure in order to tempt [Jefferson and Burr] to start for the plate, & thus lay the foundation of dissension between the two chiefs" that would rip apart the rival party. In addition, the Federalists might secure an agreement that would permit much of their program to survive. Nevertheless, Hamilton told those who would listen that while Burr would make accords, "he will laugh in his sleeve while he makes them and he will break them the first moment it may serve his purpose." On the other hand, Jefferson—with whom he had made the Compromise of 1790 on funding and assumption—would adhere to any accommodation he reached.[15]

The debate among Federalists could not be kept quiet. Tongues wagged and news spread like wildfire in a small town such as Washington, where politicians lived in close proximity to one another, often with twenty-five, thirty, or more, taking their meals together in a boardinghouse. Within three days of the revelation of the electoral college vote in the *National Intelligencer*, Jefferson and most Republicans knew that at least some Federalists were plotting to prevent the inauguration of a Republican president before December. Two weeks later, soon after Christmas, they also became aware that some Federalists hoped to elect Burr, an outcome that, at least according to some southern Republicans, was nothing more than a conspiracy to keep power in the hands of the same northern mercantile interests that had held sway for the past decade.[16]

Other disturbing tattle circulated that winter. Reports swirled of a Federalist conspiracy to assassinate Jefferson. In the fevered atmosphere that prevailed between Election Day and House action in mid-February, many Republicans believed the allegation. In the aftermath of the abortive Gabriel's Insurrection, the planned slave revolt in Henrico and Dinwiddie Counties in Virginia the previous summer, some southern Republicans were even willing to believe the rumor that the Federalists had armed the rebellious slaves. Some also gave credence to reports that here and there federal officials—who, of course, were Federalists—had seized arms and artillery from local militia units, presumably so they could maintain control of the government of the United States, by force if necessary. A Jeffersonian in Philadelphia reported early in February that at "no time . . . that I can remember since 1776" have so many concluded that opposition to the national government "is a duty and obedience a crime." If the Federalists prevented the accession of a Republican to the presidency, he added, that "day . . . is the first day of revolution and Civil War."[17]

When the new War Department and Treasury Department buildings were damaged in separate fires—one in November, the other in January—some Republicans concluded that these were episodes of arson arranged by anxious Federalists to keep incriminating documents from falling into the hands of the incoming administration. This was hardly likely, as the entire archives of both departments could have been comfortably burned in a small fireplace, yet there were Republicans who believed the worst and who wondered if the Federalists would go this far, to what lengths would they go to keep the Republicans from gaining power? The Republican press leaped to the offensive, especially assailing Federalist plans to thwart the will of the presidential electors.[18] Albert Gallatin, the Pennsylvania senator whom Jefferson had already approached about serving as his secretary of the Treasury, quietly proposed that the Republicans acquiesce to the Federalists holding power until December 1801, but in the interim all Republican states should nullify any Federalist laws that Congress enacted.[19] Equally ominously, Jefferson made it known to some Federalists—including President Adams—that if the Federalists attempted "to defeat the Presidential election," it would "produce resistance by force, and incalculable consequences."[20] Privately, however, there were times when Jefferson appeared ready to give up and go home. Virtually everyone in the capital exuded "bad passions of the heart," he lamented, and many of the Federalists not only hated him but were of the "violent kind." He told his daughter that he longed to be at home with his grandchildren, preferring to enjoy "their little follies . . . [to dwelling] in the wisdom of the wise."[21]

Jefferson's headaches arose not only from the actions of Federalists but from Burr's behavior as well. In mid-December Burr had disavowed a fight with Jefferson. However, two weeks later he wrote Samuel Smith, one of the three Republican congressmen from Maryland committed to Jefferson—and who thus had it within his power to deliver his state to Burr by changing his intended vote—and said that he would accept the presidency if elected by the House. Shortly thereafter, at the beginning of January, Burr met Smith and others over a two-day period in Philadelphia, where he allegedly told them that he intended to fight for the presidency. Smith sequestered his correspondence with Burr, but word leaked out nonetheless, and soon all of Washington believed that a sea change had occurred in Burr's outlook during the last half of December. Rumors buzzed that he was encouraging his Republican friends to seek allies among the Federalists and build a coalition that would result in his election.[22]

What provoked Burr's turnabout? Burr had made his initial pronouncement—the one in which he seemed to accept Jefferson's presidency—prior to the final disclosure of the electoral college balloting. At the time, he believed the Virginian had won the election. While the *National Intelligencer* reported in mid-December that Vermont had given its four electoral college votes to Adams and Pinckney, Burr had learned from ostensibly credible sources that one of the Green State electors in fact had cast his second vote for Jefferson.[23] Had Burr's information been accurate—and he believed it to be when he made his seemingly magnanimous professions about accepting the vice presidency—Jefferson would have been the outright victor by a count of seventy-four to seventy-three. Burr learned the truth—the *National Intelligencer* had correctly reported the Vermont vote—sometime near Christmas. As was true of virtually every political activist, he was terribly ambitious, and in the closing days of 1800 he realized that he had a shot at becoming the president of the United States. That turned Burr's head. Keep "the game perfectly in . . . [your] hand," a virulently anti-Jefferson Federalist advised him on Christmas Eve.[24] That was precisely what Burr now intended to do. Burr's strategy was to wait, watch, listen, and talk, and see what transpired in the countdown to February 11.

Burr had to know that he was playing a dangerous game. The safest course would have been to publicly disclaim the presidency, acknowledge that it belonged to Jefferson, and acquiesce to the vice presidency. Burr was yet a young man, just approaching his forty-fifth birthday. If Jefferson served two terms, Burr would be fifty-three at the time of the election of 1808, when he likely would be seen by Republicans as the heir apparent. He certainly would not be too old for the presidency in eight years. Washington had been fifty-seven and Adams sixty-one when they entered the office. What is more, given Jefferson's penchant for retiring to Monticello—he had done so in 1776, 1781, and 1793—there was a good chance that Burr would be his party's standard-bearer as soon as 1804.

However, other considerations militated against a safe course. While the odds were good that Burr would live another twenty years, dying young was not uncommon in the eighteenth century. In fact, Burr's mother and father had died at ages twenty-seven and forty-two, respectively, while his wife, Theodosia, had passed away at age forty-seven. Furthermore, Burr like every other activist, was all too aware of the vagaries of politics. Any politician who attempted to plan career moves eight or even four years down the road was on shaky ground. Any veteran of the American Revolution would have known as much, having seen the political landscape turn topsy-turvy by the overthrow of British rule and the demise of the Articles of Confederation. For that matter, within a six-month span in 1798 the Federalist Party had fallen from the giddy heights of supremacy to division and despair, and in two years John Adams had gone from being hailed as the equal of Washington in popularity to a defeated president who was being sent packing.

But if Burr tried, and failed, to beat out Jefferson, he risked political suicide, for he surely would forfeit southern support for all time. Even if he succeeded, Burr almost certainly would be viewed as a usurper, and his presidency might be in shambles before he took the oath of office. However, it must be remembered that the political parties in existence in 1800 were not entrenched institutions like those of today. They were less than a decade old and only recently had become reasonably well-disciplined entities. Both parties had members who shifted to the other side as new issues emerged or as the political wind changed direction. In fact, in the run-up to the canvass of 1800 many had been convinced that a party restructuring was under way. There had been much talk in 1799 and early 1800 that Adams and Jefferson would conclude a bargain that resurrected the so-called Adams-Lee Junto, the Virginia–New England alliance that had controlled the Continental Congress during the first several years of the American Revolution. Such a turn of affairs had probably never been in the works, but even some savvy politicians had believed it and suspected that a new party might supplant one of the two in existence or that a third party might come into being.[25] In January and February some who pushed Burr's candidacy appeared to believe—and to welcome— his presidency as the means of restructuring the existing parties along sectional lines. If so, it would not have been inconceivable for Burr to have had the solid backing of a viable new party.

Burr's intrigue was not the only game in town. Many Federalists rallied behind the bargain that Hamilton had proposed: support for Jefferson in return for his pledge to meet their demands. Jefferson subsequently mentioned that not only was he approached on the matter by Gouverneur Morris, a Federalist senator from New York, and Dwight

Foster, a Massachusetts congressman, but in a meeting with the chief executive late in January or early in February, Adams told Jefferson that the presidency would be his "in an instant" should he accept the Federalist conditions. All these individuals, and doubtless others as well, told Jefferson that if he consented to such an accord, Vermont's Federalist congressman, Lewis Morris, would switch sides, giving Jefferson nine states and victory on the first ballot in the House of Representatives. However, Jefferson rejected such a deal, saying that he "should never go into the office of President by capitulation, nor with my hands tied by any conditions which should hinder me from pursuing the measures" he preferred.[26]

Jefferson was skating on thin ice. Like the president, who sourly deplored the carnival of "Party intrigue and corruption" afoot in the capital, he too knew that men in both parties were on the make.[27] Jefferson believed that "Burr . . . has agents here at work" who were dickering with congressmen from both parties, and he suspected that bribes had been offered to seduce his supporters over to Burr.[28] On the other hand, Jefferson had to know that he had several advantages over his rival. He had to win over only one additional state to gain the presidency, whereas Burr had to pry three states into his column, likely a monumental undertaking. He also had to know that many congressmen—believing that the general electorate, together with most state legislators, who had voted Republican in 1800 had done so in the hope of electing Jefferson—were unwilling to act contrary to popular sentiment. Jefferson additionally knew from press reports that the Federalists had caucused on January 9 "for the express purpose of organizing measures for defeating the election of Mr. Jefferson" but that the meeting "broke up without concluding upon any decisive measures." This told him that Federalist support for Burr was tenuous.[29] Finally, the prevailing wisdom in the capital was that Jefferson's eight-state margin was firm and that those Republican congressmen who were committed to the Virginian were "determined to resist the election of *Burr* at every hazard."[30]

Given the high stakes and the unmistakable deadlock, one can imagine the pressures that were applied, the blandishments ladled out, and the tempting deals proffered between Christmas and mid-February to persuade congressmen to change their votes. Those in the deadlocked delegations from Maryland and Vermont must have been courted daily, but in all likelihood no one was lobbied more aggressively than James Bayard, Delaware's lone congressman. He held in his hands the sole determination of how his state would vote. Bayard, who was thirty-three years old, had been raised the son of a physician in Philadelphia and educated at Princeton before choosing to practice law in Wilmington. A Federalist, he was first elected to the House four years earlier, and quickly emerged as a partisan leader who urged a pugnacious stand toward France in 1797 and heartily supported the Alien and Sedition Acts in 1798. During the election of 1800 he had privately endorsed Pinckney, telling others that he was put off by Adams' "gusts of passion [that were] little short of phrenzy" and that he believed the president's "little jealousies and little animosities" had "palsied the sinews of the [Federalist] party."[31] When the election ended in a tie, Bayard at first was uncertain how he would vote. He would ultimately act "upon the maturest and soundest view I can take of the subject," he grandly proclaimed, but he was no less interested in first discovering what stance the Federalist Party would take and in allowing time for bargaining to get under way.[32] Bayard eventually climbed aboard Burr's bandwagon. He bristled with resentment of Virginians, including Jefferson. He saw Republican slave owners as hypocrites who "count[ed] in their train a hundred slaves," lived "like feudal barons," and looked on their neighbors as "the humblest vassals" while posturing as the "high priests of liberty."[33] Furthermore, once it became clear that "the inclination is much in favor of Burr" within the Federalist Party, Bayard chose to adhere to the majority opinion within his faction. Early on he announced that he would vote for Burr, the lesser of the evils and the one most likely to consent to maintain the Federalist program.[34]

The nation's second Election Day was February 11. It was a Wednesday. Inauguration Day, March 4, was only three weeks away. As February 11 approached, there was no sign of movement that could break the election deadlock. That was not unexpected: the pot was sure to be sweetened after the voting began.

Residents of the capital awakened to a violent snowstorm on the morning of February 11. Shortly before noon, the members of the House left their warm boardinghouses and climbed Capitol Hill, trudging through windblown drifts of snow to take up their lofty responsibility. By noon they had pushed into the overcrowded, stuffy Senate chamber to watch as the electoral college ballots were officially tabulated. It fell to Vice President Jefferson, the Senate's president, to announce the vote of each state, followed by the final tally. He treated the exercise as a mere formality. Indeed, when the tellers, those appointed to help with the count, suggested a possible irregularity with Georgia's ballot, Jefferson hurriedly moved on. Had Georgia's four votes not been allowed due to an abnormality, Jefferson and Burr would have received sixty-nine votes, one short of a majority. The House then would have had to decide the contest from among the five who had received electoral votes, opening the possibility that Adams or Pinckney might be elected. Vice President Jefferson perhaps acted from partisanship in moving on quickly and not taking up the issue of Georgia's vote, but recent scholarship has demonstrated that his decision was justified. He correctly understood that the defect in Georgia's ballot was the result of a frontier lawyer's mistake and not due to corruption.[35] When the counting was completed, Jefferson announced the official electoral vote: seventy-three votes for himself, seventy-three for Burr. It was precisely what the country had believed the vote to be for the past seven weeks.

As soon as Jefferson announced the totals, the House members hurried to their chamber. Two days earlier they had agreed to remain in session until the election was decided and to take up no other business until the president was elected. When the House came to order, it was discovered that the snowstorm had hardly affected attendance. Only one of the 105 House members was not present, and his absence would not change his delegation's tally. At least one congressman had gone to considerable pains to be in attendance. Joseph Nicholson, a thirty-year-old Maryland representative who was seriously ill, knew that his attendance would be crucial. A Republican, Nicholson was aware that if he did not vote, Maryland would ballot four to three for Burr, making the overall tally eight to seven for Jefferson, with Vermont yet deadlocked. Rather than permit such an occurrence, with the temptations that would be dangled before the congressmen whose switch-about could determine the contest for Burr, Nicholson arranged to have friends carry him on a stretcher through the swirling snow from his residence two miles away. His wife accompanied him and remained at his side as he lay on a pallet in an anteroom. With each vote, Nicholson scribbled "Jefferson" on his ballot, and his wife carried it to Speaker Sedgwick for tabulation.[36]

The House wasted no time. The moment it was gaveled into session, it voted. Only a few minutes were required for each congressman to complete his ballot and for the votes to be counted. Sedgwick announced the outcome: Jefferson eight, Burr six, two states (Maryland and Vermont) deadlocked. Of the six states that voted for Burr, only South Carolina had awarded him electoral votes. Maryland and Vermont had voted, but their delegations, as expected, were equally divided and thus deadlocked. Thus, all sixteen states had voted. Jefferson was one vote short of victory.

The House immediately voted again, allowing no time for "out of doors" maneuvers. Rumors had circulated that a vote or two might change after an initial, symbolic vote. However, if any votes changed—the records of the voting within each delegation did not survive—the outcome was not affected. Then another vote was taken, and another, and still more through the long afternoon, until the gray light of day faded and a jet-black darkness enveloped the capital. By six o'clock, nearly five hours after the initial vote, fifteen ballots had been taken. The tally never changed.

The House recessed at that point. Its members had not eaten since breakfast, and the congressmen scattered through the ice and slush to their boarding houses and nearby taverns. They returned two hours later to their warm, ill-lit chamber, and the voting resumed immediately. No change. Now the rapid pistonlike pace of voting that had prevailed through the day gave way to long delays between ballots, a sign that fresh bargaining had commenced. Only four votes were taken in the seven-hour session on that dark night. The last ballot—the nineteenth of the day—was tabulated at three in the morning. No movement had occurred in the fourteen hours since the initial ballot. The exhausted congressmen called it a day, agreeing to convene again at noon, only nine hours away.

The House voted only once on Thursday. No change. Nor did the two ballots taken on Friday, or the three on Saturday, bring any change. As night shrouded the Capitol on Saturday, February 14, the House had cast thirty-three ballots over four days. A numbing stasis prevailed, but while the House was idle on Sunday, some of its members were extremely busy on that day of rest.

Warnings had been commonplace for weeks that drastic steps might be taken if the Federalists denied the Republicans, or Jefferson, the presidency. After four days of gridlock in the House, the threats seemed more ominous. All along talk had swirled that Virginia would secede if Jefferson was not elected. Now some Republicans cautioned that if the Federalists prevented Jefferson's election, they would call another constitutional convention "to re-organize the government, & to amend it" so that it reflected the proper "democratical spirit of America." Threats of the use of force were heard as well. Governor Monroe, for instance, threatened to convene the Virginia legislature should the Federalists, by hook or crook, prevent a Republican from assuming the presidency. Many took his menacing remarks to mean that Virginia would use force to see that Jefferson took office. Some were also aware that Monroe had been in direct contact with Pennsylvania's new Republican governor, Thomas McKean, about acting in concert should the need arise. McKean, in fact, told Jefferson that he could arm twenty thousand militiamen and was prepared to use force. Rumors were rampant that Republicans in the mid-Atlantic states would take up arms if the Federalists did not relinquish power on March 4. On the Sunday of the hiatus in voting, word swept the capital that a huge mob had stormed the arsenal in Philadelphia, seizing weapons and preparing to march on Washington to drive out the defeated Federalists. That report was bogus and may have been hatched in Richmond and delivered to Washington by "a chain of expresses" that Monroe cobbled together and kept busy. But one story out of Richmond was true. Monroe had ordered his militia to guard the arsenal at New London, Virginia, supposedly so that its cache of four thousand arms could not fall into the hands of any army that the Federalists might use to preserve their power. Jefferson pitched in as well, sometimes pleading that he could not restrain his supporters and alternatively warning that the provocative actions of the Federalists threatened "a dissolution" of the Union. Sometime on Saturday Jefferson called on Adams and mentioned the possibility of resisting a Federalist coup d'état—he called it a "legislative usurpation"—with force. The next day he reported to Monroe that the campaign of blunt threats "shook" the Federalists and that the talk of a new, democratic constitution "gives them the horrors."[37] Adams was one who was shaken. Subsequently he confessed that at the time he had believed the two sides had come to the "precipice" of disaster and that "a civil war was expected."[38]

In addition to these orchestrated threats, there appear to have been sporadic incidents aimed at intimidating carefully targeted Federalists. A French informant in Washington reported that between the last ballot on Saturday and the resumption of voting on Monday, "two Federalist members of the House received anonymous notes threatening them with death if they did not vote according to the will of the people." He added that "stones were thrown against the houses where other [Federalist] representatives of the same party were living."[39]

The first break in the electoral deadlock occurred sometime after Saturday's final ballot: Delaware's congressman Bayard blinked. Knowing full well that he had it in his "power to terminate the contest"—it was a fact that he spoke of often—Bayard, probably on that Saturday night, opted to see if he could arrange a deal that would enable him to abandon Burr and allow Jefferson's election. He sought out a Republican who was close to the vice president, almost certainly John Nicholas, a member of Virginia's House delegation, and proposed a bargain. Should he, Bayard, abstain from voting—which, with only fifteen states balloting, would reduce the magic number for victory to eight states, the number that the vice president had garnered all along—would Jefferson in turn accept the terms that Hamilton and other Federalists had long since bandied about: "First, . . . the support of the public credit; secondly, the maintenance of the naval system; and lastly, that subordinate public officers employed only in the execution of details established by law shall not be removed from office on the ground of their political character, nor without complaint against their conduct"? Nicholas responded that these conditions were "very reasonable" and that he could vouch for Jefferson's acceptance. However, he did not approach Jefferson with the terms of the bargain.[40] Likely that same evening, or at the latest on Sunday morning, Bayard privately spelled out to Speaker Sedgwick, and possibly other Federalist leaders in Congress, what had transpired. He indicated that he would abstain from voting when the House reconvened on Monday. Sedgwick immediately asked Bayard not to divulge his plans until the Federalists could caucus and consider matters.

Bayard ultimately offered numerous reasons for his change of heart. His continued political career—he remained in public life until his death in

James Bayard by C. B. J. Fevret de Saint-Mémin. Bayard was thirty-three when this portrait was painted in 1801. As Delaware's sole congressman, he was in a unique position to determine the outcome of the election of 1800 within the House of Representatives.

1815—may have encouraged mendacity or at best a mottled recollection on his part, and this has prompted scholars to treat his various explanations warily. On one occasion Bayard claimed that he and the five other Federalists who held in their hands the power to determine the election—the four from Maryland and the one from Vermont—never lost "sight for a moment of the necessity of a president being chosen" by March 4. Consequently, before the House balloting commenced they supposedly entered into a bargain to support Burr until it was manifestly clear that he could not be elected, then to "give our votes to Mr. Jefferson." Bargains of this sort, he claimed, had been entered into by some House members on the other side of the aisle. Supposedly, a handful of Republicans from New York, New Jersey, and Tennessee, together with the lone Republican from Vermont, were committed to scuttling Jefferson should it become evident that he could not be elected.[41] On another occasion, Bayard also insisted that he had acted from what he called "imperious necessity" to prevent a civil war or disunion.[42] In later years he claimed to have been swayed by public opinion, which clearly preferred that Jefferson assume the presidency. At the time he made his decision Bayard provided an altogether different reason for his behavior: "Burr has acted a miserable paultry part. The election was in his power, but he was determined to come in as a Democrat." Bayard's contemporaneous remark strongly suggests that Burr had refused any bargain that included a sellout of the principles of his party.[43] In contrast, Bayard subsequently insisted that Jefferson had entered into "such a deal."[44]

Be that as it may, Jefferson had not agreed to any bargain as a result of the meeting between Bayard and Nicholas. He had not been approached by the Virginia congressman and, from all that can be determined, was unaware of what had transpired. Indeed, on Sunday, sometime after Bayard and Nicholas had talked, Jefferson wrote to Governor Monroe: "Many attempts have been made to obtain terms & promises from me. I have declared to them unequivocally, that I would not receive the government on capitulation, that I would not go into it with my hands tied."[45]

Also on that Sunday, February 15, Sedgwick summoned the congressional Federalists to a closed-door caucus. When Bayard's decision was announced, it touched off a firestorm, an unlikely occurrence had Jefferson in fact already formally agreed to a deal. Cries of "Traitor! Traitor!" rang down on Bayard, who at the time described the acrid meeting as one in which the "clamor was prodigious. The reproaches vehement." Many old colleagues were "furious" with him, he remarked. Two issues appear to have roiled his comrades. Some were furious that Bayard had broken ranks before it was known definitively what kind of deal Burr might be willing to cut. Some also were more than a bit uneasy that nothing had been heard from Jefferson, who indeed had not even been approached by Nicholas. A vexatious debate ensued for nearly an hour, according to Bayard's later recollection, after which "we broke up in confusion." In all likelihood the Federalist leadership called a recess in the hope that it could privately, and in a less hyperbolic climate, piece together a strategy. Later in the day, probably after night had fallen, the Federalists were called into a second caucus. That meeting was "no happier" than the first, the harried Bayard said.[46] Not much more is known of what transpired, as it too was a secret session, and those who attended guarded their secrets with remarkable craft. However, it appears that two decisions were reached. As letters from Burr were expected any day, Bayard agreed not to change his vote until the contents of the New Yorker's correspondence were known. Second, the caucus directed Bayard—he subsequently said that he had been "authorized"—to ask Nicholas to speak with Jefferson and secure his categorical assent to a bargain. Within a day or two, it was presumed, the Federalists would know whether Burr or Jefferson would compromise, and if so, who would offer the most.

Bayard's second conversation with Nicholas—probably on Sunday evening—went nowhere. When Bayard demanded that "the points . . . be understood as conceded by Mr. Jefferson"—that is, that the vice president assure Nicholas, the intermediary, that he would abide by the Federalists' conditions—Nicholas refused to approach Jefferson. Bayard shot back that this "was not sufficient—that we should not surrender" without a better guarantee.[47] However, Bayard did not give up. Shortly thereafter, almost certainly later on that same busy night, he sought out Samuel Smith, the Maryland Republican who had discussed matters with Burr in Philadelphia several weeks earlier. Smith was close to the vice president—he was a fellow boarder at Conrad and McMunn's—and was widely viewed as Jefferson's spokesman during the House imbroglio. Smith, who at age forty-eight remained trim and handsome, was a wealthy Baltimore merchant who had been a Federalist until his outrage at the Jay Treaty led him to change parties. Since then he had voted with the Federalists on commercial and foreign policy matters about as often as he had sided with his new comrades. Smith heard out Bayard on that cold evening and quickly provided the same assurances that Nicholas had given. Bayard responded that he "should not be satisfied or agree to yield till I had the assurance of Mr. Jefferson himself." Smith, according to Bayard, promised to speak with Jefferson on that Sunday evening and to return with the vice president's answer the following morning.[48]

On Monday morning, Bayard later recollected, Smith "informed me that he had seen Mr. Jefferson, and stated to him the points mentioned, and was authorized by him to say that they corresponded with his views and intentions, and that we might confide in him accordingly."[49] The deal was made, at least to Bayard's satisfaction. Unless Burr offered more, Jefferson would be the next president of the United States.

When the House met at noon on Monday, it balloted two additional times, its thirty-fourth and thirty-fifth votes. No change had occurred since Saturday's votes. An hour or so after convening, the House adjourned for the day.

Sometime in the next few hours, probably late on that cold afternoon, the deadlock was resolved. The communiqués from Burr arrived. What Burr said, or did not say—his missives were apparently destroyed soon after they reached Washington, and their contents remain a mystery—disappointed his Federalist proponents. At the time, Bayard told his wife that Burr had declined to meet the terms that the Federalists demanded. Bayard also confided to Hamilton that Burr "was determined not to shackle himself with federal principles."[50] That same Monday evening a dejected Speaker Sedgwick, who passionately hated Jefferson, notified friends at home: "the gigg is up."[51] Jefferson was to be the next president.

On Tuesday, February 17, an air of anticipation existed in the capital. The long electoral battle was to end, and anticlimactically, as everyone in Washington knew that the deadlock had been broken, though few were aware of the labyrinthine maneuvering that had transpired. The end came quickly. The House gathered at noon, and as it had on thirty-five previous occasions over the past six days, it voted with little ceremony.

The thirty-sixth vote was dramatically different. Delaware did not vote, which in itself was sufficient to elect Jefferson. In addition, however, none of the Federalists from Maryland, Vermont, and South Carolina cast votes. This altered voting pattern put Maryland and Vermont in Jefferson's column, and as there were no Republicans in South Carolina's congressional delegation, that state—like Delaware—abstained. The final tally was:

Jefferson	10 states
Burr	4 states (Massachusetts, New Hampshire, Rhode Island, and Connecticut)
Abstain	2 states (South Carolina and Delaware)

Jefferson had been elected, but had he won the presidency through a bargain with members of the Federalist party? He ever afterward steadfastly insisted that allegations that he had entered into a deal of any sort were "absolutely false."[52] The evidence suggests otherwise. Within days of the resolution of the disputed election, Burr was told by friends in the capital that Jefferson had struck a bargain to win the presidency.[53] In a letter written on the very day of the climactic House vote, and five years later while testifying under oath in a libel suit, Bayard insisted that Smith divulged to him that Jefferson had agreed to accept the Federalists' terms.

Smith, also while testifying under oath many years later, corroborated Bayard's story.[54] Furthermore, Bayard's account was subsequently backed by a friend who had served with him in Maryland's congressional delegation in 1801. But most telling, perhaps, was a letter that Bayard wrote at the time the deal was allegedly cut. He told a Federalist officeholder, who feared losing his position should Jefferson take office, "I have taken good care of you. . . . [Y]ou are safe."[55]

Jefferson's actions as president also lend credence to the allegations that a bargain was made. Despite having fought against the Hamiltonian economic system for nearly a decade, Jefferson acquiesced to it once in office, never touching the Bank of the United States, faithfully discharging the national debt, and tolerating continued borrowing by the federal government. Nor did he remove Federalist officeholders. Jefferson did seek naval reductions, but within the discretionary limits set by Federalist legislation passed late in Adams' presidency. His actions would prompt some friends to suspect that he had made a deal with the Federalists, leading some such as George Clinton, his stalwart Republican ally in New York, to despair that President Jefferson had become an "accommodating trimmer."[56]

Jefferson's friends who had been present tried to cover for him, but their stories often were less than convincing. Until he testified under oath, Smith always publicly denied that a bargain had been made. Thereafter, sheepishly and improbably, he embraced the story that Jefferson had agreed to the terms without realizing what he was consenting to. Nearly a half century after the disputed election, Albert Gallatin offered the bizarre claim that Smith had believed that Jefferson had consented to a bargain but that the Maryland congressman had misunderstood the vice president.[57]

The mystery is not why Jefferson would deny making such an accord but why had he compromised after so many declarations that he would never bend. Unaware of Bayard's change of heart, and with Inauguration Day barely two weeks away, Jefferson had to have concluded that he had no other good choice if he wished to become president by peaceful means. To do nothing and to permit the balloting to spin on was to hazard seeing the presidency slip from his hands and into those of Burr. Jefferson knew that a majority of the Federalists favored Burr, and he had to believe that they would make the New Yorker the same offer they were dangling before him.[58] He also must have fretted over the staying power of his backers. On the second day that the House voted, in fact, Jefferson noted that some Republicans were meeting privately with Federalists and that Bayard had urged the ubiquitous Samuel Smith to desert him, an act that would have thrown Maryland's vote to Burr.[59] Furthermore, if the Federalist Bayard was aware of a pact among some capricious Republican congressmen to desert Jefferson should it become apparent that he could not be elected, the vice president almost certainly would have known of their covenant. In addition, not only did Jefferson believe that Burr's agents were in town working for his election, but he must have known of the hot and heavy rumors swirling about the capital that New York's Edward Livingston, a silk-stocking Republican with tenuous ties to his party's southern wing, was purportedly scheming to deliver both his state and New Jersey to Burr.[60] Indeed, Jefferson appears to have already offered Livingston's brother, Robert, a cabinet position, and he may have held out a federal appointment to Edward as well.[61] Finally, while Jefferson was undoubtedly mortified by thoughts of capitulation, he was not in reality conceding that much. Hamilton's fiscal program, now a decade old, was so entrenched and so important to powerful interests in the urban North that Jefferson had to know that any attempt to undo it would put at jeopardy the Union itself. Furthermore, he probably already planned to keep most of the Federalist bureaucrats in office, at least for a time. They were experienced hands who could keep day-to-day government operations functioning smoothly, and besides, as new offices were created Jefferson would be free to appoint Republicans. In fact, within two years of Jefferson's inauguration, half of all federal officeholders were members of his party. Only a deal over the navy would have truly irked Jefferson, but it was a relatively small price to pay for the prize he would receive in turn.

Burr's misbegotten behavior is even more enigmatic. He had decided to make a play for the presidency, only to refuse the Federalist terms that might have led to his election. The reasons for his action have been lost in a confounding tangle of furtive transactions and deliberately destroyed evidence. As some Federalists doubtless feared the South's response to Burr's election, they may have demanded more of him than they did of Jefferson. Burr may have concluded that those terms were impossible to meet, or may have found it unpalatable to strike a bargain with ancient enemies, including the hated Hamilton circle. Or Burr might have been unwilling in 1801 to spurn principles to which he had been committed throughout his political career. His greatest misreckoning, it seems, was not in contesting Jefferson, but in flinching in the heated battle that he had agreed to join.

Burr's stumbling performance left open the door for the Federalists' putative bargain with Jefferson that resolved the election. With it, the prospect of mayhem, menacingly threatened by numerous Republicans, including Jefferson, immediately disappeared. The final, unsolvable mystery of the election is whether Jefferson and his backers would have sanctioned the use of force had he been denied the presidency. Force would have been unlikely had Burr been elected, and altogether inconceivable had he won out with help from Republican congressmen who defected from Jefferson to push him over the top. The possibility is greater that Jefferson might have used force had the Federalists thwarted the election of both Republicans. Still, it is more probable that Jefferson would have tried a peaceful tack. Soon after he became president, Jefferson claimed that "[t]here was no idea of [using] force." His remark proves little, as it was uttered while he was attempting to restore unity in the wake of the turbulent election. Yet during the ongoing battle in the House he alternately spoke of simply acceding to the Federalists' misconduct, in the belief that their egregious behavior would ruin them, and of calling a second Constitutional Convention to radically amend the Constitution.[62] He probably would have chosen one of these courses before he risked bloodshed and the end of the Union, a fate that would have rendered the presidency that he so passionately sought an empty vessel.

It was over. For most, the campaign had begun fifteen months earlier. For Jefferson, the battle to win the presidency had probably begun as early as two months into Adams' term, when he listened to the president's hard-line speech in May 1797 to the special session of Congress. The vote of the House of Representatives had made Jefferson "the chair of the US," as he curiously put it. While relieved and happy, he was also angry. He was bitter toward Burr for not having conceded the election, and soon, in fact, Jefferson acted to block his vice president's patronage recommendations for New York. Jefferson additionally, and presciently, regarded the vote for Burr by the four New England states "as a declaration of perpetual war" against him and his pending administration. On the other hand, he was gratified that so many Federalists in the mid-Atlantic states had voted for him. Not only did it lead him to believe that he could work harmoniously with them, but he saw it as evidence of a fatal division among his adversaries.[63] Indeed, during the crucial weekend when the election of 1800 was finally decided, Jefferson may have come to understand that by bargaining with the Federalists he could tear additional fissures in the already tattered opposition party, a prospect that made palatable the deal he had sworn never to make.

13

"The Creed of Our Political Faith"

Jefferson's Inauguration

IT IS A RARE OCCASION when the president of the United States becomes invisible, but John Adams virtually disappeared after mid-December, when the *National Intelligencer* broke the news of his defeat. With eighty days remaining in his term, and power slipping from his hands, Adams was shunned by many within his party. The remainder of his vanishing act was his own doing, as he sequestered himself within the President's House. Immobilized by what he called the "shower of ennui" that accompanied his shattering loss, and racked with grief over his late son and guilt over his own behavior toward him, Adams had almost lost interest in the presidency. He wished to see only those who were truly close to him, and he confided to nearly all with whom he spoke that he was desperately eager to leave for home. He took a daily walk along Pennsylvania Avenue, if the weather permitted, and he and Abigail worshiped on Sunday mornings at the Anglican services in the House of Representatives chamber. Otherwise he remained out of sight, counting the days, as he put it, until he became "a farmer. John of Stony field and nothing more (I hope nothing less) for the rest of my life."[1] Above all, he said, he looked forward to escaping "all intrigues, and . . . all the great and little [political] passions that agitate the world."[2]

Adams played no role in the House of Representatives' resolution of the election of 1800. He hoped that Jefferson would be chosen, privately remarking that it would be mortifying to "old patriots" and men of "splendid talents" should Burr, through the chicanery, triumph over merit.[3] The First Lady thought Jefferson would win, largely because "neither party can tolerate Burr," and she probably would have agreed with her son Thomas Boylston, who declared that while Burr's talents were equal to those of Jefferson, the Virginian was a more honest man.[4] As the House prepared to ballot, she proclaimed that Burr, like Napoleon, was dangerously ambitious, "a much more dangerous Man than Mr. Jefferson."[5]

One area in which Adams remained active was the campaign to secure Senate ratification of the Treaty of Mortefontaine, or Convention of 1800, as many would call it. He thought it a generally good treaty, as it established peace with France, defined the terms of contraband—commodities that could not be traded with belligerents—and recognized the right of the neutral United States to trade noncontraband items with France's enemies. The pact did not provide for indemnification for the American property that France had destroyed during the Quasi-War Crisis, but as it would resolve the anguishing conflict with France that had colored all his years in the presidency, Adams considered it an honorable treaty and urged ratification.[6]

Ratification required the approval of two-thirds of the Senate, which enabled the Ultra-Federalists to declare that they would approve the pact only if France agreed to pay indemnification. On January 23 the Senate rejected the original treaty, but ten days later it approved the accord with the reservation that French indemnities be paid. Adams was delighted. The preservation of United States neutrality and the frustration of those who had long sought an Anglo-American alliance meant that his presidency had brought the ship of state "into a peaceable and safe port," Adams told his son.[7] Years later he declared that he hoped his tombstone would be engraved: "Here lies John Adams, who took upon himself the responsibility of the peace with France in the year 1800."[8]

When the Federalists enacted the Alien and Sedition Acts, they had set their expiration dates for March 4, 1801. With a Republican administration now set to take office on that date, the Federalist Congress gave no thought to extending the repressive acts, but it did enact the Judiciary Act of 1801. Two years before, Adams had urged revisions to the federal judiciary system, but Congress had not acted. Now, knowing that they would lose control of Congress in three weeks, the Federalists moved to double the number of circuit courts and to create twenty-three new federal judgeships. Adams welcomed the legislation and set to work at once to fill the vacancies. A legend materialized that he remained at his desk past midnight on his final night in office signing the paperwork to pack the judiciary with Federalist magistrates, and the new justices soon were ridiculed as "midnight judges." Jefferson believed the story and condemned what he called the "indecent conduct" of his predecessor.[9] But that tale was only half true. Adams did appoint Federalists almost exclusively, including Oliver Wolcott, who was named to the Second Circuit Court, a selection that smacks either of a payback for the deliverance of Connecticut's electoral vote or of incredible forbearance on the part of the president. Otherwise, Adams made almost all of the appointments during the week of February 20 and had completed the task eight days before Inauguration Day.[10]

The First Lady had contemplated leaving for Quincy early in February so that she might have the house ready when her husband arrived, but weather and illness delayed her departure.[11] Sometime during her final week in Washington, Jefferson called to say goodbye. He came uninvited, a gracious gesture of friendship and caring, and doubtless one that he hoped might be a first step toward healing the breach with her and her husband. However, the president never reciprocated and never again saw Jefferson.

Abigail finally set out for home on February 13, just prior to Bayard's defection from Burr. She reached Philadelphia just as the city learned of Jefferson's victory. In a remark suggesting that her farewell meeting with the vice president may have been icy, Abigail registered her horror at hearing church bells toll with joy in celebration of the election of what she called "an Infidel President."[12] President Adams, meanwhile, was alone during his last nineteen days in Washington. His final state dinner—given to honor a delegation of Native Americans—occurred on the frenetic Monday when Burr's letters arrived and Congressman Smith allegedly presented Jefferson with the Federalist terms for a compromise.[13]

With little work left to be completed, Adams devoted much of his remaining time in office to writing a response to Hamilton's deeply afflicting *Letter*. Not only did Adams believe the pamphlet had been a "calamity" for his candidacy, but he knew that several of Hamilton's charges were untrue. When driven by a wild fury, Adams was barely susceptible to restraint. In this instance, he drafted an eighty-nine-page handwritten response to Hamilton's allegations and included charges of his own. He depicted the New Yorker as devious, duplicitous, calculating, and above all dangerous.[14] But for all his hurt and vehemence, Adams in the end chose not to immediately publish his tract. "I am not about to write lamentations or jeremiads over my fate [or] panegyrics upon my life and conduct," he loftily declared, but in fact he was concerned that what he wrote might someday harm the political future of John Quincy, like himself a Federalist.[15] After he returned to Quincy, Adams from time to time worked on his answer to Hamilton, as if writing was therapy for his lacerated spirit. But it was not until 1809, soon after John Quincy switched to the Republican Party, that Adams published his assault on his hated nemesis in a lengthy series in a Boston newspaper.[16]

Jefferson as well was busy writing in the days that followed his election. He composed his Inaugural Address. He had only two weeks to complete the task, but he was a wordsmith and such a rapid writer that his task was not daunting. While he worked, Jefferson continued to reside at Conrad and McMunn's, where he had a small parlor adjacent to his room, a convenient site for greeting visitors. He persisted too in dining at the common table with the numerous congressmen—and the wives of one or two—who ate regularly at Conrad's. It was a busy period for the president-elect. In addition to writing his speech, he contemplated his choices for the cabinet and diplomatic posts, met with a steady stream of eager office seekers, and tended to his correspondence. Nor did he ignore his business interests at Monticello, as he purchased clover seed for the farm and kept a record of his recent tobacco sales. Two days before he was to take office, Jefferson rented a coach, perhaps as a getaway for a few hours to collect his thought and escape the seemingly unbroken line of happy well-wishers and persistent job seekers. On March 3 and Inauguration Day, March 4, Jefferson did not spend a cent, the rarest of occurrences when he was away from Monticello.[17]

It did not snow or rain on March 4. Someone would have recorded such unpleasantness had it occurred. In all likelihood, the weather was unexceptional, which for Washington at that time of the year would have meant a high temperature slightly to one side or the other of the high forties.

Nothing is known of Jefferson's day before late morning. However, he ordinarily retired early and rose early (he once claimed that he had not slept past sunrise in more than fifty years), and on Inauguration Day he was probably out of bed before the first streaks of light penetrated the dark eastern sky. He was accustomed to breakfast at eight o'clock at Monticello, and even though he was living in a boardinghouse, he was probably able to adhere to this regimen.[18] In the couple of hours before he emerged from his apartment, Jefferson would have shaved and dressed, and may have soaked his feet in a pail of ice water, a practice he regularly endured for medicinal reasons. He would have been assisted by a trusted slave, who resided elsewhere in less comfortable quarters and who would have risen in the gloomy darkness of night to prepare for tending his master. While Jefferson awaited breakfast, he often dealt with his correspondence or read, and on this day it is likely that he re-read the speech he would soon deliver.

When he came to the breakfast table that morning, Jefferson was prob-ably greeted by his fellow diners—old friends and trusted colleagues—with the customary good-natured banter. He likely ate his usual breakfast of bread or corn cakes with cold ham and either coffee or tea.[19] Thereafter, a couple of hours remained before the day's festivities. Jefferson may have greeted some supporters in his parlor, easily making small talk, after which he retired for his final preparations. Already the sound of drum and fife could be heard, and now and then the thump of distant artillery, fired by militiamen who were practicing for the day's events.

Finally, it was time. Jefferson emerged around eleven o'clock wear-ing a plain suit, the same attire chosen by his predecessors. Unlike Wash-ington and Adams, however, he had neither powdered his hair nor strapped a sword to his waist. Jefferson wanted a ceremony without pomp or pageantry, in keeping with his belief in limited government free of formalities. He wished for his inauguration to be illustrative of what he thought was a crucial difference between his party and the contemptu-ous hauteur of his opponents. Thus he chose not to ride to his inaugural in a carriage, a vehicle that was too expensive for almost all Americans. He would walk, accompanied by the Alexandria militia, several United States marshals, those members of Adams' cabinet who chose to partici-pate, and all the Republican congressmen and senators, some of whom had begun to assemble in front of Conrad and McMunn's at midmorning.

While the festivities were beginning in Washington, celebrations were unfolding elsewhere. For some, the rejoicing was due not solely to Jefferson's accession to the presidency but to the fact that the bitterly fought election had been resolved peacefully. Power was being trans-ferred bloodlessly that day from one party to another that stood for dis-tinctly different principles, an occurrence virtually without precedence. Too, for many this day was nothing less than the consummation of the American Revolution. Poems and songs lauding Jefferson had been ap-pearing in the press since December, and especially since his victory in the House of Representatives two weeks previously, but the real celebra-tion was reserved for March 4. On that gray morning Philadelphia held a parade that featured a float in the shape of a schooner—christened the *Thomas Jefferson*—and drawn by sixteen horses, one for each state. Several towns had pageants in which a young woman dressed as Liberty was besieged variously by kings, soldiers, or even clergymen. She was always saved by a man playing Jefferson, who usually was summoned by the blast of a trumpet.[20] Killingsworth, Connecticut, celebrated by firing eight cannons, one for each state that had supported Jefferson from the outset in the House contest. After thirty-six minutes—for the number of ballots that had been cast in the recent House election—two cannons were fired for Maryland and Vermont, whose votes awarded the victory to the Virginian. Thirty-six minutes later two more cannons boomed, these for South Carolina and Delaware, which had abstained from voting for Burr. And finally, after another thirty-six minutes, the final four cannon shots were fired in honor of the remaining states.[21]

Back in Washington, Jefferson stood impatiently with those who would march as the assemblage was organized. Soon, however, the pro-

An 1800 election banner that celebrates Jefferson's victory. The in-coming chief executive is surrounded by the words: "T. JEFFERSON President of the United States of AMERICA" and "JOHN ADAMS is no MORE."

The Capitol building by watercolorist William Birch. It shows the unfinished Capitol at the time of Jefferson's inauguration. Only the Senate wing was completed by March 4, 1801, so the new president was inaugurated in that chamber.

cession set off from in front of Conrad and McMunn's, with the militia in the front ranks. Their trek was short, not more than a quarter mile, and likely did not take more than fifteen minutes. The president-elect's party traversed unpaved streets dotted with tree stumps, each marcher carefully stepping around mud holes formed by recent rains. Behind them, on the blue Potomac, numerous small craft could be seen. Ahead, all about Capitol Hill, forests mingled with open rolling land, some cleared by farmers in earlier times, some more recently by the developers who were chasing a bonanza in the embryonic capital. The inaugural train climbed the gentle slope toward the Capitol, past the wooden barnyard fence that encircled it, and on to the summit, a vantage point that permitted a glimpse of the President's House far to the west.

When Jefferson was escorted to the Capitol's entrance, he must have been surprised to discover that the outgoing president was not there to greet him, as Washington had waited on Adams in March 1797. Instead, Adams had risen early on this morning and in the cold, still darkness caught the four o'clock stage out of town. Although his term would not end for another eight hours, Adams could not bear to witness the celebration of

Jefferson's triumph and his defeat. When Jefferson entered the Capitol, Adams was already several miles north of Washington, en route to what he knew would be a permanent retirement and feared would be obscurity and oblivion.

Just before noon, the scheduled time to begin, the president-elect was led into the dim Senate chamber, where he had presided over recent sessions. Smaller than the House chamber, it contained galleries in the rear and along the sides. The low murmur of voices changed to applause as Jefferson was escorted to the dais, where Burr and stolid John Marshall, the new chief justice and the man who would administer the oath, waited. Jefferson must have greeted each perfunctorily. The events of the past seventy-five days had produced grievous strains in his relationship with Burr. Marshall, on the other hand, not only despised Jefferson, who had lived sumptuously at Monticello while he had suffered with the Continental Army, but was contemptuous of his fellow Virginian's ideology of decentralization and greater state autonomy. Jefferson, in turn, thought Marshall had betrayed Virginia by embracing the Federalist Party.

The packed chamber was warm and stuffy. Most senators and House members were present, though some Federalists who could not abide Jefferson, such as Speaker Sedgwick, had already left for home or, as was the case with three-fifths of Adams' cabinet, had simply chosen not to participate in the festivities. Foreign diplomats who were posted in Washington were in attendance, and so too were the members of the Supreme Court. Numerous government workers and local residents lucky enough—or, more likely, with sufficient influence—to obtain a pass crowded in as well and stood beneath the balconies along the circular walls.

Unlike recent inaugurals, the plan in 1801 was for Jefferson to speak, after which would come the swearing-in. At noon, it was the lot of Vice President Burr, who had been sworn in earlier that morning, to introduce Jefferson. The incoming president was greeted enthusiastically by the members of his own party and cordially by many Federalists. For Jefferson, who was shy and uncomfortable before an audience of any size, the most difficult moment of his day was at hand. Noticeably nervous, he began his address in a nearly inaudible voice that one observer characterized as "almost femininely soft."[22]

Jefferson's speech broadly addressed three main themes. He began by offering reassurances to the members of the opposition. He hoped that the vitriol of the recent presidential canvass could be laid to rest and that the nation could "unite in common efforts for the common good." What is more, he hoped his fellow citizens might "restore to social intercourse that harmony and affection without which liberty and even life are but dreary things." The first step, he said obliquely, would be the termination of the Alien and Sedition Acts. The American Revolution had "banished from our land ... religious intolerance," he claimed. He hoped no less that "political intolerance as despotic, as wicked, and capable of as bitter and bloody persecutions" might also be expelled. He also sought to persuade his countrymen that they were less divided than many believed. "We are all republicans, we are all federalists," he said. He was not alluding to the political parties, for tellingly he had not capitalized the words *republicans* and *federalists*. Jefferson used the term *republicans* as a clear reference to the citizenry's overwhelming embrace of republicanism, while by *federalists* he meant either the federal system in which power was shared by the national and state governments, the federal union, or both. Jefferson amplified that all Americans adhered to the Union, which "has so far kept us free" and safe from Europe's formidable powers. With regard to the Old World, Jefferson stressed his commitment to an independent America free of the fetters of foreign nations. To expunge any lingering concerns regarding his alleged Francophilia, he lamented the bloody carnival of "exterminating havoc" that gripped Europe. To the mercantile community, which feared him, Jefferson comfortingly explained his conviction that commerce was the "handmaiden" of agriculture and essential to the well-being of the new nation. He did not mention the navy, nor did he comment on Hamilton's public credit system. Though discursive, he pledged his adherence to the "honest payment of our debts and the sacred preservation of the public faith." Finally, he added a prayer of sorts to "that Infinite Power which rules the destinies of the universe."

Following his long introduction, Jefferson outlined his ideology and expectations. There was no need to strengthen the national government. The interests of the American people were more secure than those of any other people in any other land. America was the only nation "where every man, at the call of the law, would fly to the standard of the law, and meet invasions of the public order as his own personal concern." He wished for less government. A "wise and frugal Government" was best, and the best governors were the people. Under his administration, he pledged, the reach of the national government should be "compress[ed] ... within the narrowest compass." The states should exercise all those powers that did not explicitly belong to the federal government. He advocated "[e]qual and exact justice to all men." He insisted on an "absolute acquiescence in the decisions of the majority" but cautioned that "to be rightful" the popular will "must be reasonable," for "the minority possess their equal rights, which equal law must protect, and to violate would be oppression." Civil authorities must be supreme over the military, he said, and he advocated a diminutive national army, as the militia was "our best reliance" for security.

Lastly, Jefferson explained his electoral victory as the triumph of the American Revolution. At last, he appeared to say, the ends that most of the citizenry had sought in 1776 had been secured. Those "principles . . . which . . . guided our steps through an age of revolution" were republicanism, national union, and representative government, and continued adherence to those tenets would preserve "peace, liberty and safety." The revolutionaries had fought to free themselves from the waste and bloodshed of Europe's habitual warfare. Their hope had been "peace, commerce, and honest friendship with all nations, entangling alliances with none." Those sentiments remained the popular conviction, as demonstrated by the election of 1800. Finally, said Jefferson, the "wisdom of our sages and the blood of our heroes" were devoted to the securing of individual liberties—"freedom of religion, freedom of the press, and freedom of person under the protection of the habeas corpus and trial by juries impartially selected." To secure these ends, the patriots of 1776 had risked all. "These principles form the bright constellation" for which the United States stands, and they must be "the creed of our political faith" and "the touchstone by which to try the services of those [leaders] we trust" with authority.[23]

With that, Jefferson closed. The speech had consumed less than thirty minutes. Once the applause died down, Jefferson took the oath of office. It was official. Given the "approbation implied by your suffrage," as Jefferson the literary stylist had just awkwardly put it, he was now the third president of the United States.[24] The ceremony, such as it was, had concluded. Jefferson, according to popular legend, immediately returned to Conrad and McMunn's, where he stood with fellow boarders awaiting a chair so that he might have his dinner.[25]

Epilogue

"The Revolution of 1800"

IN THE TWO WEEKS THAT FOLLOWED his inauguration, Jefferson behaved like a person who had been called on suddenly to speak but later regretted not having said things a bit differently. Or perhaps he simply wished to broach ideas that he had thought were better left unsaid in his conciliatory Address. While still residing at Conrad and McMunn's—he remained there during the first fifteen days of his presidency, while work continued on the President's House—Jefferson wrote to many of the surviving signers of the Declaration of Independence, and to Thomas Paine, who had been the first to publicly broach the idea of independence, to expand on several themes.[1]

Jefferson expressed pride in the Revolutionary generation, which, like its predecessors, had sacrificed to preserve liberty. We have "done our part" and deserve the "embraces of our fathers," he boasted. He hoped that America would serve as a beacon to the oppressed everywhere and that "the condition of man over a great portion of the globe" would be ameliorated through "our example [of] a free government." He reflected a bit on the recent election, characterizing it as a "recovery from delusion," for his party's victory signaled that the nation had overcome its rapture for militarism, monarchy, commercialism, corrupt stockjobbery, infringements on civil liberties, and a reunion with Great Britain. To Paine, who had forecast in 1776 that the American Revolution was the birthday of a new world, Jefferson in 1801 exalted that his election meant that the American Revolution would be fulfilled. Breaking with Great Britain had been filled with risk, he added, but now the "storm is over, and we are in port." The new "chapter in the history of man" that Paine had foreseen was at last about to begin.[2]

Jefferson never stopped reflecting on the meaning of the election of 1800. Nearly twenty years later, when he was seventy-six years old, he offered his most memorable observation on his victory. The election of 1800 was tantamount to "the revolution of 1800." It was "as real a revolution in the principles of our government as that of 1776 was in its form; not effected indeed by the sword, as that, but by the rational and peaceful instruments of reform, the suffrage of the people."[3]

Not all of Jefferson's contemporaries agreed with his premise that Americans had wanted a revolution of 1800 or even that Jefferson should have been elected.[4] Some Federalist newspapers immediately charged that he never would have been elected had it not been for the three-fifths rule that had unjustly inflated the number of electors allocated to the South. A New England journal said that Jefferson had ridden "into the temple of Liberty on the shoulders of slaves," and Pickering labeled him the "Negro President."[5] John Adams let that charge pass, but he insisted that because the electoral vote had been so closely divided between Federalists and Republicans, it was impossible to read into the outcome a popular repudiation of his party or his presidency. Adams ever after objected to the notion that the American nation had been unalterably reshaped by the Jeffersonians after 1801, and he said as much to Jefferson. History had witnessed many true revolutions—Adams pointed to the Crusades, the spread of Islam, the Reformation, the Thirty Years' War, the American Revolution, and the French Revolution as examples—but he thought it was going too far to claim that Jefferson's victory had set in motion radical change.[6]

Jefferson, who abhorred confrontation, sidestepped a clash with Adams. It would be unseemly for the two former presidents to "become the Athletae of party, and exhibit ourselves, as gladiators, in the Arena of the newspapers," he remarked. But he did tell Adams that what he had meant was that the American Revolution had been about who would be supreme: the people or a small elite. That question, he said, had not been fully answered until the election of 1800. Throughout history where free governments existed, he went on, the "same political parties which now agitate the U.S. have existed thro' all time." One party exists in "favor of the many," the other "of the few." Jefferson added that he had never believed that Adams was a friend of aristocratic rule. Indeed, from 1776 forward he had regarded Adams as his soul mate in favoring "the rights of our countrymen," while the other side "cherished the monarchy of England." The election of 1800, he went on, was in reality a triumph over the "old tories," and as such it was a pivotal event in history, for it finally determined the outcome of the American Revolution and the destiny of the American people and their new nation.[7]

Beyond a doubt, Jefferson's presidency and those of his Republican successors, Madison and Monroe, ushered in significant changes. As president, Jefferson consciously set out to banish every trace of monarchy and aristocracy that he believed had defiled Federalist rule. He eschewed a carriage and liveried servants while traveling about the capital, preferring simply to ride horseback. Levees were also a thing of the past, and he greeted diplomats wearing casual attire. He abandoned the practice of appearing before Congress to deliver the State of the Union message, a style that smacked of royalty, he thought. Despite reservations about the constitutionality of the treaty in which France offered to sell Louisiana to the United States, Jefferson consented to the pact, a stroke that appeared to portend that the Republic would remain a yeoman's country for generations—centuries, even—to come. Each of the three Republican presidents, moreover, chipped away at Federalist land legislation, steadily bringing down the price of western lands, until under the Land Act of 1820 a farmer could acquire eighty acres for about $130, a sum that was easily obtained by most who practiced husbandry. Jefferson had bloodlessly acquired and made accessible a vast domain, a feat that some Ultra-Federalists had dreamed of accomplishing through the use of force. What is more, the revenue generated by land sales and the tariff eliminated the necessity of direct federal taxation. Much of Jefferson's presidency was conducted in the shadow of Napoleonic warfare, but like Washington and Adams before him, he maintained the peace, giving the infant Republic more time to find its legs.

Although Jefferson's claim of a "revolution of 1800" was exaggerated, his famous postmortem was not absurd. While his election was not as revolutionary as independence had been in 1776, Republican governance came with a new tone, a new style, and a new ideology that enabled the nation to move piecemeal from the habits of 1800, laced as they yet were with restrictive customs that had persisted from colonial days, toward egalitarianism and democratization. It was a transformation that many of the consolidationists had sought to inhibit through the Constitution of 1787 and that the Federalists had eagerly attempted to forestall when they fought to thwart Jefferson's election in the House of Representatives. Sooner or later a democratic revolution almost certainly would have occurred, but it would not have been during an era of Federalist hegemony, and had Adams or Pinckney been elected in 1800, the Federalists might have controlled both the executive and judicial branches of the national government for a very long time. In this sense, the election of 1800 consummated the American Revolution, resolving what had not been settled in the initial upheaval and fulfilling the dreams of those who, like Paine, long had yearned for the "birthday of a new world."[8]

By July 4, 1826, the fiftieth anniversary of independence, the nation was substantively different from what it had been during the troubled election year of 1800. In the quarter century since Jefferson's election the population had more than doubled, topping eleven million. Philadelphia, with sixty-one thousand inhabitants, had been the largest city on Jefferson's Inauguration Day. Twenty-five years later it had been surpassed by New York City, which boasted a population of more than 150,000, larger than that of either Delaware or Rhode Island. Every state had grown in population during the past twenty-five years, but the most spectacular growth had occurred in the western region. When Washington had been inaugurated as president, fewer than a hundred thousand settlers had lived beyond the mountains; by 1826 more than 2.5 million lived in trans-Appalachia.[9]

Other changes had occurred as well, and some were set in motion by Hamiltonianism. In 1826 New York City was the commercial hub of what historian Gordon Wood called the "most thoroughly commercialized nation in the world."[10] Over 40 percent of the nation's imports entered through its busy port, and on some days more ships bobbed in its harbor than had visited the city annually on the eve of the American Revolution. Banks fostered an entrepreneurial spirit that had moved America into a capitalist and industrial age. Textile mills dotted the northern landscape, churning out cheap manufactured cloth, which together with other commodities was transported to backcountry markets by steamship, canals, and wagons that plied thousands of miles of toll roads. In the ascendancy was a bourgeois republic in which the businessman was taking up a position alongside the yeoman.

There was a different feel to life in America by 1826, and while some of it was the legacy of Hamilton, more of it—or so, at least, contemporaries believed—was their inheritance from Jefferson. Social distinctions had blurred, and the fashions that once had set one class apart from another had largely disappeared. A pervasive egalitarian spirit had taken root, and despite wide inequities in the distribution of wealth, most free citizens believed they enjoyed the same rights and opportunities as all other free men. The country was more democratic. In the year of Jefferson's inauguration, Maryland abandoned property qualifications for voting and instituted the secret ballot in its elections. Others followed, until by 1826 universal manhood suffrage—which was not as encompassing as it sounded, as neither women nor African Americans could vote—was widespread. In 1800 property qualifications kept free men from voting in a majority of states, but a quarter century later only one-third of the states yet maintained property qualifications, and some of those had pared down their restrictions or waived them altogether in return for militia service or paying taxes. In 1800 the members of the electoral college had been chosen by state legislatures in three-fourths of the states. Twenty-five years later electors were popularly elected in three-fourths of the states. What is more, the electoral college operated differently, and it had since the election of 1804. The Twelfth Amendment, ratified that year, limited each elector to one vote for president and a distinct vote for the vice presidency. Never again would the nation face an ordeal akin to that brought about by the tie between Jefferson and Burr.[11]

More than any other single public figure, Jefferson deserved credit for the social and political reforms that had been achieved by 1826. In the Declaration of Independence he had outlined a vision of an attainable new world that was free of privilege and tyranny. Thereafter, he proposed liberating changes in education, religion, land ownership, and the treatment of criminals. He was among the first to divine the reactionary threat posed by the extreme conservatives in the early days of the new Republic, and he was the first major official to take steps to organize an opposition to the peril. While today his resistance to the economic changes that have shaped our world may seem archaic, he may have been the first to grasp the menace to republican governance that was posed by great wealth. He understood the hazards that lurked to peace, independence, and civil liberties in the spirit of the Ultra-Federalists, and he took the lead in the fight to resist those dangers. Far more so than subsequent generations, the great majority of those who were alive in 1826 recognized Jefferson's achievements in breaking many of the fetters that had existed before 1776.

Long before 1826 many of the major players in the election of 1800 had disappeared from public life, including even the Federalist Party. It enjoyed some successes after 1800, but it never again came close to winning control of the national government. Adams' long public career ended with his defeat in 1800, which he knew to be the case when he stole out of Washington in the predawn darkness of Jefferson's Inauguration Day. The election of 1800 was also the swan song for both Hamilton and Burr as national political figures. Hamilton's *Letter* had ruined him with many Federalists, making it unlikely that he could ever again hold high office. Yet at age forty-four in 1801 he was young and resourceful. Biding his time, he founded a newspaper and practiced law, and in 1804 he fought vigorously—and successfully—against Burr's attempt to win the governorship of New York. However, it was a Pyrrhic victory for Hamilton. Burr harbored a festering resentment of Hamilton, feeling that the former Treasury secretary had been instrumental in his defeat on three occasions—when he was turned out of the Senate in the mid-1790s, when he lost the presidency in the House of Representatives in 1801, and in the gubernatorial contest. He seized on word that Hamilton had slandered him during the governor's contest by allegedly calling him "a dangerous man" who did not deserve to hold important office. Burr demanded an apology, and eventually a duel, and killed Hamilton at Weehawken, New Jersey, on July 11, 1804.[12] Thereafter, grand juries in New York and New Jersey indicted Burr. Having already burned his bridges in Jefferson's Republican Party, Burr seemingly no longer had a future in electoral politics. He subsequently engaged in mystifying behavior in the western country that finished him altogether in public life. He eventually returned to a successful legal practice in New York and lived on to 1836, dying at age eighty.

Of the principal candidates, only Charles Cotesworth Pinckney was not hurt by the election. He served in South Carolina's senate until 1804, but his hopes of election to the United States Senate were frustrated by the Republican Party's control of the state legislature. When South Carolina redistricted late in 1804, he lost his state office and never again held an elective post. The Federalist Party nominated him once again in the presidential election of 1804, but he was buried beneath an avalanche of support for Jefferson, winning only 14 electoral votes to the Virginian's 162. The Federalists tried with Pinckney yet again in 1808. This time he was overwhelmed by Madison and failed to carry either his state or Charleston. That was Pinckney's final electoral contest, although he remained active in Charleston thereafter, dabbling in medicine, science, and a Bible society. Pinckney died in the summer of 1825 at the age of eighty.

On Independence Day in 1826, ninety-year-old John Adams and eighty-three-year-old Thomas Jefferson lay near death, insensible to the happy festivities all across the land. Adams had retired to Peacefield in March 1801, Jefferson to Monticello in 1809. Retirement had been more traumatic for Adams. Not only had he been sent home against his will, but he suffered through the inescapable reality that Jefferson was a popular president. "I am buried and forgotten," he lamented, and in a slough of despair he exclaimed that if he had his life to live over, it would not be as a public servant. He privately poured out vitriol at Washington and Hamilton, and sniped at Jefferson as well, though less petulantly. In his darkest moments Adams despaired that the American Revolution had changed the world for the better. Rather than having ushered in an age of reason, the years after 1776 had been an "age of Folly, Vice, Frenzy, Fury, Brutality, Daemons," he raged.[13]

In time, however, Adams changed. He discovered that he enjoyed life at home. Abigail was at his side, as were several grandchildren, and he was free of the cares that accompanied officeholding. He reestablished ties with his brother, who lived on a nearby farm, and the two grew close for the first time. Adams stayed quite busy, mingling work in his study with long daily walks through Peacefield's rolling green acres. He wrote his memoirs, intending their posthumous publication by his descendants, and he toiled with a voluminous correspondence, carefully preserving what he wrote in the hope that it too would be published and illumine future generations as to his service and sacrifices.

During his first decade at home the post relentlessly brought tidings of the passing of the Revolutionary generation: John Dickinson, Thomas Paine, and Samuel Adams were among those who were gone before 1810. The demise of old Revolutionary friends and foes changed his perspective. Adams mellowed, and he softened even more as dignitaries increasingly traveled to Quincy after 1810 to pay homage to him. He drew sustenance too from the career of John Quincy, who was elected to the Senate in 1803 and appointed minister to Russia in 1809 by President Madison, and who still later would head the State Department before winning the presidency in 1824. Adams believed that his son's political success offered proof that the public had come to approve of his own public service, including his presidency. By the time Adams had been home for fifteen years and had passed his eightieth birthday, the United States had survived the War of 1812 and its independence at last appeared to be safe. With that, Adams came to believe that the American Revolution had succeeded, and he once again was proud that he had played a major role in such an epic occurrence.

But it was Adams' rapprochement with Jefferson in 1812 that completed his transformation. Mutual friends persuaded each man that the
other was ready to forget old enmities. Once the ground was readied,
Adams took the first step, writing cautiously to Jefferson. The Virginian
quickly responded, and a remarkable correspondence began that resulted
in the exchange of over 150 letters in fourteen years. Both men seemed
moved by the reestablishment of their once amicable relationship, but it
was especially important to Adams, who was gratified at being embraced
as an equal by the man who had beaten him in 1800 and who had come
to occupy a seat in the American pantheon alongside Washington and
Franklin.

Unlike Adams, Jefferson had never wavered in his belief that the
American Revolution had been a glorious success. The "flames kindled
on the 4th of July 1776 have spread over too much of the globe to be
extinguished by the feeble engines of despotism," he remarked in 1821,
adding that "light and liberty are on a steady advance."[14] In his final letter, written in 1826, Jefferson reiterated his belief that the American Revolution had been, and would continue to be, "the signal arousing men to
burst the chains" that bound them and to secure the "blessings and security of self-government."[15]

Jefferson had been content with retirement from the outset, but he
too coped with cares, though of a different sort than those that nettled
Adams. Jefferson's insurmountable debt pressed hard on him during his
last years. In 1819 it exceeded $40,000, and he had to find $1,200 annually merely to service the interest charges. Indeed, had anyone other than
Jefferson inhabited Monticello, creditors likely would have seized the
estate before 1815. As it was, Jefferson was compelled to sell land, slaves,
and even his magnificent library to stay afloat, and all the while he lived
with the reality that his beloved mountaintop mansion would inevitably be lost to his descendants following his demise.[16]

After 1815, both Adams and Jefferson declined physically. Adams'
hearing deteriorated, and his eyesight grew so clouded that grandchildren and friends were pressed into reading to him and taking his dicta-
tion. In 1818 he lost Abigail to typhoid fever. By 1820 he was weak and
gnarled, barely able to leave the house and hardly mobile within it.
Jefferson suffered painfully with arthritis, an enlarged prostate, and intermittent gastroenterological disorders. While in his seventies he remarked that he was akin to a watch that was winding down, and at age
eighty-two, in 1825, he quipped that he had "one foot in the grave, and
the other uplifted to follow it." With the end closing in, he told Adams

that he welcomed the "friendly hand of death," and Adams in turn said that he neither hated life nor feared death.[17]

The end came for each man on Independence Day in 1826, the day of jubilee, a coincidence so striking that many contemporaries saw the hand of God in the occurrence. Jefferson passed away first, early in the afternoon. Adams died five hours later as the first long shadows of late day enveloped Peacefield.[18] They left a world that was startlingly different from that of 1800 and radically unlike the one in which they had come of age before the American Revolution. It was not precisely the world that either had sought to make during the long, sometimes dangerous, and always trying years of revolution and partisan strife. However, when Jefferson and Adams died on that festive July 4, each was celebrated by the surviving generation—the majority of whom had been born after the election of 1800—as Founders who had extricated America from a foreign grip and brought to it republican liberty.[19] The coincidence of the nearly simultaneous deaths of these two old revolutionaries led eulogists to dwell on their roles in the American Revolution. There was much talk of Washington, Adams, and Jefferson having been the great triumvirate of the American Revolution: Washington was its sword, it was said, Adams its tongue who had shepherded independence into being, and Jefferson its pen who had written the cherished national creed. Not much was said about Adams' service after the War of Independence, although one speaker noted that the "hate of *Adams*" that once had "spread to every shore" had faded now into "an adoration." But Jefferson was remembered both for the Declaration of Independence and as a president and party leader who had been "a mighty reformer." The tenor of most eulogies was that Jefferson was a greater man than Adams and that among the Founders he was surpassed only by Washington.[20] The eulogists, of course, were celebrating the world they inhabited, and they radiated the conviction that the new nation had reached a stage of purity and perfection unequaled by any other people. Above all, Americans on the fiftieth anniversary of the Declaration of Independence believed—as Thomas Paine in 1776 had predicted would be the case should the American Revolution succeed—that the example set by the United States was a moral influence for all the world to follow.[21] And while they believed that Adams and Jefferson, through their service in the American Revolution, had given birth to their world, it was Jefferson who had delivered to them an America that was finally free of the shackles of the colonial era, cutting those repressive cords in the course of a presidency set in motion by the election of 1800.

Abbreviations

The following abbreviations are used in the notes to designate frequently cited publications, libraries, and individuals.

AA   Abigail Adams

AAS   American Antiquarian Society

AFC   L. H. Butterfield, Wendell D. Garrett, and Marjorie E. Sprague, eds., *Adams Family Correspondence* (Cambridge: Belknap, 1963–93)

AFP   Adams Family Papers, Massachusetts Historical Society, Boston, 1954–59, microfilm edition

AH   Alexander Hamilton

AHR   *American Historical Review*

AJL   Lester J. Cappon, ed., *The Adams–Jefferson Letters: The Complete Correspondence Between Thomas Jefferson and Abigail and John Adams,* 2 vols. (Chapel Hill: University of North Carolina Press, 1961)

DAJA	L. H. Butterfield, Leonard C. Faber, and Wendell D. Garrett, eds., *Diary and Autobiography of John Adams*, 4 vols. (Cambridge, Mass.: Belknap Press, 1961)
FLTJ	Edwin Morris Betts and James A. Bear, eds., *The Family Letters of Thomas Jefferson* (Columbia: University of Missouri Press, 1966)
GW	George Washington
JA	John Adams
JER	*Journal of the Early Republic*
JM	James Madison
JMB	James A. Bear and Lucia Stanton, eds., *Jefferson's Memorandum Books: Accounts, with Legal Miscellany, 1767–1826*, 2 vols. (Princeton: Princeton University Press, 1997)
JQA	John Quincy Adams
LDC	Paul H. Smith, ed., *Letters of Delegates to Congress, 1774–1789* (Washington, D.C.: Library of Congress, 1976–2000)
MHS	Massachusetts Historical Society
MPP	James D. Richardson, comp., *A Compilation of the Messages and Papers of the Presidents of the United States*, 20 vols. (Washington, D.C.: U.S. Government Printing Office, 1897–1917)
PAH	Harold C. Syrett and Jacob E. Cooke, eds., *Papers of Alexander Hamilton*, 26 vols. (New York: Columbia University Press, 1961–79)
PGW: Confed Ser	W. W. Abbot et al., eds., *The Papers of George Washington: Confederation Series*, 6 vols. (Charlottesville: University Press of Virginia, 1992–97)
PGW: Pres Ser	Dorothy Twohig et al., eds. *The Papers of George Washington: Presidential Series* (Charlottesville: University Press of Virginia, 1987–)

PGW: Ret Ser	Dorothy Twohig et al., eds., *The Papers of George Washington: Retirement Series*, 4 vols. (Charlottesville: University Press of Virginia, 1998–99)
PJA	Robert J. Taylor, Mary-Jo Kline, and Gregg L. Lint, eds., *Papers of John Adams* (Cambridge, Mass.: Belknap Press, 1977–)
PJM	William T. Hutchinson et al., eds., *Papers* [of James Madison] (Chicago: University of Chicago Press; Charlottesville: University Press of Virginia, 1962–)
PCAB	Mary-Jo Kline, ed., *Political Correspondence and Public Papers of Aaron Burr* (Princeton: Princeton University Press, 1983–)
PTJ	Julian P. Boyd et al., eds., *The Papers of Thomas Jefferson* (Princeton: Princeton University Press, 1950–)
TBA	Thomas Boylston Adams
TJ	Thomas Jefferson
WJA	Charles Francis Adams, ed., *The Works of John Adams, Second President of the United States: With a Life of the Author*, 10 vols. (Boston: Little, Brown, 1850–56)
WMQ	*William and Mary Quarterly*
WTJ	Paul Leicester Ford, ed., *The Writings of Thomas Jefferson*, 10 vols. (New York: G. P. Putnam's Sons, 1892–99)
WTJ (L & B)	A. A. Lipscomb and A. E. Bergh, eds., *The Writings of Thomas Jefferson*, 20 vols. (Washington, D.C.: Thomas Jefferson Memorial Association of the United States, 1900–4)
WW	John C. Fitzpatrick, ed., *The Writings of Washington*, 39 vols. (Washington, D.C.: United States Government Printing Office, 1931–34)

Notes

Chapter 1

1. *DAJA* 1:140n; AA to JA, Feb. 11, 1784, *AFC* 5:303, 305n; AA to Mary Cranch, Aug. 9, 1789, Dec. 11, 1799, Stewart Mitchell, ed., *New Letters of Abigail Adams* (Boston, 1947), 20, 221.
2. John H. B. Latrobe, *The Capitol and Washington at the Beginning of the Present Century* (Baltimore, 1881), 5.
3. Eric Sloane, *Our Vanishing Landscape* (New York, 1955), 57, 62–64; Jack Larkin, *The Reshaping of Everyday Life, 1790–1840* (New York, 1988), 157, 161, 212, 216.
4. AA to Mary Cranch, Nov. 21, 1800, Feb. 7, 1801, Mitchell, *New Letters of Abigail Adams*, 256, 264.
5. *JMB* 2:1021n; Dumas Malone, *Jefferson and His Times* (Boston, 1948–81), 3:209, 477; Jack McLaughlin, *Jefferson and Monticello: The Biography of a Builder* (New York, 1988), 94, 258, 271.
6. McLaughlin, *Jefferson and Monticello*, 109–13; Malone, *Jefferson*, 3:453–54; Merrill D. Peterson, *Thomas Jefferson and the New Nation* (New York, 1970), 634.
7. *WTJ* 7:475–77.
8. Peterson, *Jefferson and the New Nation*, 641.
9. TJ to James Monroe, Sep. 20, 1800, *WTJ* 7:457–58.
10. Quoted in Malone, *Jefferson*, 3:477.
11. McLaughlin, *Jefferson and Monticello*, 143; *JMB* 2:878n, 1047n. 1031.
12. *JMB* 2:1031, 1031n.
13. Jack N. Rakove, "The Political Presidency: Discovery and Invention," in James Horn, Jan Ellen Lewis, and Peter S. Onuf, eds., *The Revolution of 1800: Democracy, Race, and the New Republic* (Charlottesville, 2002), 35–36; Clinton Rossiter, *1787: The Grand Convention* (New York, 1966), 198–200, 218–21.

14. On the height of adult males in this period, see John Ferling, "Soldiers for Virginia: Who Served in the French and Indian War?" *Virginia Magazine of History and Biography* 94 (1986): 307–28; Kenneth L. Sokoloff and George C. Villaflor, "The Early Achievement of Modern Stature in America," *Social Science History* 6 (1982): 435–81.

15. The profile of Burr is based on Milton Lomask, *Aaron Burr: The Years from Princeton to Vice President, 1756–1805* (New York, 1979). See also Roger G. Kennedy, *Burr, Hamilton, and Jefferson: A Study in Character* (New York, 2000), 58, and Mary-Jo Kline, "The 1796 Presidential Election: Editorial Note," in *PCAB* 1:266–70.

16. Quoted in Marvin R. Zahniser, *Charles Cotesworth Pinckney: Founding Father* (Chapel Hill, 1967), 224.

17. The quotations in this paragraph can be found in ibid., 22, 47, 49.

18. Ibid., 65, 80.

19. Quoted in Clinton Rossiter, *1787: The Grand Convention* (New York, 1966), 79.

20. Ibid., 249. See also Zahniser, *Pinckney*, 87–106.

21. Quoted in Zahniser, *Pinckney*, 98.

22. GW to Timothy Pickering, Jul. 11, 1798, *WW* 36:325; GW to AH, Jul. 14, 1798, ibid., 36:332.

23. The profile of Pinckney is based on Zahniser, *Pinckney*, but also see Stanley Elkins and Eric McKitrick, *The Age of Federalism* (New York, 1993), 559–61, and David Hackett Fischer, *The Revolution of American Conservatism: The Federalist Party in the Era of Jeffersonian Democracy* (New York, 1965), 2–28.

24. Quoted in Gordon S. Wood, *The Radicalism of the American Revolution* (New York, 1992), 305.

25. Peter Kolchin, *American Slavery, 1619–1877* (New York, 1993), 76–92; Ira Berlin, *Many Thousands Gone: The First Two Centuries of Slavery in North America* (Cambridge, Mass., 1998), 228–55.

26. David McCullough, *John Adams* (New York, 2001), 551.

27. AA to Cranch, Nov. 21, 1800, Mitchell, *New Letters of Abigail Adams*, 257, 259.

Chapter 2

1. JA to TJ, Jul. 29, 1791, *AJL* 1:250.

2. JA to James Warren, Aug. 27, 1784, *PTJ* 7:382n; JA to TJ, May 26, 1777, ibid., 5:204; AA to TJ, Jun. 6, 1785, *AJL* 1:28.

3. Quoted in John H. Hazleton, *The Declaration of Independence: Its History* (New York, 1906), 161–62.

4. TJ to AA, Sep. 25, 1785, *AJL* 1:70; TJ to JM, Jan. 30, 1787, *PTJ* 11:94–95.

5. Adams and Jefferson are the subjects of countless biographies and character studies. On JA see Gilbert Chinnard, *Honest John Adams* (Boston, 1933); Page Smith, *John Adams*, 2 vols. (New York, 1962); Peter Shaw, *The Character of John Adams* (Chapel Hill, 1976); John Ferling, *John Adams: A Life* (Knoxville, 1992); Joseph Ellis, *Passionate Sage: The Character and Legacy of John Adams* (New York, 1993); and McCullough, *Adams*. On TJ see Malone, *Jefferson*; Peterson, *Thomas Jefferson and the New Nation*; Fawn Brodie, *Thomas Jefferson: An Intimate History* (New York, 1974); Page Smith, *Jefferson: A Revealing Biography* (New York, 1976); Noble E. Cunningham, *In Pursuit of Reason: The Life of Thomas Jefferson* (Baton Rouge, 1987); Saul K. Padover, *Thomas Jefferson* (New York, 1942); Willard Sterne Randall, *Thomas Jefferson* (New York, 1992); Andrew Burstein, *The Inner Jefferson: Portrait of a Grieving Opti-*

mist (Charlottesville, 1995); Joseph Ellis, *American Sphinx: The Character of Thomas Jefferson* (New York, 1997); Michael Knox Beran, *Jefferson's Demons: Portrait of a Restless Mind* (New York, 2003); R. B. Bernstein, *Thomas Jefferson* (New York, 2003). For a comparative study of JA, TJ, and George Washington, see John Ferling, *Setting the World Ablaze: Washington, Adams, Jefferson and the American Revolution* (New York, 2000). For bibliographical guides, see John Ferling, ed., *John Adams: A Bibliography* (Westport, Conn., 1993); Frank Shuffelton, ed., *Thomas Jefferson: A Comprehensive Annotated Bibliography of Writings About Him* (New York, 1983); and Frank Shuffelton, ed., *Thomas Jefferson, 1981–1990: An Annotated Bibliography* (New York, 1992).

6. TJ to Chevalier de Chastellux, Sep. 21, 1785, *PJJ* 8:468.

7. TJ to Vine Utley, Mar. 21, 1819, *WTJ* 9:126; TJ to William Duane, Oct. 1, 1812, *WTJ* (L&B) 2:420–21; Malone, *Jefferson*, 1:56–57; Randall, *TJ*, 37, 41–42; TJ to John Page, Oct. 7, 1763, *PTJ* 1:11.

8. *DAJA* 1:24–25, 78, 118, 132, 168, 337–38; JA to Jonathan Sewall, Feb. 1760, *PJA* 1:41–42; Charles McKirdy, "Massachusetts Lawyers on the Eve of the American Revolution: The State of the Profession," in *Law in Colonial Massachusetts, 1630–1800* (Boston, 1984), 333–36; John Murrin, "The Legal Transformation: The Bench and Bar of Eighteenth-Century Massachusetts," in Stanley N. Katz and John M. Murrin, eds., *Colonial America: Essays in Politics and Social Development* (New York, 1983), 541–42, 548–53.

9. On JA's legal career, see Ferling, *Setting the World Ablaze*, 20–21, 25–27, and John Ferling, "Before Fame: Young John Adams and Thomas Jefferson," in Richard A. Ryerson, ed., *John Adams and the Founding of the Republic* (Boston, 2001), 72–102. JA wrote of his early trials as a lawyer in his diary and memoirs. See *DAJA* 1:45–138; 3:270–73. On JA's marriage, see Ferling, *Adams*, and Ferling, *Setting the World Ablaze*, 55–57.

10. On the legal practices of TJ and JA, see Brodie, *Jefferson*, 71; Malone, *Jefferson*, 1:114, 122–23; Douglass Adair, *Fame and the Founding Fathers: Essays*, ed. Trevor Colbourn (New York, 1974), 7, 13–16, 19; Frank Dewey, *Thomas Jefferson, Lawyer* (Charlottesville, 1986), 29, 34, 44, 83–93; Cunningham, *In Pursuit of Reason*, 12–13; Randall, *Jefferson*, 95, 98, 102, 104, 109; Edmund Randolph, *Essays on the Revolutionary History of Virginia, 1774–1782*, in *Virginia Magazine of History and Biography* 43 (1935): 115, 368; John W. Davis, "Thomas Jefferson: Attorney at Law," *Proceedings, Virginia State Bar Association*, 38 (1926): 369; TJ to Page, Dec. 25, 1762, *PTJ* 1:5; TJ to Fleming [Oct. 1763], ibid., 1:13; Daniel R. Coquillette, "Justinian in Braintree: John Adams, Civilian Learning and Legal Elitism, 1758–1775," in *Law in Colonial Massachusetts*, 369–82; Kinvin Wroth and Hiller Zobel, eds., *Legal Papers of John Adams* (Cambridge, Mass., 1965), 1:xxxi–xciv.

11. *DAJA* 1:349, 352; 2:74; 3:290–91; 2:34–35, 55, 80, 119; John Adams, "The Letters of Novanglus" (Jan.–Apr. 1775), *PJA* 2: 256–57, 277–78, 284, 370.

12. On JA's long battle over political activism, and his transformation in 1773, see Ferling, *Adams*, 39–85, and Ferling, *Setting the World Ablaze*, 41–88.

13. TJ to John Randolph, Aug. 25, 1775, *PTJ* 1:241; TJ to Page, Feb. 21, 1770, ibid., 1:35–36; Ellis, *American Sphinx*, 27. On the causes of TJ's inner turmoil, see Ferling, *Setting the World Ablaze*, 36–39.

14. TJ to Martha Jefferson Randolph, Apr. 4, 1790, *FLTJ*, 51; TJ to Mary Jefferson Eppes, Jan. 7, 1788, ibid., 152.

15. TJ, "Autobiography," *WTJ* 1:5, 7–8; TJ to Edward Coles, Aug. 25, 1814, in *The Portable Jefferson*, ed. Merrill Peterson (New York, 1975), 544; TJ to Thomas Adams, Feb. 20, 1771, *PTJ* 1:61; [Thomas Jefferson], *A Summary View of the Rights of British America* (Williamsburg, 1774), ibid., 1:123–24, 133, 135; Timothy Breen, *Tobacco Culture: The Mentality of the Great Tidewater Planters on the Eve of the Revolution* (Princeton, 1985), 127–28, 159; Ellis, *American Sphinx*,

32–34; Peterson, *Jefferson and the New Nation*, 45–65; Bernard Bailyn, *The Ideological Origins of the American Revolution* (Cambridge, Mass., 1967), 55–143; Gordon S. Wood, *The Creation of the American Republic* (Chapel Hill, 1969), 10–45; Wood, *Radicalism of the American Revolution*, 97–107.

16. JA to Timothy Pickering, Aug. 6, 1822, *WJA* 2:512.

17. JA to Shelton Jones, Mar. 11, 1809, ibid., 9:612; JA to Tudor, Apr. 18, 1815, ibid., 10:245; JA to AA, Feb. 9, 1799, AFP, reel 393; JA to F. A. Vanderkemp, Apr. 18, 1815, ibid., reel 322; *DAJA* 2:362–63.

18. Carol Berkin, *Jonathan Sewall: Odyssey of an American Loyalist* (New York, 1974), 142; Shaw, *Character of John Adams*, 95; Ellis, *Passionate Sage*, 42–43.

19. *The Autobiography of Benjamin Rush. His "Travels Through Life" Together with the Commonplace Book for 1789–1813*, ed. George W. Corner (Westport, Conn., 1970), 140.

20. Ibid., 140, 141, 142; David Hawke, *Benjamin Rush: Revolutionary Gadfly* (Indianapolis, 1971), 164–65; G. S. Rowe, *Thomas McKean: The Shaping of a Republican* (Boulder, Colo., 1978), 164–65.

21. Harry S. Randall, *The Life of Thomas Jefferson* (New York, 1858), 1:34–35; 3:364; Ellis, *American Sphinx*, 120; Cunningham, *In Pursuit of Reason*, 22; Padover, *Jefferson*, 180, 334–35, 339, 411–12; Randall, *Jefferson*, 100; McLaughlin, *Jefferson and Monticello*, 4.

22. TJ to GW, May 8, 1791, *PTJ* 20:292.

23. *DAJA* 3:335–36.

24. Samuel Ward to Henry Ward, Jun. 22, 1775, *LDC* 1:535; JA to Timothy Pickering, Aug. 6, 1822, *WJA* 2:512; Ellis, *American Sphinx*, 41.

25. Pauline Maier, *American Scripture: Making the Declaration of Independence* (New York, 1997), 99–105. For JA's version of how TJ became the principal author, see JA to Pickering, Aug. 6, 1822, *WJA* 2:514, and *DAJA* 3:335–37.

26. JA to Rush, Jun. 21, 1811, in *The Spur of Fame: Dialogues of John Adams and Benjamin Rush, 1805–1813*, ed. John A. Schutz and Douglass Adair (San Marino, Calif., 1966), 182.

27. Thomas Paine, *Common Sense*, in *The Complete Writings of Thomas Paine*, ed. Philip Foner (New York, 1945), 1:45.

28. JA to Hezekiah Niles, Feb. 13, 1818, *WJA* 10:282; JA to TJ, Aug. 24, 1815, *AJL* 2:455.

29. JA to AA, Apr. 28, 1776, *AFC* 1:401.

30. John Adams, *Thoughts on Government* (1776), *PJA* 4:86–93.

31. JA to TJ, Nov. 15, 1813, *AJL* 2:402.

32. JA to Patrick Henry, Jun. 3, 1776, *PJA* 4:235.

33. Ellis, *American Sphinx*, 293–300.

34. TJ to JM, Dec. 20, 1787, *PTJ* 12:442.

35. Malone, *Jefferson*, 1:274–80; Thomas Jefferson, *Notes on the State of Virginia*, ed. William Peden (New York, 1972), 130–49, 159–60; TJ to JM, Dec. 16, 1786, *PTJ* 10:603–4; TJ, "Bills No. 79, 80, 81, 82," ibid., 2:526–47, 549–50n; TJ to Edward Carrington, Jan. 16, 1787, ibid., 11:49; TJ to JA, Oct. 28, 1813, *AJL* 2:389; TJ, "Autobiography," *WTJ* 1:67–69.

36. On TJ and slavery in this period, see Ferling, *Setting the World Ablaze*, 161–63.

37. On TJ's problems as governor, see John Ferling, "Jefferson's War," *American History* 35 (Feb. 2001): 37–44.

38. "Charges Advanced by George Nicholas with Jefferson's Answers" [after Jul. 31, 1781], *PTJ* 6:106–09; TJ to Edward Randolph, Sept. 15, 1781, ibid., 6:116–17.

39. See John Ferling, "John Adams, Diplomat," *WMQ* 51 (1994): 227–52.

40. Quoted in William Howard Adams, *The Paris Years of Thomas Jefferson* (New Haven, 1997), 181.

41. JA to TJ, Jan. 22, 1825, *AJL* 2:606–7.

42. Bernstein, *Thomas Jefferson*, 57; Edward Dumbauld, "Jefferson and Adams' English Garden Tour," in William Howard Adams, ed., *Jefferson and the Arts: An Extended View* (Washington, 1976), 135–57.

43. JA to Jonathan Sewall, Feb. 1760, *PJA* 1:41–42; JA to Wythe, Apr. 1776, *WJA* 4:200; JA to Jay, Sep. 22, 1787, ibid., 8:451.

44. C. Bradley Thompson, *John Adams and the Spirit of Liberty* (Lawrence, Kans., 1998), 94–95, 241–49.

45. JA to TJ, Dec. 10, 1787, *AJL* 1:214–15.

46. Thompson, *Adams and the Spirit of Liberty*, 176, 179, 195–96, 212–15, 247.

47. Ibid., 221; John Adams, *Defence of the Constitutions of the United States of America* [1787], in *WJA* 4:585; 5:473; 6:186–87. See also John Ferling, "'Father and Protector': President John Adams and Congress in the Quasi-War Crisis," in Kenneth R. Bowling and Donald R. Kennon, eds., *Neither Separate Nor Equal: Congress in the 1790s* (Athens, Oh., 2000), 300–304.

48. TJ to JA, May 25, 1785, Aug. 2, 1788, *AJL* 1:23, 230; JA to TJ, Jan. 2, 1789, ibid., 1:234; Malone, *Jefferson*, 2:7.

49. Malone, *Jefferson*, 2:12–13, 17, 19.

50. Beran, *Jefferson's Demons*, 42–44.

51. TJ to Maria Cosway, Oct. 12, 1786, *PTJ* 10:445–46, 450. On the affair, see Brodie, *Thomas Jefferson*, 252–92; Ellis, *American Sphinx*, 93–97.

52. TJ to Cosway, Oct. 12, 1786, *PTJ* 10:447–49.

53. TJ to Cosway, Apr. 24, Jul. 27, Sep. 26, 1788, Jan. 14, May 21, Jul. 25, Sep. 11, Oct. 14, 1789, ibid., 13:103–4, 423–24, 639; 14:446; 15:143, 305, 414, 521.

54. TJ to Carlo Bellini, Sep. 30, 1785, ibid., 8:568–69; TJ to JM, Oct. 28, 1785, Jan. 30, 1787, ibid., 8:681–82; 11:92–93; TJ to David Ramsay, Aug. 4, 1787, ibid., 11:687; TJ to John Rutledge, Aug. 6, 1787, ibid., 11:701; TJ to Jay, Oct. 8, 1787, ibid., 12:218; TJ to Wythe, Aug. 13, 1786, ibid., 10:244–45; TJ to GW, May 2, 1788, ibid., 13:128.

55. TJ to John Page, May 4, 1786, ibid., 9:445; TJ to Monroe, Jun. 17, 1785, ibid., 8:233. TJ never fleshed out his views on the European commercial revolution, but for excellent analyses of his outlook on the inequities inherent in an urban manufacturing society, see Peter Onuf, *Jefferson's Empire: The Language of American Nationhood* (Charlottesville, 2000), 69–79, and Drew McCoy, "Political Economy," in Merrill D. Peterson, ed., *Thomas Jefferson: A Reference Biography* (New York, 1986), 106–12. On the changing economic conditions in eighteenth-century Great Britain, see John M. Murrin, "The Great Inversion, or Court Versus Country: A Comparison of the Revolution Settlements in England (1688–1721) and America (1776–1816)," in J.G.A. Pocock, ed., *Three British Revolutions: 1641, 1688, 1776* (Princeton, 1980), 379–81.

56. TJ to GW, Dec. 4, 1788, *PTJ* 14:330; TJ to Jay, Aug. 6, 1787, May 23, 1788, ibid., 11:698; 13:190; TJ to Paine, Jul. 11, 1789, ibid., 15:268; TJ to JM, Jan. 12, 1789, ibid., 14:437.

57. TJ to Lafayette, May 6, Jun. 3, 1789, ibid., 15:97–98, 165–66; Lafayette to TJ, Jun. 3, 1789, ibid., 15:166–67.

58. TJ to Jay, Jun. 29, Jul. 19, 1789, ibid., 15:221–23, 290; TJ to JM, Jul. 22, 1789, ibid., 15:299, 300–1; TJ to Cosway, Sep. 11, 1789, ibid., 15:414; TJ to Thomas Paine, Sep. 13, 1789, ibid., 15:424.

59. TJ to Maria Cosway, May 21, Oct. 14, 1789, ibid., 15:142, 521; TJ to JM, Aug. 29, 1789, ibid., 15:369.

60. Cunningham, *In Pursuit of Reason*, 129, 159.

61. JA to TJ, Nov. 10, Dec. 6, 10, 1787, Mar. 1, 1789, *AJL* 1:210, 213–14, 237.

62. The quotation is from Malone, *Jefferson*, 2:228. For TJ's views on the friendliness of the revolutionaries, see TJ to JM, Aug. 28, 1789, *PTJ* 15:366–67.

63. Malone, *Jefferson*, 2:161, 164; TJ to JA, Nov. 13, 1787, *AJL* 1:212.

64. TJ to JM, Dec. 20, 1787, *PTJ* 12:439–40; TJ to William Smith, Nov. 13, 1787, ibid., 12:356.

Chapter 3

1. GW, "Circular to the States," Jun. 8, 1783, *WW* 26:483–96.

2. AH to GW, Sep. 1788, *PAH* 5:220–22. On entreaties to GW and the general's answers, see Robert Livingston to GW, Oct. 21, 1788, *PGW: Pres. Ser.* 1:56; John Trumbull to GW, Oct. 28, 1788, ibid., 1:80; Samuel Vaughn to GW, Nov. 4, 1788, ibid., 1:165–66; John Armstrong to GW, Jan. 27, 1789, ibid., 1:254; Benjamin Harrison to GW, Feb. 26, 1788, ibid., 1:345; GW to Benjamin Lincoln, Oct. 26, 1788, ibid., 1:6; GW to William Gordon, Sep. 24, 1788, ibid., 1:1–2; GW to AH, Oct. 3, 1788, ibid., 1:32.

3. AH's biographers are about equally divided between the years of 1755 and 1757 as his birth year.

4. AH to Edward Stevens, Nov. 11, 1757, *PAH* 1:4.

5. AH to Tobias Lear, Jan. 2, 1800, ibid., 24:155.

6. Richard Brookhiser, *Alexander Hamilton: American* (New York, 1999), 49.

7. GW to president of Congress, Oct. 16, 1781, *WW* 23:228.

8. Maier, *American Scripture*, 59–69, 225–34.

9. Jesse Root to Jonathan Trumbull, Aug. 23, 1779, *LDC* 13:400.On the desperate economic crisis, see James Ferguson, *The Power of the Purse: A History of American Public Finance, 1776–1790* (Chapel Hill, 1961), 34–100; John Ferling, *A Leap in the Dark: The Struggle to Create the American Republic* (New York, 2003), 209–46.

10. GW to Mason, Mar. 27, 1779, *WW* 14:300; GW to John Armstrong, May 18, 1779, ibid., 15:97; GW to Edmund Randolph, Aug. 1, 1779, ibid., 16:97.

11. Jack Rakove, *The Beginnings of National Politics: An Interpretive History of the Continental Congress* (Baltimore, 1979), 292–93, 313, 315.

12. Alexander Hamilton, *The Continentalist*, in *PAH*, 2:649–50, 664, 665; 3:103, 106.

13. Rakove, *Beginnings of National Politics*, 322, 337–38.

14. AH to John Jay, Mar. 14, 1779, *PAH* 2:18; "Memorial to Abolish the Slave Trade," Mar. 13, 1786, ibid., 3:654n.

15. Robert Henrickson, *Hamilton: 1757–1789* (New York, 1976), 409, 411.

16. E. M. Cunningham, ed., *Correspondence Between the Hon. John Adams, Late President of the United States, and the Late William Cunningham, Esq.* (Boston, 1823), 47.

17. On AH see Jacob Cooke, *Alexander Hamilton* (New York, 1982); Forrest McDonald, *Alexander Hamilton* (New York, 1979); John C. Miller, *Alexander Hamilton: Portrait in Paradox* (New York, 1959); Adrienne Koch, *Power, Morals, and the Founding Fathers: Essays in the Interpretation of the American Enlightenment* (Ithaca, 1961), 50–80; Brookhiser, *Hamilton*; Richard B. Morris, *Seven Who Shaped Our Destiny: The Founding Fathers as Revolutionaries* (New York, 1973), 221–58; Joseph J. Ellis, *Founding Brothers: The Revolutionary Generation* (New York, 2000), 60; Willard Sterne Randall, *Alexander Hamilton: A Life* (New York, 2003).

18. JA to AA, Jul. 3, 1776, *AFC* 2:28; JA to Richard Cranch, Aug. 2, 1776, ibid., 2:74.; TJ to Franklin, Aug. 3, 1777, *PTJ* 2:26.

19. Wood, *Radicalism of the American Revolution*, 232. See also Wood's extended essay on the changes brought on by the American Revolution in ibid., 169–324.

20. Quoted in Merrill Jensen, *The American Revolution Within America* (New York, 1974), 104–5.

21. James Madison, *The Federalist*, No. 57; JM to GW, Dec. 7, 24, 1786, Feb. 21, 1787, *PJM* 9:200, 224, 286; JM to TJ, Dec. 4, 1786, Feb. 15, 1787, ibid., 9:190, 267; JM to Edmund Randolph, Feb. 24, 25, 1787, ibid., 9:295, 299; [James Madison], "Vices of the Political System of the United States" [Apr. 1787], ibid., 9:351, 353; Jensen, *The American Revolution Within America*, 109, 115, 119.

22. Monroe to TJ, Aug. 19, 1786, *PTJ* 10:277; Monroe to JM, Aug. 14, Sep. 3, 1786, *PJM* 9:104, 113.

23. For biographies of JM, see Rakove, *Madison and the Creation of the American Republic*; Irving Brant, *James Madison*, 6 vols. (Indianapolis, 1941–61); Ralph Ketchum, *James Madison: A Biography* (New York, 1971); Robert A. Rutland, *James Madison and the Search for Nationhood* (Washington, D.C., 1981); Robert A. Rutland, *James Madison: Founding Father* (New York, 1987); Harold Schultz, *James Madison* (New York, 1970); Garry Wills, *James Madison* (New York, 2002).

24. The evolving nature of JM's thought has been the subject of considerable scholarly study. See Lance Banning, *The Sacred Fire of Liberty: James Madison and the Founding of the Federal Republic* (Ithaca, 1995); Jack Rakove, *Original Meanings: Politics and Ideas in the Making of the Constitution* (New York, 1996); Drew McCoy, *The Last of the Fathers: James Madison and the Republican Legacy* (Cambridge, Mass., 1989); William Lee Miller, *The Business of May Next: James Madison and the Founding* (Charlottesville, 1992); Marvin Myers, *The Mind of the Founder: Sources of the Political Thought of James Madison*, rev. ed. (Hanover, N.H., 1981).

25. JM, *The Federalist*, No. 10; Max Farrand, ed., *The Records of the Federal Convention of 1787* (New Haven, 1966), 1:423; JM to GW, Dec. 7, 24, 1787, *PJM* 9:200, 224, 286; JM to TJ, Dec. 4, 1786, Feb. 15, 1787, ibid., 9:190, 267; JM to Edmund Randolph, Feb. 24, 25, 1787, ibid., 9:295, 299; JM, "Vices of the Political System of the United States" [Apr. 1787], ibid., 9:351, 353.

26. JM to Randolph, Apr. 8, 1787, *PJM.*, 9:369–70; JM to GW, Apr. 16, 1787, ibid., 9:384.

27. JM, *The Federalist*, No. 10. JM's views can be interpreted many ways. For other views, see Rakove, *Original Meanings*, 161–62, 197, 235, 238, 280; Rakove, *Madison and the Creation of the Federal Republic*, 44–52; Banning, *Sacred Fire of Freedom*, 76–121; Richard K. Matthews, *"If Men Were Angels": James Madison and the Heartless Empire of Reason* (Lawrence, Kan., 1994); Neal Riemer, *James Madison: Creating the American Constitution* (Washington, D.C., 1986); Wills, *Madison*, 24–37. For a brief ready reference to JM's thought, see *James Madison's "Advice to My Country,"* ed. David B. Mattern (Charlottesville, 1997).

28. GW to David Humphreys, Dec. 26, 1786, *PGW: Confederation Ser.* 4:478; GW to Henry Knox, Dec. 26, 1786, ibid., 4:481–83; GW to Benjamin Lincoln, Feb. 24, 1787, ibid., 5:51–52; GW to Lafayette, Mar. 25, 1787, ibid., 5:106.

29. Quoted in Clinton Rossiter, *1787: The Grand Convention* (New York, 1966), 138.

30. Forrest McDonald, *Novus Ordo Seclorum: The Intellectual Origins of the Constitution* (Lawrence, Kan., 1985), 270.

31. The literature on the Constitutional Conventional is enormous. My analysis draws heavily on John P. Roche, "The Founding Fathers: A Reform Caucus in Action," *American Political Society Review* 55 (1961): 799–816; Jensen, *The American Revolution Within America*, 172–212; Rossiter, *1787*, 159–273; Forrest McDonald, *The Formation of the American Republic, 1776–1790* (Baltimore, 1968), 155–208; Wood, *Creation of the American Republic*, 519–64. On slavery at the convention, see Paul Finkleman, "Slavery and the Constitutional Convention: Making a Covenant with Death," in Richard Beeman, Stephen Botein, and Edward C. Carter II, eds., *Beyond Confederation: Origins of the Constitution and American National Identity* (Chapel Hill, 1957), 188–215; Donald Robinson, *Slavery in the Structure of American Politics,*

1765–1820 (New York, 1971), 168–246; Staughton Lynd, *Class Conflict, Slavery, and the Constitution* (Indianapolis, 1967), 185–213; William W. Freehling, "The Founding Fathers and Slavery," *American Historical Review* 77 (1972): 81–93; William M. Wiecek, "The Witch at the Christening: Slavery and the Constitution's Origins," in Leonard Levy and Dennis J. Mahoney, eds., *The Framing and Ratification of the Constitution* (New York, 1987), 167–84; Earl M. Maltz, "The Idea of the Proslavery Constitution," *JER* 17 (1997): 37–60. On the three-fifths compromise, see Garry Wills, *"Negro President": Jefferson and the Slave Power* (Boston, 2003), 50–61.

32. Speech of George Mason in the Virginia Ratifying Convention, Jun. 4, 1788, in Herbert J. Storing, ed., *The Complete Anti-Federalist* (Chicago, 1981), 5:256–58.

33. On the Anti-Federalists, see Robert Allen Rutland, *The Ordeal of the Constitution: The Anti-Federalists and the Ratification Struggle, 1787–1788* (Norman, 1966); Jackson Turner Main, *The Anti-Federalists: Critics of the Constitution* (Chapel Hill, 1961); Saul Cornell, *The Other Founders: Anti-Federalism and the Dissenting Tradition in America, 1788–1828* (Chapel Hill, 1999).

34. See *The Federalist*, Nos. 3, 6, 9, 11, 15, 22, 34, 62. See also Gottfried Dietze, *The Federalist: A Classic on Federalism and Free Government* (Baltimore, 1960), 177–254.

35. For succinct and illuminating assessments of AH's plans for laying the foundation of the commercial republic, see Peter McNamara, *Political Economy and Statesmanship: Smith, Hamilton, and the Foundation of the Commercial Republic* (DeKalb, Ill., 1998), 95–151; Robert E. Wright, *Hamilton Unbound: Finance and the Creation of the American Republic* (Westport, Conn., 2002); Karl-Friedrich Walling, *Republican Empire: Alexander Hamilton on War and Free Government* (Lawrence, Kan., 1999), 175–208.

36. Brookhiser, *Hamilton*, 86; Paul A. Gilje, "The Rise of Capitalism in the Early Republic," *JER* 16 (1996): 159–82.

37. "Conversation with George Beckwith" [Oct. 1789], *PAH* 5:488. On JM's ties to GW, see Stuart Leibiger, *Founding Friendship: George Washington, James Madison, and the Creation of the American Republic* (Charlottesville, 1999).

38. GW to TJ, Oct. 13, 1789, *PTJ* 15:519–20; TJ to GW, Dec. 15, 1789, ibid., 16:34–35; TJ to Monroe, Jun. 20, 1790, ibid., 16:536.

39. Kenneth R. Bowling, *The Creation of Washington, D.C.: The Idea and Location of the American Capital* (Fairfax, Va., 1991), 38–73. On the Compromise of 1790, see "Jefferson's Account of the Bargain on the Assumption and Residence Bills" [1792?], *PTJ* 17:206–7; Jacob E. Cooke, "The Compromise of 1790," *WMQ* 27 (1970): 523–45; Kenneth R. Bowling, "Dinner at Jefferson's: A Note on Jacob E. Cooke's 'Compromise of 1790,'" *WMQ* 28 (1971): 629–48; Norman K. Risjord, "The Compromise of 1790: New Evidence on the Dinner Table Bargain," *WMQ* 33 (1976): 309–14.

40. TJ to William Short, Jan. 8, 1825, *WTJ* 10:332–33; TJ to George Mason, Feb. 4, 1791, *PTJ* 19: 241.

41. JA to Trumbull, Mar. 12, 1790, AFP, reel 115.

42. TJ to JM, Jul. 29, 1789, *PTJ* 15:315–16.

43. All save the final essay of JA's "Discourses on Davila" [1790–91] can be found in *WJA* 6:223–404. That last essay appeared in the *Gazette of the United States*, Apr. 27, 1791.

44. Ellis, *American Sphinx*, 120.

45. TJ to GW, May 8, 1791, *PTJ* 20:291–92; TJ to JA, Jul. 17, Aug. 30, 1791, ibid., 20:302–3, 310–11; JA to TJ, Jul. 29, 1791, ibid., 20:305–7; "The Rights of Man," editor's note, ibid., 20:268–90; TJ to JM, Jul. 29, 1789, May 9, 1791, ibid., 15:315–16; 20:293; Malone, *Jefferson*, 2:259–61, 354–59. Few scholars any longer believe that Adams was a monarchist. See Thompson, *Adams and the Spirit of Liberty*, 107–25, 183–84, 264.

46. TJ to GW, May 23, 1792, *PTJ* 23:537; TJ to Paine, Jun. 19, 1792, ibid., 20:312.

47. TJ to GW, May 3, 1792, ibid., 22:536–39; TJ to George Mason, Feb. 4, 1791, ibid., 19:241–42.

48. For intriguing essays on this passionate decade, see Marshall Smelser, "The Federalist Period as an Age of Passion," *American Quarterly* 10 (1958): 391–419, and John Howe, "Republican Thought and Political Violence in the 1790s," *American Quarterly* 19 (1967): 147–65. Although it does not deal specifically with the 1790s, the following essay should be consulted as an illuminating piece on the perspective of this age: Gordon Wood, "Conspiracy and the Paranoid Style: Causality and Deceit in the Eighteenth Century," *WMQ* 39 (Jul. 1982): 401–41.

49. Elkins and McKitrick, *Age of Federalism*, 78.

50. For example, see TJ, *Anas* (Aug. 13, 1791), *WTJ* 1:169–72, 180, 185–87, 201–2. For a more extensive treatment on TJ's information-gathering practices, see Joanne Freeman, *Affairs of Honor: National Politics in the New Republic* (New Haven, 2001), 120–23.

51. TJ, "Report" [Dec. 17, 1790], *PTJ* 18:301–3; Banning, *Jeffersonian Persuasion*, 156.

52. TJ to Freneau, Feb. 28, 1791, *PTJ* 19:351; TJ to JM, May 9, Jul. 21, 1791, ibid., 20:293, 657; TJ to GW, Sep. 9, 1792, ibid., 24:356–57; Malone, *Jefferson*, 2:423–28; Noble E. Cunningham, *The Jeffersonian Republicans: The Formation of Party Organization, 1789–1801* (Chapel Hill, 1957), 17. For an excellent assessment of Fenno and Freneau, see Jeffrey L. Pasley, *"The Tyranny of Printers": Newspaper Politics in the Early Republic* (Charlottesville, 2001), 51–78.

53. TJ to Edward Rutledge, Aug. 25, 1791, *PTJ* 22:74; TJ to Robert Livingston, Feb. 4, 1791, ibid., 19:241; TJ to Mason, Feb. 4, 1791, ibid., 19:241–42; TJ to Henry Innes, Mar. 13, 1791, ibid., 19:542–43.

54. Robert Troup to AH, Jun. 15, 1791, *PAH* 8:478–79.

55. TJ, "Journal of the Tour," May 21–Jun. 10, 1791, *PTJ* 20:453–565, 434–53n; Elkins and McKitrick, *Age of Federalism*, 241. For JM's notes, see "Notes on the Lake Country Tour" [1791], *PJM* 14:25–30.

56. JM, *National Gazette*, Sep. 22, Dec. 20, 1792, *PJM* 14:371, 427.

57. Ibid., Mar. 31, 1792, ibid., 14:274–75.

58. Ellis, *American Sphinx*, 123.

59. Alexander Hamilton, "An American" [Aug. 4, 11, 18, 1792], *PAH* 12:159–60, 163–64, 381, 383–85, 393–401, 504.

60. AH to Edward Carrington, May 26, 1792, ibid., 11:430, 432, 437, 441, 442, 444.

61. Ibid., 11:442, 444.

Chapter 4

1. TJ to Brissot de Warville, May 8, 1793, *PTJ* 25:679; TJ to T. Pinckney, Apr. 12, 1793, ibid., 25:536; Ferling, *Adams*, 318; McCullough, *Adams*, 427, 441; Freeman, *Washington*, 7:8.

2. Cooke, *Hamilton*, 67; AH to Theodore Sedgwick, Oct. 9, Nov. 9, 1788, *PAH* 5:225, 231; AA to Abigail Adams Smith, Jul. 16, 1788, in Caroline Smith DeWindt, ed., *Journal and Correspondence of Miss Adams* (New York, 1841), 89; Smith, *Adams*, 2:739; Ferling, *Adams*, 298. For an excellent assessment of the battle over the vice presidency in 1792, see Alfred F. Young, *The Democratic Republicans of New York: The Origins, 1763–1797* (Chapel Hill, 1967), 324–32.

3. John P. Kaminsky, *George Clinton: Yeoman Politician of the New Republic* (Madison, Wis., 1993), 87, 126, 232–33, 230.

4. AH to JA, Jun. 25, Aug.16, Sep. 9, 1792, *PAH* 11:559; 12:209, 342.

5. AH to Charles C. Pinckney, Oct. 10, 1792, ibid., 12:544; AH to John Steele, Oct. 15, 1792, ibid., 12:567–68.

6. AH to Charles C. Pinckney, Oct. 10, 1792, ibid., 12:544; AH to Steele, Oct. 15, 1792, ibid., 12:568–69; Cooke, *Hamilton*, 124.

7. GW to David Humphries, Jul. 20, 1791, *PGW: Pres. Ser.* 8:359; GW to G. Morris, Jul. 28, 1791, ibid., 8:381–83; GW to Sir Edward Newenham, Jun. 22, 1792, *WW* 32:73.

8. Catherine Sawbridge Macaulay Graham to GW, Oct. [20], 1789, *PGW: Pres. Ser.* 4:258; Lafayette to GW, Mar. 17, 1790, ibid., 5:242; Alexander Hamilton, "The French Revolution" (1794), *PAH* 17:586; Elkins and McKitrick, *Age of Federalism*, 309–10.

9. GW to Comte de Rochambeau, Aug. 10, 1790, *PGW: Pres. Ser.* 6:231; GW to Chevalier de la Luzerne, Sep. 10, 1791, ibid., 8:517; GW to Humphreys, Jul. 20, 1791, ibid., 8:360; TJ to Lafayette, Apr. 2, 1790, *PTJ* 16:293; TJ to Mason, Feb. 4, 1791, ibid., 19:241.

10. TJ to John Mercer, Dec. 10, 1792, *PTJ* 24:757; Simon Schama, *Citizens: A Chronicle of the French Revolution* (New York, 1989), 639–43.

11. JM to George Nicholas, Mar. 15, 1793, *PJM* 14:472.

12. Schama, *Citizens*, 633, 776.

13. Fisher Ames, "[Untitled] Against Jacobins" [1794?], in Seth Ames, ed., *Works of Fisher Ames*, edited and enlarged by W. B. Allen (Indianapolis, 1983), 2:974–84; Ames to Theodore Dwight, Aug. [?], 1793, ibid., 2:964; David Waldstreicher, "Federalism, the Style of Politics, and the Politics of Style," in Doran Ben-Atar and Barbara B. Oberg, eds., *Federalists Reconsidered* (Charlottesville, 1998), 115–16.

14. Matthew Schoebachler, "Republicanism in the Age of Democratic Revolution: The Democratic-Republican Societies of the 1790s," *JER* 18 (1998): 237–62; Philip S. Foner, ed., *The Democratic-Republican Societies, 1790–1820: A Documentary Sourcebook* (Westport, Conn., 1976), 5; Eugene Link, *Democratic-Republican Societies, 1790–1800* (New York, 1942), 44–70.

15. Ames to Thomas Dwight, Sep. 11, 1794, Ames, *Works of Ames*, 2:1049; "Debates Over the Propriety of Replies to the President's Speeches" [Nov. 26, 1794], ibid., 2:1057, 1059, 1060; Keith Abour, "Benjamin Franklin as Weird Sister: William Cobbett and Federalist Philadelphia's Fears of Democracy," in Ben-Atar and Oberg, eds., *Federalists Reconsidered*, 186; Nathaniel Chipman to AH, [Jun.] 9, 1794, *PAH* 16:465–70; Alexander Hamilton, "No Jacobin, No. VII" [1793], ibid., 15:269.

16. Donald Stewart, *The Opposition Press of the Federalist Period* (Albany, 1969), 147–51.

17. AH, "No Jacobin, No. IV," *PAH* 15:228.

18. Paine, *Common Sense*, in *Complete Writings of Paine*, 1:21.

19. TJ to JM, Aug. 11, 1793, ibid., 26:652.

20. JM to TJ, Mar. 12, 14, 26, 1794, *PJM* 15:279, 284, 294–95.

21. The quotations can be found in Foner, *Democratic-Republican Societies*, 38, 105, 134.

22. James Roger Sharp, *American Politics in the Early Republic: The New Nation in Crisis* (New Haven, 1993), 113, 307n.

23. Young, *Democratic Republicans of New York*, 382–85.

24. TJ to GW, May 23, 1792, *PTJ* 23:536.

25. Thomas Slaughter, *The Whiskey Rebellion: Frontier Epilogue to the American Revolution* (New York, 1986), 109–24, 133–39, 144–57, 163–64; GW to governors of Pennsylvania, North Carolina, and South Carolina, Sep. 29, 1792, *WW* 32:169; GW to Henry Lee, Aug. 26, 1794, ibid., 33:475–79; GW to AH, Aug. 21, 1794, *PAH* 17:126; Freeman, *GW*, 7:191.

26. Slaughter, *Whiskey Rebellion*, 217–20; John C. Miller, *The Federalist Era, 1789–1801* (New York, 1960), 159.

27. JM to TJ, Nov. 30, 1794, *PJM* 15:397; Foner, *Democratic-Republican Societies*, 91–93, 99–100, 147–48.

28. GW, sixth State of the Union address, Nov. 19, 1794, *WW* 34:29–35; GW to Jay, Nov. 1[–5], 1794, ibid., 34:17–18.

29. JM, speech to Congress, Nov. 27, 1794, *PJM* 15:391; JM to TJ, Nov. 30, 1794, ibid., 15:396–97; TJ to JM, Dec. 28, 1794, *PTJ* 28:228–30.

30. Sharp, *American Politics in the Early Republic*, 101–2; Robert Kelley, *The Cultural Pattern in American Politics: The First Century* (New York, 1979), 104; Elkins and McKitrick, *Age of Federalism*, 487–88.

31. In Article XII of the Jay Treaty, London had agreed to permit American trade in the West Indies in merchant vessels of less than seventy tons, such small ships that the overhead costs likely would have consumed all potential profits. GW and the Federalist senators saw this as an affront, and the article was expunged from the treaty during the Senate's deliberations.

32. Jerald Combs, *The Jay Treaty: Political Background of the Founding Fathers* (Berkeley, 1970), 161; Miller, *Federalist Era*, 167; DeConde, *Entangling Alliance*, 112.

33. GW to AH, Jul. 3, 13, 29, 1795, *WW* 34:226–28, 237–40, 262–64; GW to Edmund Randolph, Jul. 22, 31, 1795, ibid., 34:244, 266; GW to Knox, Sep. 20, 1795, ibid., 34:310–11.

34. Stewart, *Opposition Press of the Federalist Era*, 195, 202, 211–13, 215–17; Resolution of the South Carolina–Washington District, Sep. 28, 1795, in Foner, *Democratic-Republican Societies*, 402.

35. On the Republican Party and its outlook by 1795, see Joyce Appleby, *Capitalism and a New Social Order: The Republican Vision of the 1790s* (New York, 1984), 25–87; Lance Banning, *The Jeffersonian Persuasion: Evolution of a Party Ideology* (Ithaca, 1978), 179–245; Miller, *Federalist Era*, 70–98; Elkins and McKitrick, *Age of Federalism*, 195–208, 263–70, 354–65.

36. TJ to JM, Sep. 21, 1795, *PTJ* 28:475–76. The thirty-eight essays of AH's "The Defence" are scattered throughout *PAH*, vols. 18–19.

37. Michael Durey, *Transatlantic Radicals and the Early American Republic* (Lawrence, Kan., 1997), 257.

38. GW to William Pearce, Feb. 21, 1796, *WW* 34:476.

39. Ibid.; GW to William Pearce, Feb. 21, 1796, ibid., 34:476; GW to Robert Lewis, Jun. 26, 1796, ibid., 34:99; *PAH* 20:169n.

Chapter 5

1. GW to Jay, May 8, 1796, *WW* 35:37.

2. JA to AA, Jan. 5, 1786, AFP, reel 381.

3. JA to TJ, Jan. 31, 1796, *PTJ* 28:600.

4. JA to TJ, Apr. 6, 1796, ibid., 28:59.

5. TJ, "Memoranda of Conversations with the President," Mar. 1, 1792, ibid., 23:185–86; TJ to John Syme, Sep. 17, 1792, ibid., 24:388.

6. TJ to Martha Jefferson Randolph, Dec. 22, 1793, ibid., 27:608; TJ to JM, Jun. 9, 1793, ibid., 26:239–40.

7. TJ to Horatio Gates, Feb. 3, 1794, ibid., 28:14; TJ to Cosway, Sep. 8, 1795, ibid., 28:455; TJ to Madame de Tessé, Sep. 6, 1795, ibid., 28:451; TJ to Edward Rutledge, Nov. 30, 1795, ibid., 28:541.

8. Malone, *Jefferson*, 3:167, 178–79, 196–99.

9. *JMB* 1:565n; 2:815, 827, 862; Malone, *Jefferson*, 3:3, 58–59, 178.

10. TJ to James Lyle, Jul. 10, 1795, *PTJ* 28:405; TJ to Tench Coxe, Jun. 1, 1795, ibid., 28:373; TJ to Thomas Pinckney, Sep. 8, 1795, ibid., 28:457; TJ to John Barnes, Dec. 11, 1795, ibid., 28:552; TJ to John Harvie, Feb. 22, 1796, ibid., 28:615; TJ to Daniel Hylton, Mar. 17, 1792, ibid., 23:140; *JMB* 2:915, 919, 925, 926, 933, 942, 945; Ellis, *American Sphinx*, 140.

11. TJ to JM, Apr. 27, 1795, *PTJ* 28:339; TJ to JA, Feb. 6, 1795, ibid., 28:261; TJ to Robert Morris, Feb. 19, 1795, ibid., 28:268; Malone, *Jefferson*, 3:169.

12. TJ to JM, Apr. 3, 1794, *PTJ* 28:50; TJ to Donald, May 30, 1795, ibid., 28:366; TJ to Philip Mazzei, May 30, 1795, ibid., 28:370.

13. McLaughlin, *Jefferson and Monticello*, 241, 249–63; TJ to Randolph, Nov. 28, 1796, *PTJ* 29:211; TJ to Constantine Volney, Jan. 8, 1797, ibid., 29:259.

14. TJ to David Rittenhouse, Feb. 24, 1795, *PTJ* 28:279; TJ to Giles, Apr. 27, 1795, ibid., 28:337; *JMB* 2:916n; Brodie, *Jefferson*, 285.

15. TJ to Cosway, Jun. 23, 1790, *PTJ* 16:550–51; Cosway to TJ, Apr. 6, 1790, ibid., 16:312–13.

16. TJ to Angelica Church, Jun. 7, Nov. 27, 1793, ibid., 26:215; 27:449; Church to TJ, Aug. 19, 1793, ibid., 26:723.

17. Cosway to TJ, Nov. 13, 24, 1794, ibid., 28:201, 209–10.

18. TJ to Cosway, Sep. 8, 1795, ibid., 28:455–56.

19. Cosway to TJ, Dec. 4, 1795, ibid., 28:543–44.

20. Frasier D. Neiman, "Coincidence or Causal Connection? The Relationship Between Thomas Jefferson's Visits to Monticello and Sally Hemings' Conceptions," *WMQ* 57 (2000): 198–210.

21. Several essays on the TJ–Sally Hemings issue can be found in "Forum: Thomas Jefferson and Sally Hemings Redux," *WMQ* 57 (2000): 121–210. See also Lucia Stanton, "'Those Who Labor for My Happiness': Thomas Jefferson and His Slaves," in Peter S. Onuf, ed., *Jeffersonian Legacies* (Charlottesville, 1993), 153; Joshua D. Rothman, "James Callender and Social Knowledge of Interracial Sex in Antebellum Virginia," in Jan Ellen Lewis and Peter S. Onuf, eds., *Sally Hemings and Thomas Jefferson: History, Memory, and Civic Culture* (Charlottesville, 1999), 96; Philip D. Morgan, "Interracial Sex in the Chesapeake and the British Plantation World, c. 1700–1820," in ibid., 52–84; Brodie, *Jefferson*, 493–501.

22. Joseph J. Ellis, "Jefferson: Post–DNA," *WMQ* 57:125–38. The DNA evidence can be found in E. A. Foster et al., "Jefferson Fathered Slave's Last Child," *Nature* 396 (Nov. 5, 1998): 27–28, and Eric Lander and Joseph J. Ellis, "DNA Analysis: Founding Father," *Nature* 396 (Nov. 5, 1998): 13–14. For conflicting views on the matter, see Eyler Robert Coates Sr., ed., *The Jefferson-Hemings Myth: An American Travesty* (Charlottesville, 2001) and Robert F. Turner, editor, *Jefferson-Hemings Scholars Commission Report on the Jefferson-Hemings Matter* (Thomas Jefferson Heritage Society, 2001).

23. TJ to Cosway, Oct. 12, 1786, *PTJ* 10:447–49.

24. The foregoing analysis of TJ and Sally Hemings draws on Brodie, *Jefferson*, and Annette Gordon-Reed, *Thomas Jefferson and Sally Hemings: An American Controversy* (Charlottesville, 1997). See also the valuable essays in Lewis and Onuf, eds., *Sally Hemings and Thomas Jefferson*, and in "Forum: Thomas Jefferson and Sally Hemings Redux," *WMQ* 57 (2000): 121–210.

25. TJ to JM, Apr. 27, 1795, *PTJ* 28:339.

26. TJ to Edward Randolph, Sep. 7, 1794, ibid., 28:148, 119n.

27. TJ to JM, Apr. 27, 1795, ibid., 28:339.

28. JM to TJ, Feb. 7, 1795, ibid., 28:607.

29. TJ to JM, Mar. 6, 1796, ibid., 29:7.

30. TJ to Mazzei, Apr. 24, 1796, ibid., 29:82.

31. TJ to Volney, Dec. 9, 1795, ibid., 28:551.

32. TJ to JM, Apr. 3, Sep. 21, Nov. 26, 1795, ibid., 28:50, 475, 540; TJ to François D'Ivernois, Feb. 6, 1795, ibid., 28:263; TJ to JA, Feb. 28, 1796, ibid., 28:619; TJ to Monroe, Sep. 6, 1795, ibid., 28:449; TJ to Donald, May 30, 1795, ibid., 28:366–67; TJ to Mazzei, Apr. 24, 1796, ibid., 29:81–83.

33. TJ to JA, Apr. 24, 1794, Feb. 28, 1796, ibid., 28:57, 619; JA to TJ, Apr. 4, May 11, Nov. 21, 1794, Apr. 6, 1796, ibid., 28:50, 71–72, 208, 600; 29:59.

34. JA to AA, Dec. 22, 1793, Jan. 22, Feb. 8, 1794, AFP, reels 376, 377; JA to John Quincy Adams, Jul. 9, 1789, ibid., reel 373; JA to Trumbull, Mar. 9, 1790, ibid., reel 115.

35. For a chronology of JA's travels and residences, see *JADA* 4:266–67.

36. JA to AA, Jun. 2, 1796, AFP, reel 381.

37. JA wrote one or two letters to AA each week during their separations. The citations are representative of JA's comments in dozens of missives. See JA to AA, Jan. 24, 1793, Dec. 5, 16, 1795, Apr. 1, 1796, ibid., reels 376, 378, 379, 389.

38. Roger L. Gould, "Transformation During Early and Middle Adult Years," in Neil J. Smelser and Erik H. Erikson, eds., *Themes of Work and Love in Adulthood* (Cambridge, Mass., 1980), 235–36; Daniel J. Levinson, "Toward a Conception of the Adult Life Course," in ibid., 284, 286–87; Roger L. Gould, *Transformation: Growth and Change in Adult Life* (New York, 1978), 309–19; Daniel Gutman, "An Exploration of Ego Configurations in Middle and Late Life," in Bernice L. Neugarten et al., *Personality in Middle and Later Life: Empirical Studies* (New York, 1964), 119–30.

39. For details on JA's bouts with the malady, and a more detailed analysis than what follows, see John Ferling and Lewis E. Braverman, "John Adams' Health Reconsidered," *WMQ* 55 (1998): 83–104. On thyrotoxicosis, see Lewis E. Braverman and Robert D. Utiger, "Introduction to Thyrotoxicosis," in Lewis E. Braverman and Robert D. Utiger, eds., *Werner and Ingbar's The Thyroid: A Fundamental and Clinical Text* (Philadelphia, 1991), 6454–57; Sidney Werner, "History of the Thyroid," ibid., 3–5; Robert Volpe, "Graves' Disease," ibid., 648–50; Peter C. Wybrow, Behavioral and Psychiatric Aspects of Thyrotoxicosis," ibid., 865; Henry Burch, "Ophthalmopathy," ibid., 536–52; Vaheb Fatourechi, "Localized Myxedema and Thyroid Acropachy," ibid., 553–58; Jeffrey D. Bernhard, "The Skin in Thyrotoxicosis," ibid., 595–97; Marjorie Safran and Lewis D. Braverman, "Thyrotoxicosis and Graves' Disease," *Hospital Practice* 20 (1985): 34–36; Leslie J. De Groot, *The Thyroid and Its Diseases* (New York, 1984), 2–42, 136–44; Rene Mornex and Jacques J. Orgiazzi, "Hyperthyroidism," in Michael De Visscher, ed., *The Thyroid Gland: Comprehensive Endocrinology* (New York, 1980), 279–91, 306–17; Brita Winsa et al., "Stressful Life Events and Graves' Disease," *Lancet* 338 (Dec. 14, 1991): 1475–79; Paul J. Rosch, "Stressful Life Events and Graves's Disease," ibid., 342 (Sep. 4, 1993): 566–67; A. Horsley, "On the Function of the Thyroid Gland," *Proceedings of the Royal Society of London*, 33 (1885): 5.

40. JA to Charles Adams, Feb. 7, 1795, AFP, reel 379.

41. TJ to JA, May 27, 1795, *PTJ* 28:363; *JADA* 3:225–48.

42. JA to AA, Dec. 14, 1794, AFP, reel 378.

43. "An Account of the Real Estate of John Adams," n.d., AFP, reel 607.

44. JA to Cotton Tufts, Oct. 10, 1790, AFP, reel 115; Guerrero, *John Adams' Vice Presidency*, 60–61.

45. Akers, *Abigail Adams*, 117–18, 120–22, 133–35.

46. JA to AA, Nov. 23, 1794, AFP, reel 378.

47. JA to AA, Feb. 17, Dec. 22, 30, 1793, Jan. 21, 1794, Feb. 15, 1795, Jan. 26, Feb. 8, 1796, ibid., reels 376, 377, 379, 381; JA to John Quincy Adams, Dec. 13, 1790, ibid., reel 374.

48. JA to AA, Jun. 6, 1789, Feb. 1, 8, Mar. 11, 1796, ibid., reels 372, 380, 381.

49. Shaw, *Character of John Adams*, 90–91.

50. JA to Trumbull, Mar. 31, 1791, Apr. 25, 1790, AFP, reel 115; JA to AA, Feb. 27, 1793, ibid., reel 376.

51. JA to AA, Apr. 22, Nov. 15, 1794, ibid., reels 377, 378; JA to John Quincy Adams, Dec. 2, 1794, ibid., reel 378.

52. JA to AA, Feb. 4, 1794, ibid., reel 377; John Howe, *The Changing Political Thought of John Adams* (Princeton, 1966), 196, 214; Thompson, *Adams and the Spirit of Liberty*, 181–91, 209, 264; Ellis, *Passionate Sage*, 132–36.

53. JA to AA, Jan. 9, 1794, AFP, reel 377.

54. JA to AA, Dec. 26, Feb. 23, 1793, Nov. 26, Jan. 6, 1794, Mar. 13, 1796, ibid., reels 376, 377, 378, 381.

55. TJ to JM, Jan. 22, 30, 1797, *PTJ* 29:271, 280.

Chapter 6

1. TJ to JM, Mar. 6, 1796, *PTJ* 29:7; JM to Monroe, Feb. 26, 1796, *PJM* 16:232–33; Ellis, *American Sphinx*, 157–58.

2. JA to AA, Jan. 2, 7, 20, 1796, AFP, reel 381.

3. JA to AA, Feb. 10, 1796, ibid., reel 381.

4. JA to AA, Feb. 6, 8, 10, 15, 27, Mar. 3, 1796, ibid., reel 381.

5. JA to AA, Feb. 20, Mar. 1, 12, 15, 19, 1796, ibid., reel 381.

6. JA to AA, Mar. 1, Feb. 23, 1796, ibid., reel 381.

7. JA to AA, Mar. 25, 1796, ibid., reel 381.

8. TJ to Thomas M. Randolph, Jan. 6, 12, 18, Feb. 7, Mar. 13, Apr. 11, *PTJ* 28:574, 581, 592, 607; 29:26, 63; TJ to John Barnes, Jan. 17, 1796, ibid., 28:591; TJ to John Harris, Feb. 22, 1796, ibid., 28:615.

9. TJ to Monroe, Jul. 10, 1796, ibid., 29:147.

10. Ames to Oliver Wolcott, Sep. 26, 1796, Ames, *Works of Ames*, 2:1192.

11. A vast literature exists on early American politics, but a sense of political practices in the colonial era can be discerned in the following sample: Patricia U. Bonomi, *A Factious People: Politics and Society in Colonial New York* (New York, 1971); T. H. Breen, *The Character of the Good Ruler: A Study in Puritan Political Ideas in New England, 1630–1730* (New Haven, 1970); Edward M. Cook Jr., *The Fathers of the Towns: Leadership and Community Structure in Eighteenth-Century New England* (Baltimore, 1976); Bruce C. Daniels, ed., *Power and Status: Officeholding in Colonial America* (Middletown, Conn., 1986); Lawrence H. Leder, *Robert Livingston, 1654–1728, and the Politics of Colonial New York* (Chapel Hill, 1961); Charles S. Sydnor, *Gentlemen Freeholders: Political Practices in Washington's Virginia* (Chapel Hill, 1952).

12. Joanne Freeman, "The Presidential Election of 1796," in Ryerson, ed., *John Adams and the Founding of the Republic*, 148–49; Page Smith, "The Election of 1796," in Arthur M. Schlesinger Jr., Fred L. Israel, and William P. Hansen, eds., *History of American Presidential Elections, 1789–1968* (New York, 1971), 1:71.

13. John E. Selby, *The Revolution in Virginia, 1775–1783* (Williamsburg, 1988), 36.

14. See Tables A.2 and A.3 in Alexander Keyssar, *The Right to Vote: The Contested History of Democracy in the United States* (New York, 2000); Jeffrey L. Pasley, "1800 as a Revolution in Political Culture: Newspapers, Celebrations, Voting, and Democratization in the Early Republic," in Horn, Lewis, and Onuf, eds., *The Revolution of 1800*, 127–28.

15. Chilton Williamson, *American Suffrage: From Property to Democracy, 1760–1860* (Princeton, 1960), 84–86, 89, 100, 107, 117, 122–24; Keyssar, *The Right to Vote*, 6, 7, 10, 21, 29; Jackson T. Main, *The Sovereign States, 1775–1783* (New York, 1973), 200.

16. William N. Chambers, *Political Parties in a New Nation: The American Experience, 1776–1809* (New York, 1963), 32; Miller, *Federalist Era*, 123, 125; Elkins and McKitrick, *Age of Federalism*, 521; John F. Hoadley, *Origins of American Political Parties, 1789–1803* (Lexington, Ky., 1986), 38–44; Williamson, *American Suffrage from Property to Democracy*, 44–45, 57, 76–137; Keyssar, *The Right to Vote*, 1–25. See also Robert Dinkin, *Voting in Revolutionary America* (Westport, Conn., 1982).

17. Freeman, *Affairs of Honor*, 218–20.

18. To understand how the Constitutional Convention devised the electoral college system and how it played out through the election of 1800, see Jack N. Rakove, "The Political Presidency: Discovery and Invention," in Horn, Lewis, and Onuf, eds., *Revolution of 1800*, 30–58.

19. Fischer, *Revolution of American Conservatism*, 400–401; Elkins and McKitrick, *Age of Federalism*, 524–28; Freeman, *Affairs of Honor*, 217.

20. AH to Jeremiah Wadsworth, Dec. 1, 1796, *PAH* 20:418, 419n; Manning J. Dauer, *The Adams Federalists* (Baltimore, 1953), 99–101, 103–4; Smith, "Election of 1796," in Schlesinger, Israel, and Hansen, eds., *History of American Presidential Elections*, 1:71–72.

21. JM to TJ, Dec. 5, 19, 1796, Jan. 15, 1797, *PTJ* 29:214, 226, 264; TJ to JM, Dec. 17, 1796, ibid., 29:223; Benjamin Rush to TJ, Jan. 4, 1797, ibid., 29:251; Elbridge Gerry to TJ, Mar. 27, 1797, ibid., 29:326; TJ to Gerry, May 13, 1797, ibid., 29:362.

22. AA to JA, Dec. 31, 1796, AFP, reel 382.

23. JA [to ?], Mar. 7, 1797, ibid., reel 117; JA to AA, Dec. 16, 18, 30, 1796, Jan. 9, 1797, ibid., reels 382, 383; JA to John Quincy Adams, Oct. 28, 1796, ibid., reel 382.

24. "Documents Relating to the 1796 Campaign for Electors in Virginia," *PTJ* 29:193–99. For an excellent essay on paper wars in early American electoral contests, see Freeman, *Affairs of Honor*, 113–26.

25. TJ to JM, Dec. 17, 1796, ibid., 29:223.

26. Edmond Berkeley and Dorothy Smith Berkeley, *John Beckley: Zealous Partisan in a Nation Divided* (Philadelphia, 1973), 146.

27. Quoted in Bernstein, *Jefferson*, 115.

28. Sedgwick to Rufus King, Mar. 12, 1797, Sedgwick Letterbook, MHS; Cunningham, *Jeffersonian Republicans*, 97–103; Cunningham, *In Pursuit of Reason*, 201–2; Malone, *Jefferson*, 3:283–84; Daniel Sisson, *The American Revolution of 1800* (New York, 1974), 243–46; Robert M. S. McDonald, "Was There a Religious Revolution of 1800?" in Horn, Lewis, and Onuf, eds., *Revolution of 1800*, 175–80.

29. JA to AA, Dec. 1, 1796, AFP, reel 382.

30. JM to TJ, Dec. 10, 1796, *PJM* 16:425.

31. Freeman, *Affairs of Honor*, 223.

32. JA to AA, Nov. 27, 1796, AFP, reel 382; Stephen G. Kurtz, *The Presidency of John Adams: The Collapse of Federalism, 1795–1800* (Philadelphia, 1957), 177–86; Elkins and McKitrick, *Age of Federalism*, 520–21, 860n; Freeman, "Election of 1796," 155; Berkeley and Berkeley, *John Beckley*, 148–51.

33. Mark Scherr, "The 'Republican Experiment' and the Election of 1796 in Virginia," *West Virginia History* 37 (1976):89–108.

34. Elkins and McKitrick, *Age of Federalism*, 521.

35. AH to Theodore Sedgwick, Feb. 26, 1797, *PAH* 20:521.

36. JM to James Maury, Jan. 18, 1797, *PJM* 16:462.

37. TJ to James Sullivan, Feb. 9, 1797, *PTJ* 29:289; TJ to Burr, Jun. 17, 1797, ibid., 29:438.

38. Freeman, "Election of 1796," 153–55.

39. JM to TJ, Dec. 19, 1796, *PJM* 16:432–33.

40. TJ to JM, Jan. 1, 1797, *PTJ* 29:247–48.

41. JA to AA, Dec. 1, 7, 20, 22, 1796, AFP, reel 382.

42. JA to AA, Dec. 20, 22, 1796, ibid., reel 382.

43. JA to AA, Jan. 9, 11, 28, 31, Feb. 2, 7, 1797, ibid., reel 383.

44. TJ to JM, Jan. 1, 1797, *PTJ* 29:248.

45. TJ to JA, Dec. 28, 1796, ibid., 29:235.

46. TJ, *Anas* (Mar. 2, 1797), *WTJ* 1:272–73; JA, "Correspondence Published in the *Boston Patriot*," *WJA* 9:285; JA to Knox, Mar. 30, 1797, AFP, reel 117.

47. JM to TJ, Apr. 27, 1785, *PJM* 8:270.

48. JA to Rush, Aug. 23, 1805, Apr. 22, 1812, Schutz and Adair, *Spur of Fame*, 36, 214.

49. TJ to Gerry, May 13, 1797, *PTJ* 29:362.

50. Malone, *Jefferson*, 3:277–78; McCullough, *Adams*, 467–68.

51. JA to AA, Mar. 5, 17, 1797, AFP, reel 383.

52. JA, Inaugural Address (Mar. 4, 1797), *MPP* 1:218–22.

53. TJ to Gerry, May 13, 1797, *PTJ* 29:362.

54. JA to AA, Mar. 5, 1797, AFP, reel 383.

Chapter 7

1. GW to AH, May 8, 1796, *WW* 35:39–40; GW to the secretary of state, Jul. 8, 18, 1796, ibid., 35:127, 144; GW to Pinckney, Jul. 8, 1796, ibid., 35:129–31.

2. Alexander DeConde, *The Quasi-War: The Politics and Diplomacy of the Undeclared War with France, 1797–1801* (New York, 1966), 16.

3. George Gibbs, ed., *Memoirs of the Administrations of Washington and John Adams, Edited from the Papers of Oliver Wolcott, Secretary of Treasury* (New York, 1846); Elkins and McKitrick, *Age of Federalism*, 627–28; Wolcott to AH, Nov. 6, 1796, *PAH* 20:376.

4. Bernard Steiner, *The Life and Career of James McHenry* (Cleveland, 1907).

5. AH to GW, Nov. 5, 1795, *PAH* 19:397; GW to AH, Aug. 9, 1798, *PGW: Retirement Ser.* 2:500.

6. Gerald Clarfield, *Timothy Pickering and the American Republic* (Pittsburgh, 1980); AH to GW, Mar. 5, 1796, *PAH* 20:374; Elkins and McKitrick, *Age of Federalism*, 623–26.

7. Pickering to AH, Mar. 22, 26, 1797, *PAH* 20:545, 549; Wolcott to AH, Mar. 31, 1797, ibid., 20:569–70; JA to AA, Apr. 3, 1797, AFP, reel 384.

8. AH to Pickering, May 11, 1797, *PAH* 21:81–84; AH to Wolcott, Mar. 30 and Mar. [?], 1797, ibid., 20:567–68, 574. For a succinct assessment of AH's thought and actions during the 1797–1798 phase of the Quasi-War crisis, see Walling, *Republican Empire*, 209–44.

9. DeConde, *Quasi-War*, 28–29; JA, "Correspondence Originally Published in the *Boston Patriot*," *WJA* 9:286–87; Ferling, *Adams*, 345; Sharp, *American Politics in the Early Republic*, 168.

10. JA to Uriah Forest, Jun. 20, 1797, *WJA* 8:546–47; *PTJ* 29:418n.

11. Philadelphia *Aurora*, Mar. 16, 14, 1797; Tagg, *Benjamin Franklin Bache*, 296; Walt Brown, *John Adams and the American Press: Politics and Journalism at the Birth of the Republic* (Jefferson, N.C., 1995), 79–87. The last of these sources provides useful details on the press throughout JA's presidency.

12. Tagg, *Benjamin Franklin Bache*, 315–17.

13. Ibid., 319–21.

14. The quotations are from Kurtz, *Presidency of John Adams*, 237, and Stewart, *Opposition Press of the Federalist Period*, 283, respectively.

15. TJ, "Notes on a Paragraph by John Henry" [after Mar. 1, 1797], *PTJ* 29:309; TJ, "Notes on Alexander Hamilton," n.d., ibid., 29:517–18; TJ, "Notes on Conversations with John Adams and George Washington" [after October 13, 1797], ibid., 29:551–53; TJ, "Notes on a Conversation with Tench Coxe" [Dec. 27, 1979], ibid., 29:596; James Callender to TJ, Sep. 28, 1797, ibid., 29:536–37; TJ to John Barnes, Oct. 8, 1797, ibid., 29:544; Barnes to TJ, Oct. 19, 1797, ibid., 29:561–62; TJ, "Notes on Conversations with Andrew Baldwin, John Brown, and John Hunter," Mar. 11, 1798, ibid., 30:172–73; TJ, "Notes on Senators' Comments about House Impeachment Committee," Mar. 12, 1798, ibid., 30:176; TJ, "Notes of Presidential Appointments," May 3, 1798, ibid., 30:325; TJ, "Notes on Comments by John Adams" [Jan. 1–14, 1799], ibid., 30:608; TJ, "Notes on Comments of Timothy Pickering and John Adams," Jan. 14, 1799, ibid., 30:621; TJ, "Notes on a Letter from Thomas Tingey to the Secretary of the Navy," Jan. 27, 1977, ibid., 30:659–60. The best source for TJ as the covert and artful politician is Freeman, *Affairs of Honor*, 85–89.

16. Ralph Adams Brown, *The Presidency of John Adams* (Lawrence, Kans., 1975), 42–43; DeConde, *Quasi-War*, 30–35.

17. TJ to Gerry, Jun. 21, 1797, and Jan. 26, 1799, *PTJ* 29:448, 30:647; TJ to Coxe, Jul. 10, 1796, ibid., 29:146.

18. TJ to Gerry, May 13, 1797, ibid., 29:365n. TJ deleted this sentence in the final draft of his missive.

19. TJ to Gerry, Jun. 21, 1797, ibid., 29:448.

20. TJ to Gerry, May 13, 1797, ibid., 29:363; TJ to Sullivan, Feb. 9, 1797, ibid., 29:289.

21. TJ to Giles, Dec. 31, 1795, ibid., 28:566–67; TJ, "Notes on a Conversation with Tench Coxe," Dec. 27, 1797, ibid., 29:596; TJ to Mazzei, Apr. 24, 1796, ibid., 29:82; TJ, "Notes on Conversations with John Adams and George Washington" [after Oct. 13, 1797], ibid., 29:552; Malone, *Jefferson*, 3:261–66.

22. Gerald Stourzh, *Alexander Hamilton and the Idea of Republican Government* (Stanford, 1970), 189–205; AH to GW, Sep. 15, 1790, *PAH* 7:48–49.

23. AH to Pickering, Mar. 22, 29, 1797, *PAH* 20:546, 557; AH to Wolcott, Mar. 20, Apr. 5, 13, ibid., 20:567; 21:22, 47; AH to William Laughton Smith, Apr. 5, 10, 1797, ibid., 21:21, 30, 32, 33, 37; AH to McHenry, Apr. 29, 1797, ibid., 21:65.

24. TJ to Thomas M. Randolph, Dec. 14, 1797, *PTJ* 29:583; TJ to Monroe, Dec. 27, 1797, ibid., 29:594; TJ to JM, Feb. 8, Mar. 2, 1798, ibid., 30:87–88, 156–57; DeConde, *Quasi-War*, 61.

25. TJ to Martha J. Randolph, Dec. 27, 1797, *PTJ* 29:596; TJ to Edward Rutledge, Jun. 24, 1797, ibid., 29:456–57; TJ to JM, Feb. 15, 1798, ibid., 30:111–12; JM to TJ, Mar. 4, 1798, *PJM* 17:89; Malone, *Jefferson*, 3:363–64; Elkins and McKitrick, *Age of Federalism*, 706–11.

26. Gerald H. Clarfield, *Timothy Pickering and American Diplomacy, 1795–1800* (Columbia, Mo., 1969), 194; JA to the Senate, Mar. 5, 1798, *MPP* 1:263–64.

27. AH to McHenry [Jan. 27–Feb. 11], 1798, *PAH* 21:341; Steiner, *McHenry*, 291–95; McHenry to JA, AFP, reel 387; DeConde, *Quasi-War*, 64–65.

28. AH to Pickering, Mar. 17, 1798, *PAH* 21:364–67, 379–80; Pickering to AH, Mar. 25, 1798, ibid., 21:370–78; JA, "Message" [Mar. 1798], AFP, reel 387; JA, Message to Congress, Mar. 19, 1798, *MPP* 1:264–65; Smith, *Adams*, 2:953–54; DeConde, *Quasi-War*, 67–68.

29. AH to Pickering, Mar. 27, 1798, *PAH*, 21:379; [Alexander Hamilton], "The Stand," ibid., 21:383, 386–87; TJ to JM, Mar. 21, 29, Apr. 5, 26, May 3, 1798, *PTJ* 30:189–90, 227–28, 244–45, 299–300, 322–24; JM to TJ, Feb. 18, 1798, *PJM* 17:82; TJ to Tench Coxe, May 21, 1799, *WTJ* 7:380–81.

30. TJ to JM, Apr. 12, 1798, *PTJ* 30:268; TJ to Pendleton, Apr. 2, 1798, ibid., 30:241; JM to TJ, Apr. 2, 15, 22, 1797, *PJM* 17:105, 113–14, 118; Brown, *Presidency of Adams*, 51.

31. TJ to JM, Apr. 6, 12, 1798, *PTJ* 30:250–51, 268.

32. The addresses can be found scattered through AFP, reels 388–392, and many are contained in *WJA*, vol. 9.

33. Sedgwick to King, Apr. 9, Jul. 2, 1798, King, *Life and Correspondence of Rufus King*, 2:312, 354.

34. Sedgwick to Harry Van Schaack, Dec. 14, 1797, Sedgwick Papers, MHS; Sedgwick to Ephraim Williams, Jan. 29, 1797, ibid.; Robert Troup to King, Jul. 10, 1798, King, *Life and Correspondence of Rufus King*, 2:363; AA to Thomas B. Adams, May 1, Jul. 20, 1798, AFP, reels 388, 390; AA to Mary Cranch, May 10, 1798, Mitchell, *New Letters of Abigail Adams*, 171–72; DeConde, *Quasi-War*, 81; McCullough, *Adams*, 501.

35. Quoted in Brown, *Presidency of Adams*, 56.

36. DeConde, *Quasi-War*, 90–91, 96.

37. Benjamin Rosseter to Sedgwick, Mar. 30, 1798, Sedgwick Papers, MHS; Sedgwick to Williams, Jan. 4, 1798, ibid.

38. Dauer, *Adams Federalists*, 183; Brown, *Presidency of Adams*, 58; DeConde, *Quasi-War*, 80, 83, 89–98.

39. Quoted in Tagg, *Bache*, 319.

40. TJ to JM, Mar. 29, Apr. 26, 1798, *PTJ* 30:299–300. Also see Richard Rosenfeld, *American Aurora: A Democratic Republican Returns* (New York, 1997), 324–25, and Stewart, *Opposition Press in the Federalist Period*, 293–309, 311, 317.

41. TJ to JM, Apr. 26, Jun. 7, 1798, *PTJ* 30:300, 393; Elkins and McKitrick, *Age of Federalism*, 591–93. On the Alien and Sedition Acts, see also James Morton Smith, *Freedom's Fetters: The Alien and Sedition Acts and American Civil Liberties* (Ithaca, 1956), and John C. Miller, *Crisis in Freedom: The Alien and Sedition Acts* (Boston, 1951).

42. AH to Wolcott, Jun. 5, 29, 1798, *PAH* 21:485, 522; AH to Pickering, Jun. 7, 1798, ibid., 21:495; AH to GW, May 19, 1798, ibid., 21:467. AH subsequently defended the Sedition Act and government's right to protect itself from those who sought to limit its authority. See James H. Read, *Power Versus Liberty: Madison, Hamilton, and Jefferson* (Charlottesville, 2000), 55–87. For a discussion of AH's thinking in a legal and philosophical context, see Walling, *Republican Empire*, 245–51.

43. Sedgwick [to ?], Mar. 7, 1798, Sedgwick Papers, MHS; Ames to Wolcott, Apr. 22, 1798, Ames, *Works of Ames*, 2:1273; Ames to Pickering, Jun. 4, 1798, ibid., 2:1277–78.

44. Quoted in Smith, *Freedom's Fetters*, 15.

45. Quoted in Dauer, *Adams Federalists*, 165.

46. Quoted in Smith, *Freedom's Fetters*, 26, 277.

47. TJ to JM, Apr. 26, Jun. 21, 1798, *PTJ* 30:299–300, 417–18; TJ to Samuel Smith, Aug. 22, 1798, ibid., 30:484–86; TJ to John Taylor, Jun. 4, 1798, ibid., 30:387–89.

Chapter 8

1. AH to Rufus King, Aug. 22, 1798, *PAH* 22:154; AH to Harrison Gray Otis, Jan. 26, 1799, ibid., 22:441; AH to Francisco de Miranda, Aug. 22, 1798, ibid., 22:156. For AH's history with Miranda, see ibid., 21:1n.

2. On this episode, see Ferling, *A Leap in the Dark*, 435–38; Ferling, *Adams*, 357–63.

3. DeConde, *Quasi-War*, 99.

4. Quoted in ibid., 97; TJ to Thomas M. Randolph, Feb. 2, 1800, *WTJ* 7:423.

5. AA to JA, Jan. 28, 1797, Dec. 31, 1796, AFP, reels 383, 382.

6. Malone, *Jefferson*, 2:287.

7. JA to Vanderkemp, Jan. 25, 1808, AFP, reel 118; JA to AA, Jan. 9, 1797, ibid., reel 383.

8. JA to Rush, Aug. 23, Sep. 30, Dec. 4, 1805, Jan. 25, 1806, Sep. 2, Nov. 11, 1807, Aug. 18, 1808, Aug. 28, 1811, in Schutz and Adair, *Spur of Fame*, 34–35, 42, 45, 47–48, 94–95, 98–99, 113, 192; JA to Trumbull, Jul. 23, Nov. [?], 1805, AFP, reel 118; JA to Benjamin Waterhouse, Jul. 12, 1811, in *Statesman and Friend: Correspondence of John Adams and Benjamin Waterhouse, 1784–1822*, ed. Worthington C. Ford (Boston, 1927), 65; JA to William Cunningham, Oct. 15, 1808, in *Correspondence Between the Hon. John Adams . . . and the Late William Cunningham*, 44; Shaw, *Character of John Adams*, 304.

9. TJ to Samuel Smith, Aug. 22, 1798, *PTJ* 30:484–86; TJ to John Taylor, Nov. 26, 1798, ibid., 30:588–90; Onuf, *Jefferson's Empire*, 94.

10. TJ to Monroe, Sep. 7, 1797, *PTJ* 29:526–27.

11. TJ, "Draft of the Kentucky Resolution of 1798" [before Oct. 4, 1798], ibid., 30:536–41. See also the editor's introductory note, ibid., 30:529–35.

12. Cunningham, *In Pursuit of Reason*, 219. The resolutions, as passed, can be found in *WTJ* 8:458–79.

13. JA to JQA, Oct. 16, 1798, APF, reel 119; Abigail Adams Smith to JQA, Sep. 28, 1798, ibid., reel 391; Levin, *Abigail Adams*, 354.

14. JA to GW, Oct. 9, 1789, AFP, reel 119; JA to Pickering, Aug. 25, Oct. 15, 1798, ibid., reel 119; JA to McHenry, Aug. 29, Oct. 22, 28, 1798, ibid., reel 119; McCullough, *Adams*, 508.

15. JA to McHenry, Oct. 22, 1798, AFP, reel 119; JA to Pickering, Oct. 20, 1798, ibid; Abigail Adams Smith to JQA, Sep. 28, 1798, ibid., reel 391.

16. JA to McHenry, Oct. 22, 1798, ibid., reel 119; JA to AA, Nov. 13, 15, 1798, ibid., reel 392; Ferling, *Adams*, 369–70; McCullough, *Adams*, 515–16.

17. TJ to JM, Jun. 21, 1798, *PTJ* 30:417–18; JM to TJ, May 13, 1798, *PJM* 17:130; Henry Tazewell to JM, Jun. 28, 1798, ibid., 17:159; Malone, *Jefferson*, 3:377.

18. Quoted in McLaughlin, *Jefferson and Monticello*, 265–68; TJ to Maria Eppes, Jul. 13, 1798, *FLTJ*, 167.

19. TJ to Gerry, Jan. 26, 1799, *PTJ* 30:649; TJ to Pendleton, Jan. 29, 1799, ibid., 30:661; TJ to Monroe, Jan. 23, 1799, ibid., 30:635; TJ to JM, Jan. 30, 1799, ibid., 30:665; TJ to Thomas M. Randolph, Jan. 30, 1799, ibid., 30:668.

20. TJ to JM, Jan. 3, 1799, ibid., 30:610; *JMB* 2:995.

21. JA to McHenry, Aug. 29, Sep. 13, 1798, AFP, reel 119.

22. JA to Gerry, Dec. 15, 1798, *WJA* 8:617; Kurtz, *Presidency of John Adams*, 341.

23. JA to Wolcott, Oct. 27, 31, 1797, AFP, reel 119; *Correspondence of the Late President Adams, Originally Published in the Boston Patriot* (Boston, 1809), 10.

24. Murray to JA, Jul. 1, 17, 22, Aug. 3, 20, Oct. 7, 1798, *WJA* 8:677–91; GW to JA, Feb. 1, 1799, *WW* 37:119–20; DeConde, *Quasi-War*, 147–48, 154–68; Samuel Flagg Bemis, *John Quincy Adams and the Foundation of American Foreign Policy* (New York, 1956), 99.

25. Adams, Second Annual Address, Dec. 8, 1798, *MPP* 1:261–65; Ferling, *Adams*, 373–78; DeConde, *Quasi-War*, 173, 178; TJ to Archibald Stuart, Feb. 13, 1799, *WTJ* 7:352.

26. AH to Otis, Dec. 27, 1798, Jan. 26, 1799, *PAH* 22:394, 441; AH to Sedgwick, Feb. 2, 1799, ibid., 22:452–53; Elkins and McKitrick, *Age of Federalism*, 615–17.

27. "Correspondence Originally Published in the *Boston Patriot*," *WJA* 9:305–6.

28. JA to the Senate, Feb. 18, 1799, *MPP* 1:282; TJ to JM, Feb. 19, 1799, *WTJ* 7:363.

29. Quoted in Henry Cabot Lodge, *Life and Letters of George Cabot* (Boston, 1877), 221.

30. Cabot to King, March 10, Sep. 7, 1799, in King, *Life and Correspondence of King*, 2:551; 3:101; Troup to King, Apr. 19, 1799, ibid., 2:596.

31. TJ to Edmund Pendleton, Feb. 19, 1799, *WTJ* 7:364; Sedgwick to King, Jan. 20–27, March 20, Dec. 29, 1799, Sedgwick Family Papers, MHS; Peter Van Schaack to Sedgwick, March 12, 1799, ibid.; Sedgwick to AH, Feb. 7, 1799, *PAH* 22:471; Miller, *Hamilton*, 493–94.

32. Troup to King, Jun. 5, 1799, in King, *Life and Correspondence of King*, 3:35; Sedgwick to King, Nov. 15, 1799, ibid., 3:146; Charles Gore to King, May 14, 1800, ibid., 3:242.

33. Brown, *Presidency of John Adams*, 97; DeConde, *Quasi-War*, 182; Sedgwick to Van Schaack, Feb. 26, 1799, Jan. 4, 1800, Sedgwick Family Papers, MHS; Sedgwick to John Rutherford, March 1, 1799, ibid., JA to AA, Feb. 27, 1799, AFP, reel, 393; TJ to JM, Feb. 26, 1799, *WTJ* 7:370–71.

34. McCullough, *Adams*, 526.

35. AA to TBA, Apr. 2, Jul. 15, 1799, AFP, reel 395; AA to JQA, Dec. 30, 1799, ibid., reel 396; AA [to ?], Nov. 13, 1799, ibid., reel 396; Smith, *Adams*, 2:1006, 1010, 1014; Shaw, *Character of John Adams*, 257–58.

36. Smith, *Freedom's Fetters*, 159–87.

37. JA to Pickering, Aug. 6, 1799, AFP, reel 120; DeConde, *Quasi-War*, 216.

38. Stoddert to JA, Aug. 29, Sep. 13, 1799, *WJA* 9:18–19, 26–29; JA to Cunningham, Nov. 9, 1808, AFP, reel 118.

39. JA to AA, Oct. 12, 1799, Dec. 17, 31, 1798, AFP, reel, 396, 392, 393; McCullough, *Adams*, 411; Ferling, *Adams*, 322–23, 386.

40. JA to AA, Oct. 24, 1799, AFP, reel 396; JA to Cunningham, Nov. 9, 1808, ibid., reel 118; JA [to ?], Nov. 26, 1812, ibid., reel 118; Dauer, *Adams Federalists*, 233–34; Miller, *Federalist Era*, 255.

41. *Correspondence of the Late President Adams*, 29–30; JA [to ?], Nov. 26, 1812, AFP, reel 118. JA's account, as well as that of AA, which was contemporaneous, can also be found in *PAH* 23:546–47n.

42. AA to William Cranch, Feb. 3, 1800, AFP, reel 397; AA to JQA, Dec. 2, 1798, ibid., reel 392; Shaw to AA, Jan. 21, 1799, ibid., reel 393; TBA to AA, Aug. 12, 1799, ibid., reel 396.

43. Peter Henriques, *He Died as He Lived: The Death of George Washington* (Mount Vernon, Va., 2000), 27–36.

44. AA to Mary Cranch, Dec. 30, 1799, Mitchell, *New Letters of Abigail Adams*, 225; JA to the Senate, Dec. 23, 1799, *MPP* 1:299; McCullough, *Adams*, 533.

45. Murray to JA, Feb. 7, 1800, AFP, reel 397; AA to Hannah Cushing, Apr. 2, 1800, ibid., reel 397.

46. Adams, Third Annual Address, Dec. 3, 1799, *MPP* 1:289–92; AA to Mary Cranch, Dec. 11, 1799, Mitchell, *New Letters of Abigail Adams*, 220.

Chapter 9

1. DeConde, *Quasi-War*, 265–66; Dauer, *Adams Federalists*, 240–42.

2. AA to Mary Cranch, Dec. 11, 1799, in *New Letters of Abigail Adams*, ed. Mitchell, 221.

3. TJ to Archibald Stuart, Feb. 13, 1799, *WTJ* 7:351, 354; TJ to Burr, Feb. 11, 1799, ibid., 7:348; TJ to Pendleton, Feb. 14, 1799, ibid., 7:356.

4. Dauer, *Adams Federalists*, 232–36.

5. AA to Mary Cranch, May 5, 1800, in *New Letters of Abigail Adams*, ed. Mitchell, 251; John Dawson to JM, May 4, 1800, *PJM* 17:386.

6. AH to King, May 4, 1796, *PAH* 20:158.

7. William Merrill and Sean Wilentz, eds., *The Key of Liberty: The Life and Democratic Writings of William Manning, "A Laborer," 1747–1814* (Cambridge, Mass., 1993), 59, 63–64, 73–74, 112, 126. On status and work, see the essay in Wood, *Radicalism of the American Revolution*, 24–42.

8. Quoted in Linda K. Kerber, "The Federalist Party," in Arthur M. Schlesinger Jr., *History of U.S. Political Parties* (New York, 1973), 1:17.

9. Gordon Wood, "The Enemy Is Us: Democratic Capitalism in the Early Republic," *JER* 16 (1996): 293–308; David Waldstreicher, "Federalism, the Styles of Politics, and the Politics of Style," in Ben Atar and Oberg, eds., *Federalists Reconsidered*, 99–117; Steven Watts, "Ministers, Misanthropes, and Mandarins: The Federalists and the Culture of Capitalism," ibid., 157–75; Alan Taylor, "From Fathers to Friends of the People: Political Personae in the Early Republic," ibid., 225–45; David Waldstreicher, *In the Midst of Perpetual Fetes: Nationalism, 1776–1820* (Chapel Hill, 1997), 129, 131, 136–37, 140, 145, 158, 204, 239–40; Simon P. Newnam, *Parades and Politics of the Street: Festive Culture in the Early American Republic* (Philadelphia, 1997), 57, 89, 94, 125, 160–63, 176, 180–81; Fischer, *Revolution of American Conservatism*, 23; Robert Ernst, *Rufus King: American Federalist* (Chapel Hill, 1968), 83, 86; Samuel E. Morison, *Harrison Gray Otis, 1765–1848: The Urbane Federalist* (Boston, 1969), 88; Ames, "The Republican," X, Ames, *Works of Ames*, 1:264.

10. TJ to Charles Pinckney, Oct. 29, 1799, *WTJ* 7:398; TJ to Monroe, Jan. 16, 1800, ibid., 7:402.

11. Lomask, *Burr*, 1:238–46; Freeman, *Affairs of Honor*, 231–33; Wills, *Negro President*, 70.

12. Lomask, *Burr*, 241–43; Kurtz, *Presidency of John Adams*, 379; AH to McHenry, Jan. 2, 13, Mar. 9, 1800, *PAH* 24:155–56, 185, 306–7; AH to William Smith, Jan. 3, 1800, ibid., 24:157–58; AH to C. C. Pinckney, Feb. 25, 1800, ibid., 24:252; AH, General Orders, Jan. 4, 1800, ibid., 24:164–65; AH to Nathan Rice, Jan. 6, 1800, ibid., 24:171–72; AH to King, Jan. 5, 1800, ibid., 24:169.

13. Young, *Democratic Republicans of New York*, 474–76; Paul A. Gilje and Howard B. Rock, eds., *Keepers of the American Revolution: New Yorkers at Work in the Early Republic* (Ithaca, 1992), 17–19. The raw data for the vote in New York, and much in this book that subsequently chronicles the results elsewhere, can be found in the Lampi Collection of Early American Electoral Data, compiled by Philip Lampi at the American Antiquarian Society in Worcester, Massachusetts.

14. Quoted in Edwin G. Burrows and Mike Wallace, *Gotham: A History of New York City to 1898* (New York, 1999), 328.

15. AA to TBA, Nov. 13, 1800, in *Letters of Mrs. Adams, the Wife of John Adams. With an Introductory Memoir*, ed. Charles Francis Adams (Boston, 1841), 2:238; AA to JQA, May 15, 1800, AFP, reel 397. See also *PAH* 24:453n.

16. AH to Jay, May 7, 1800, *PAH* 24:464–66, 467n.

17. AH to Sedgwick, May 4, 1800, ibid., 24:453.

18. TJ to Thomas M. Randolph, May 7, 1800, in "The Jefferson Papers," *Collections of the Massachusetts Historical Society*, 7th ser. (Boston, 1900), 1:77; Zahniser, *Pinckney*, 216.

19. AA to Malcolm, May 18, 1800, AFP, reel 397.

20. "A Friend" to JA, Mar. 19, 1800, ibid., reel 397; Sedgwick to King, May 11, Sep. 26, 1800, Sedgwick Family Papers, MHS; Ames to Sedgwick, Dec. 14, 1800, ibid.; Richard E. Welch, *Theodore Sedgwick, Federalist: A Political Portrait* (Middlebury, Conn., 1965), 208–18; Miller, *Federalist Era*, 263; Elkins and McKitrick, *Age of Federalism*, 734–36; Brown, *Presidency of John Adams*, 177, 179.

21. Wolcott to Ames, Dec. 29, 1799, in Gibbs, *Memoirs of the Administrations of Washington and Adams*, 2:239; Sedgwick to AH, May 13, 1800, *PAH* 24:482. See also *PAH* 24:484n.

22. McHenry to JA, May 31, 1800, AFP, reel 397; McHenry to AH, May 31, 1800, *PAH* 24:552–65.

23. JA to Pickering, May 10, 12, 1800, AFP, reel 120; Pickering to JA, May 12, 1800, ibid., reel 397; JA to Stoddert, Nov. 16, 1811, ibid., reel 118.

24. Stewart, *Opposition Press of the Federalist Era*, 262; Sedgwick to AH, May 7, 10, 1800, *PAH* 24:467, 475.

25. AH to Sedgwick, Feb. 27, 1800, *PAH* 24:270; AH to Henry Lee, Mar. 7, 1800, ibid., 24:299; AH to McHenry, May 15, 1800, ibid., 24:490; AH to GW, May 19, 1798, ibid., 21:467; Esmond Wright, *Fabric of Freedom, 1763–1800* (New York, 1961), 224–25; Brown, *Presidency of John Adams*, 118–19.

Chapter 10

1. AA to Mary Cranch, Nov. 26, 1799, in *New Letters of Abigail Adams*, ed. Mitchell, 217. The Philadelphia *Aurora* confirmed her assessment. See Cunningham, "Election of 1800," in Schlesinger, *History of American Presidential Elections*, 1:107.

2. Bernard Weisberger, *America Afire: Jefferson, Adams, and the Revolutionary Election of 1800* (New York, 2000), 235; John Beckley to Tench Coxe, Jan. 24, 1800, in *Justifying Jefferson: The Political Writings of John James Beckley*, ed. Gerard W. Gawalt (Washington, D.C., 1995), 164.

3. Miller, *Crisis in Freedom*, 213–14.

4. The sketch of Callender draws on Michael Durey, *"With the Hammer of Truth": James Thomson Callender and America's Early National Heroes* (Charlottesville, 1990); Durey, *Transatlantic Radicals and the Early American Republic*; Beran, *Jefferson's Demons*, 158.

5. TJ to Monroe, Jul. 15, 1803, *WTJ* 9:388–89; TJ to Callender, Oct. 6, 1799, ibid., 7:393–95; Malone, *Jefferson*, 3:331–32; 468–70; Cunningham, *In Pursuit of Reason*, 222. Most of TJ's correspondence with Callender was published in the *New England Historical and Genealogical Register* 50 (1896): 321–33, 445–58.

6. James T. Callender, *The Prospect Before Us* (Richmond, 1800), in the Early American Imprint Series, Nos. 37083, 37084. See 1:3, 10, 18, 24, 25, 28–30, 73, 85, 93, 124, 160; 2:50.

7. AA to JQA, May 19, 1800, AFP, reel 397.

8. Ferling, *Adams*, 402–3; Marcus Cunliffe, *American Presidents and the Presidency* (New York, 1972), 46.

9. William Shaw to AA, Jun. 8, 1800, AFP, reel 398; JA to James Lloyd, Mar. 31, 1815, AFP, reel 122; Kurtz, *Presidency of John Adams*, 398; Cunningham, "Election of 1800," in Schlesinger, *History of American Presidential Elections*, 1:115–16.

10. JA to AA, Jun. 13, 1800, AFP, reel 398; Smith, *Adams*, 2:1036–37; McCullough, *Adams*, 541–42.

11. JA to AA, Jun. 13, 1800, AFP, reel 398.

12. Alexander White to JA, Jan. 15, 1800, AFP, reel 397; Stoddert to White, Jan. 2, 1800, ibid., reel 397; [?] Law to JA, Apr. 9, 1800, ibid., reel 397.

13. JA to AA, Jul. 12, 1800, ibid., reel 398; Cunningham, "Election of 1800," Schlesinger, *History of American Presidential Elections*, 1:115; Kurtz, *Presidency of John Adams*, 399.

14. TJ to JM, Mar. 4, Apr. 4, May 12, 1800, *WTJ* 7:430–34, 446–47.

15. Malone, *Jefferson*, 3:461, 467–72.

16. TJ to Gerry, Jan. 26, 1799, *PTJ* 30:645–50; Cunningham, "Election of 1800," in Schlesinger, *History of American Presidential Elections*, 1:114, 118–19; Cunningham, *In Pursuit of Reason*, 223–24.

17. TJ to Thomas M. Randolph, May 7, 1800, *Collections of the Massachusetts Historical Society*, 7th ser., 1:77–78.

18. Wolcott to AH, Sep. 3, 1800, *PAH* 25:104–10; Cabot to AH, Oct. 11, 1800, ibid., 25:148–49. See also the editor's note in ibid., 25:176–77n.

19. Alexander Hamilton, *Letter from Alexander Hamilton, Concerning the Public Conduct and Character of John Adams* (1800), in ibid., 25:186–234. The quotations are on pages 190, 192, 196, 210, 214, 216, 222, and 233.

20. Ibid., 25:170n, 172–73n.

21. AH to Sedgwick, May 10, 1800, ibid., 24:475.

22. Pickering to William L. Smith, May 7, 1800, ibid., 24:451n.

23. AA to TBA, Jul. 12, 1800, AFP, reel 398.

24. AH, *Letter from Alexander Hamilton*, in *PAH* 25:194.

25. Zahniser, *Pinckney*, 217–21.

26. TJ to JM, Feb. 7, 1799, *PJM* 17:227; Freeman, *Affairs of Honor*, 234; Cunningham, *Jeffersonian Republicans*, 106–74, 197; Sisson, *American Revolution of 1800*, 354.

27. Jeffrey L. Pasley, *"The Tyranny of Printers": Newspaper Politics in the Early Republic* (Charlottesville, 2001), 157.

28. The quotations are taken from Cunningham, *Jeffersonian Republicans*, 153–54, 160.

29. Carl E. Prince, *New Jersey's Jeffersonian Republicans: The Genesis of an Early Party Machine, 1789–1817* (Chapel Hill, 1964), 41–61. The quotations are on pages 46 and 58.

30. Fischer Ames, "Laocoon," No. 1, Ames, *Works of Ames* 1:194–95.

31. William Smith to Ralph Izard, May 23, 1797, in "South Carolina Federalist Correspondence," ed. Ulrich B. Phillips, *AHR* 14 (1909): 787; Cunningham, *Jeffersonian Republicans*, 147–66.

32. *Baltimore American*, Jul. 16, 1800.

33. TJ to JA, Jun. 15, 1813, *AJL* 2:332; *Aurora*, Feb. 17, May 7, 9, 1800; *Constitutional Telegraphe*, May 10, Jun. 25, Sep. 6, 1800; *Baltimore American*, Jun. 30, 1800; Weisberger, *America Afire*, 251.

34. *Aurora*, Sep. 11, 1800; Zahniser, *Pinckney*, 208, 223, 225–26.

35. *Constitutional Telegraphe*, Jun. 25, 1800.

36. *Aurora*, May 20, 1800; *Constitutional Telegraphe*, Aug. 20, 1800; *Independent Chronicle*, May 15, Jul. 24, 1800; *Baltimore American*, Jul. 17, 1800.

37. Quoted in Sisson, *American Revolution of 1800*, 389.

38. Quoted in Noble E. Cunningham, "The Jeffersonian Republican Party," in Schlesinger, *History of U.S. Political Parties*, 1:254.

39. *Aurora*, Feb. 4, 8, 12, 13, Mar. 5, Apr. 12, 19, May 1, 1800; *Independent Chronicle*, Apr. 14, 1800; John Beckley, *Address to the People of the United States with an Epitome and Vindication of the Public Life and Character of Thomas Jefferson* (1800), in *Justifying Jefferson*, ed. Gawalt, 166. The quotation "whether we shall have at the head of our executive" can be found in Bernstein, *Jefferson*, 113.

40. *Constitutional Telegraphe*, Jan. 29, 1800.

41. The quotations are from Sisson, *American Revolution of 1800*, 402, and John Beckley, *To the Author of a Pamphlet entitled "Serious Considerations on the Election of a President . . ."* (1800), in *Justifying Jefferson*, ed. Gawalt, 207.

42. *Aurora*, Mar. 5, 12, Sep. 20, 1800.

43. *Constitutional Telegraphe*, Apr. 5, 1800.

44. *Aurora*, Dec. 3, Apr. 24, 1800. See also the *Constitutional Telegraphe*, Mar. 29, May 12, 31, 1800.

45. *Aurora*, Mar. 4, May 19, 1800.

46. *Aurora*, Oct. 14, 1800. This article is reprinted in full in Cunningham, *Jeffersonian Republicans*, 213–14.

47. *Independent Chronicle*, May 29, 1800.

48. Waldstreicher, *In the Midst of Perpetual Fetes*, 187.

49. *Aurora*, Oct. 4, 1800.

50. Quoted in Cunningham, *Jeffersonian Republicans*, 217.

51. Beckley, *Address to the People*, in *Justifying Jefferson*, ed. Gawalt, 167.

52. *Independent Chronicle*, May 12, Jun. 2, 16, 30, Aug. 29, Sep. 8, 15, 22, 1800; *Constitutional Telegraphe*, Jan. 25, 1800; Miller, *Federalist Era*, 266; Pasley, "1800 as a Revolution in Political Culture," in Horn, *Revolution of 1800*, 142.

53. Quoted in Cunningham, *Jeffersonian Republicans*, 219.

54. *Constitutional Telegraphe*, Feb. 15, 1800.

55. *Independent Chronicle*, Jan. 23, May 12, 1800.

56. Kerber, "Federalist Party," in Schlesinger, *History of U.S. Political Parties*, 1:19.

57. *Gazette of the United States*, May 10, 20, Sep. 13, Oct. 14, 1800; *Commercial Advertiser*, Jan. 20, 1800; *Connecticut Courant*, Sep. 1, 1800; *Columbian Sentinel*, May 10, 1800; Henry De Saussure, *Address to the Citizens of South Carolina on the Approaching Election* (Charleston, 1800), 7; James Cheetham, *An Answer to Alexander Hamilton's Letter Concerning John Adams* (New York, 1800), 19, 24.

58. *Connecticut Courant*, Jan. 20, 1800.

59. Quoted in McCullough, *Adams*, 546.

60. *Gazette of the United States*, Oct. 14, 1800; De Saussure, *Address*, 7.

61. De Saussure, *Address*, 30, 32, 34.

62. *Gazette of the United States*, Jan. 20, 24, 28, May 20, Sep. 6, 1800; *Commercial Advertiser*, Jan. 20, 1800.

63. *Gazette of the United States*, Jan. 9, Mar. 24, 1800; *Connecticut Courant*, Sep. 29, 1800; *Columbian Sentinel*, Feb. 22, 1800; Sisson, *Revolution of 1800*, 352, 396.

64. *Commercial Advertiser*, Apr. 29, 30, 1800.

65. *Gazette of the United States*, Sep. 16, Nov. 29, 1800; *Commercial Advertiser*, Mar. 17, Apr. 29, 30, 1800; William Linn, *Serious Considerations on the Election of a President* (New York, 1800), 5–8; *Connecticut Courant*, Jun. 23, Aug. 18, 25, Sep. 1, 15, 1800.

66. *Gazette of the United States*, Jul. 3, 10, Aug. 1, Oct. 8, 13, 1800; McCullough, *Adams*, 543.

67. TJ to Philip Mazzei, Apr. 24, 1796, *PTJ* 29:81–83. See also the useful editor's note, ibid., 29:73–81, and Malone, *Jefferson*, 3:302–7.

68. *Gazette of the United States*, Aug. 4, 11, 14, 1800; *Columbian Sentinel*, Jul. 19, 1800; Linn, *Serious Considerations*, 24.

69. The quotations are from "Editor's Note," *PTJ* 29:79.

70. TJ, *Notes on the State of Virginia*, 159.

71. McDonald, "Was There a Religious Revolution of 1800?" in Horn, *Revolution of 1800*, 180–84.

72. McCullough, *Adams*, 543; Miller, *Federalist Era*, 264–65.

73. *Gazette of the United States*, Sep. 16, 1800.

74. John Ward Fenno, *Desultory Reflections on the New Political Aspects of Public Affairs in the United States of America* (New York, 1800), 5.

75. *Connecticut Courant*, Sep. 22, 1800.

76. *Commercial Advertiser*, Apr. 26, 28, 1800.

77. JA, Fourth Annual Address, Nov. 22, 1800, *MPP* 1:308.

78. Waldstreicher, *In the Midst of Perpetual Fetes*, 138, 164, 177–245. The quotations are on pages 184 and 204.

79. Newman, *Parades and the Politics of the Streets*, 175–76.

80. Gordon-Reed, *Thomas Jefferson and Sally Hemings*, 63.

81. *PJM* 17:251n.

82. Quoted in Cunningham, *Jeffersonian Republicans*, 145.

83. Philip J. Lampi, "Election of 1800 Revisited," paper presented at the American Historical Association, Chicago, Jan. 9, 2000, 1 (used with the author's permission); Cunningham, *Jeffersonian Republicans*, 146–47.

84. Waldstreicher, *In the Midst of Perpetual Fetes*, 198; Ronald P. Formisano, "Federalists and Republicans: Parties Yes—System, No," in Paul Kleppner et al., eds., *The Evolution of American Electoral Systems* (Westport, Conn., 1981), 46.

85. Harry M. Tinkcom, *The Republicans and Federalists in Pennsylvania, 1789–1800: A Study in National Stimulus and Local Response* (Harrisburg, 1950), 243–45, 247–53.

86. John Trumbull to JA, Sep. 24, 1800, AFP, reel 398; AA to TBA, Aug. 15, Oct. 12, 1800, ibid., reel 398, 399; Bushrod Washington to Wolcott, Nov. 1, 1800, *PAH* 25:249–50n; JM to Monroe, Nov. 10, 1800, *PJM* 17:434; JM to TJ, Nov. 11, 1800, ibid., 17:437; Brown, *Presidency of John Adams*, 176–85.

87. Ferling, *Adams*, 398–99; JA to Pinckney, Oct. 27, 1800, AFP, reel 399; AH, *Letter from Alexander Hamilton*, *PAH* 25:197–204: Zahniser, *Pinckney*, 218–20.

88. Charles Pinckney to TJ, Nov. 22, 1800, *AHR* 4 (1898): 119.

89. C. Pinckney to TJ, Oct. 12, December [?], 1800, ibid., 4:115, 122; Zahniser, *Pinckney*, 224.

90. Waldstreicher, *In the Midst of Perpetual Fetes*, 184.

91. Zahniser, *Pinckney*, 227–28.

92. C. Pinckney to TJ, Oct. 12, 1800, *AHR*, 4:114; C. Pinckney to JM, Oct. 26, 1800, ibid., 4:116–17.

93. James Gunn to AH, Dec. 13, 1800, *PAH* 25:254; JM to Monroe, Nov. 23, 1800, *PJM* 17:439; AA to TBA, Nov. 13, 1800, AFP, reel 399.

94. DeConde, *Quasi-War*, 283.

95. TJ to Thomas M. Randolph, Dec. 12, 1800, *Collections of the Massachusetts Historical Society*, 7th ser., 1:80.

96. TJ to T. M. Randolph, Nov. 30, 1800, ibid., 1:78, 80.

Chapter 11

1. TBA to JQA, Dec. 6, 1800, AFP, reel 399.

2. JA to TBA, Dec. 17, 1800, ibid., reel 399; Levin, *Abigail Adams*, 385–86; Ferling, *Adams*, 406.

3. Quoted in Malone, *Jefferson*, 3:492.

4. TJ to Thomas M. Randolph, Dec. 12, 1800, *Collections of the Massachusetts Historical Society*, 7th ser., 1:80.

5. Peter H. Argersinger, "Electoral Processes," in Jack P. Greene, ed., *Encyclopedia of Political History* (New York, 1984), 2:490.

6. First Democracy Project, AAS.

7. GW to John Trumbull, Jul. 21, 1799, *PGW: Retirement Ser.* 4:202.

8. TJ, *Notes on the State of Virginia*, 165. See also Ferling, *Setting the World Ablaze*, 50–52.

9. Charles Pinckney to TJ, Jan. 24, 1801, Oct. 12, 1800, *AHR* 4 (1898): 128, 114.

10. Zahniser, *Pinckney*, 228–33. The Ames quotation is on page 218.

11. William Freehling, *The Road to Disunion: Secessionists at Bay, 1776–1854* (New York, 1990), 146–48; Sharp, *American Politics in the Early Republic*, 247.

12. First Democracy Project, AAS; Lampi, "Election of 1800 Revisited," 4–5, 12; Michael A. Bellesiles, "'The Soil Will Be Soaked with Blood': Taking the Revolution of 1800 Seriously," in Horn, *Revolution of 1800*, 63.

13. Lampi, "Election of 1800 Revisited," 3, 10.

14. JA to TBA, Jan. 16, 1800, AFP, reel 400.

15. *PAH* 25:185n, 180n.

16. AH to James Ross, Dec. 18, 1800, ibid., 25:264–65.

17. Pasley, "1800 as a Revolution in Political Culture," in Horn, *Revolution of 1800*, 127.

18. First Democracy Project, AAS.

19. Ibid.; Lampi, "Election of 1800," 10.

20. Formisano, "Federalists and Republicans," in Kleppner, ed., *Evolution of American Electoral Systems*, 40, 53; Prince, *New Jersey's Jeffersonian Republicans*, 31, 65; Cunningham, *Jeffersonian Republicans*, 134, 246–47.

21. *Historical Statistics of the United States, Colonial Times to 1957* (Washington, D.C., 1960), 14.

22. TJ to Priestley, Mar. 21, 1800, *WTJ* 8:22; TJ to Spencer Roane, Sep. 6, 1819, ibid., 12:136.

23. Pasley, "1800 as a Revolution in Political Culture," in Horn, *Revolution of 1800*, 122.

24. Morris to AH, Dec. 19, 1800, *PAH*, 25:267.

Chapter 12

1. Jack N. Rakove, "The Political Presidency: Discovery and Invention," in Horn, *Revolution of 1800*, 36.

2. James E. Lewis Jr., "'What Is to Become of Our Government?': The Revolutionary Potential of the Election of 1800," ibid., 16.

3. TJ to JM, Dec. 19, 1800, *PJM* 17:444–45.

4. Sharp, *American Politics in the Early Republic*, 265.

5. JM to TJ, Jan. 10, 1801, *PJM*, 17:453–54, 471n.

6. TJ to Burr, Dec. 15, 1800, *WTJ* 7:466–68; TJ, *Anas* (Jan. 26, 1804), ibid., 1:302; Burr to TJ, Dec. 23, 1800, *PCAB* 1:469–74; Burr to Samuel Smith, Dec. 16, 1800, ibid., 1:471.

7. TJ to Burr, Feb. 1, 1801, *WTJ* 7:485.

8. Lewis, "'What Is to Become of Our Government?'" in Horn, *Revolution of 1800*, 14.

9. Ibid., 16–17.

10. Bellesiles, "'The Soil Will Be Soaked with Blood,'" ibid., 67.

11. Sedgwick to AH, Jan. 10, 1801, *PAH* 25:310–13.

12. Morris to AH, Jan. 26, 1801, *PAH*, 25:329–30; John Rutledge Jr. to AH, Jan. 10, 1801, ibid., 25:308. The Harper quotation is from Joseph W. Cox, *Champion of Southern Federalism: Robert Goodloe Harper of South Carolina* (Port Washington, N.Y., 1972), 192.

13. Morris to AH, Jan. 16, 1801, *PAH* 25:324–25.

14. AH to Wolcott, Dec. 16, 1800, ibid., 25:257; AH to James Bayard, Dec. 27, 1800, Jan. 16, 1801, ibid., 25:276–77, 319–24; AH to John Rutledge Jr., Jan. 4, 1801, ibid., 25:293–98. See also Kennedy, *Burr, Hamilton, and Jefferson*.

15. AH to McHenry, Jan. 4, 1801, *PAH* 25:292–93; AH to Wolcott, Dec. 16, 1800, ibid., 25:258; AH to Bayard, Dec. 27, 1800, ibid., 25:277.

16. TJ to Burr, Dec. 15, 1800, *WTJ* 7:466–68; Sharp, *American Politics in the Early Republic*, 255; Cunningham, *Jeffersonian Republicans*, 242.

17. Beckley to Albert Gallatin, Feb. 4, 15, 1801, in *Justifying Jefferson*, ed. Gawalt, 231, 232–33.

18. Beckley to Littleton Tazewell, Jan. 25, 1801, ibid., 228; Berkeley and Berkeley, *Beckley*, 211–16; Bellesiles, "'The Soil Will Be Soaked with Blood,'" in Horn, *Revolution of 1800*, 64; Sharp, *American Politics in the Early Republic*, 250–52.

19. Albert Gallatin, "Plan at Time of Balloting for Jefferson and Burr, Communicated to Nicholas and Mr. Jefferson" [late Jan.–early Feb. 1801], in *The Writings of Albert Gallatin*, ed. Henry Adams (Philadelphia, 1879), 1:18–20.

20. TJ, *Anas* (Apr. 15, 1806), *WTJ* 1:313.

21. TJ to Martha Jefferson Randolph, *Collections of the Massachusetts Historical Society*, 7th ser., 1:85.

22. TJ subsequently hinted that he knew immediately of Burr's remarks in Philadelphia. See TJ, *Anas* (Jan. 2, 1804), *PTJ* 1:301.

23. Lomask, *Burr*, 1:270–71, 276–77, 285–86; Elkins and McKitrick, *Age of Federalism*, 747.

24. Robert Goodloe Harper to Burr, Dec. 24, 1800, *PCAB* 1:474–76.

25. *PAH* 24:483–86n.

26. TJ, *Anas* (Apr. 15, 1806), *WTJ* 1:312–13.

27. JA to Gerry, Dec. 30, 1800, *WJA* 9:577–78.

28. TJ, *Anas* (Feb. 12, 14, 1801), *WTJ* 1:291.

29. *PAH* 25:302–3n.

30. Gunn to AH, Jan. 9, 1801, ibid., 25:303; Sharp, *American Politics in the Early Republic*, 264.

31. Bayard to AH, Aug. 18, 1800, *PAH* 25:71. On Bayard's background, see Morton Borden, *The Federalism of James A. Bayard* (New York, 1955), 8–46.

32. Bayard to Richard Bassett [?], Jan. 3, 1801, in *Annual Report of the American Historical Association for the Year 1913* (Washington, D.C., 1915), 117.

33. Quoted in Miller, *Federalist Era*, 107.

34. Bayard to AH, Jan. 7, 1801, *PAH* 25:300–301; Bayard to Caesar Rodney [?], Jan. 5, 1801, *Annual Report of the American Historical Association for the Year 1913*, 118.

35. Bruce Ackerman and David Fontana, "How Jefferson Counted Himself In," *Atlantic Monthly*, 293 (Mar. 2004): 84–95.

36. Miller, *Federalist Era*, 271.

37. TJ to Monroe, Feb. 15, 1800, *WTJ* 7:491; TJ, *Anas* (Apr. 15, 1806), ibid., 1:313; TJ to JM, Feb. 18, 1801, ibid., 7:494; Lewis, "'What Is to Become of Our Government,'" Horn, *Revolution of 1800*, 20; Bellesiles, "'The Soil Will Be Soaked with Blood,'" ibid., 65; Sharp, *American Politics in the Early Republic*, 267–71.

38. JA to James Lloyd, Feb. 6, 1815, *WJA* 10:115.

39. The full text of the informant's letter can be found in Sisson, *American Revolution of 1800*, 463–68. The quotations are on page 467.

40. "Deposition of James A. Bayard," Apr. 3, 1806, in *Memoirs of Aaron Burr: With Miscellaneous Selections from His Correspondence*, ed. Matthew L. Davis (New York, 1971), 2:125, 130–31.

41. Ibid., 2:125–26; John S. Pancake, *Samuel Smith and the Politics of Business, 1752–1839* (Tuscaloosa, Ala., 1972), 57; Frank A. Cassell, *Merchant Congressman in the Young Republic: Samuel Smith of Maryland, 1752–1839* (Madison, Wis., 1971), 99–101.

42. Quoted in Bordon, *Federalism of Bayard*, 91.

43. Bayard to Bassett, Feb. 16, 1801, *Annual Report of the American Historical Association for the Year 1913*, 126.

44. "Deposition of James A. Bayard," in *Memoirs of Aaron Burr*, ed. Davis, 2:122–33; Bordon, *Federalism of Bayard*, 85–93.

45. TJ to Monroe, Feb. 15, 1801, *WTJ* 7:491.

46. Bayard to Samuel Bayard, Feb. 22, 1801, *Annual Report of the American Historical Association for the Year 1913*, 2:131–32.

47. "Deposition of James A. Bayard," in *Memoirs of Aaron Burr*, ed. Davis, 2:131.

48. Ibid., 2:131–32.

49. Ibid., 2:132.

50. Borden, *Federalism of Bayard*, 84; Bayard to AH, Mar. 8, 1801, *PAH* 25:344.

51. Sedgwick to Theodore Sedgwick Jr., Feb. 16, 1801, Sedgwick Papers, MHS.

52. TJ, *Anas* (Apr. 15, 1806), *WTJ* 1:312.

53. Burr to Albert Gallatin, Feb. 25, 1801, *PCAB* 1:509.

54. Bayard to Allan McLane, Feb. 17, 1801, *Annual Report of the American Historical Association for the Year 1913*, 128; "Deposition of James A. Bayard," in *Memoirs of Aaron Burr*, ed. Davis, 2:122–33; "Deposition of Samuel Smith," Apr. 1806, ibid., 2:133–37.

55. Borden, *Federalism of Bayard*, 91. The quotation is on page 84.

56. The quotation is in Beran, *Jefferson's Demons*, 156.

57. Ibid., 92–93.

58. TJ to Thomas M. Randolph, Jan. 29, 1801, *Collections of the Massachusetts Historical Society*, 7th ser., 1:88.

59. TJ, *Anas* (Feb. 12, 1801), *WTJ* 1:291.

60. Freeman, *Affairs of Honor*, 244–45; Bellesiles, "'The Soil Will Be Soaked with Blood,'" in Horn, *Revolution of 1800*, 68; William B. Hatcher, *Edward Livingston: Jeffersonian Republican and Jacksonian Democrat* (Baton Rouge, 1940), 18–25, 69.

61. Wills, *Negro President*, 86.

62. TJ to Joseph Priestley, Mar. 21, 1801, *WTJ* 8:22; Malone, *Jefferson*, 4:9; Bellesiles, "'The Soil Will Be Soaked with Blood,'" in Horn, *Revolution of 1800*, 73–81.

63. TJ to Henry Dearborn, Feb. 18, 1801, *WTJ* 7:495; TJ to Thomas M. Randolph, Feb. 19, 1801, ibid., 7:497; TJ to Thomas Lomax, Feb. 25, 1801, ibid., 7:500.

Chapter 13

1. JA to William Tudor, Jan. 20, 1801, AFP, reel 400; AA to TBA, Dec. 25, 1800, ibid., reel 399.

2. JA to Boudinot, Jan. 26, 1801, *WJA* 9:94.

3. JA to Gerry, Dec. 30, 1800, ibid., 9:577–78.

4. AA to TBA, Jan. 3, 1801, AFP, reel 400; TBA to AA, Jan. 9, 1801, ibid., reel 400.

5. AA to TBA, Jan. 26, 1801, ibid., reel 400.

6. DeConde, *Quasi-War Crisis*, 223–58.

7. JA to TBA, Jan. 24, 1801, AFP, reel 400.

8. Quoted in Zoltán Haraszti, *John Adams and the Prophets of Progress* (New York, 1964), 263.

9. TJ to Benjamin Rush, March 24, 1801, *WTJ* 8:32; TJ to Knox, Mar. 27, 1801, ibid., 8:37.

10. McCullough, *Adams*, 562–63.

11. Levin, *Abigail Adams*, 389–90.

12. AA to JA, Feb. 21, 1801, AFP, reel 400.

13. McCullough, *Adams*, 563–64.

14. JA's first draft can be found under "Draft of a Reply to the Pamphlet of Alexander Hamilton" in AFP, reel 499.

15. JA to Tudor, Jan. 20, 1801, ibid., reel 400.

16. For an insightful essay on JA's paper war, see Freeman, *Affairs of Honor*, 105–58.

17. *JMB* 2:1034–35.

18. TJ to C. C. Pinckney, March 6, 1801, *WTJ* 8:7.

19. The foregoing on TJ's habits draws on McLaughlin, *Jefferson and Monticello*, 9.

20. Malone, *Jefferson*, 4:29–32.

21. Waldstreicher, *In the Midst of Perpetual Fetes*, 187–93.

22. Margaret Bayard Smith, *The First Forty Years of Washington*, ed. Gaillard Hunt (New York, 1906), 26.

23. Thomas Jefferson, First Inaugural Address (Mar. 4, 1801), *MPP* 1:321–24. TJ's first draft of the speech can be found in *WTJ* 8:1–6. The Richardson copy of the speech incorrectly capitalizes the words *republican* and *federalist* in the passage: "We are all republicans, we are all federalists."

24. TJ, First Inaugural Address, *MPP* 1:324.

25. Bernstein, *Jefferson*, 136.

Epilogue

1. Malone, *Jefferson*, 4:29.

2. TJ to John Dickinson, Mar. 8, 1801, *WTJ* 8:7–8; TJ to Paine, Mar. 18, 1801, ibid., 8:18–19; TJ to Joseph Priestley, Mar. 21, 1801, ibid., 8:22; TJ to Samuel Adams, Mar. 29, 1801, ibid., 8:39.

3. TJ to Spencer Roane, Sep. 6, 1819, ibid., 12:136.

4. For an excellent summation of scholarly interpretations of the notion of a "revolution of 1800," see Sisson, *American Revolution of 1800*, 3–12.

5. The quotations are from Wills, *Negro President*, 2.

6. JA to TJ, Jun. 14, 1813, *AJL* 2:329–30.

7. TJ to JA, Jun. 27, 1813, ibid., 2:335–36.

8. A wonderfully succinct statement on TJ's revolution, and on which this paragraph draws, can be found in Joyce Appleby, "Thomas Jefferson and Psychology of Democracy," in Horn, *Revolution of 1800*, 155–72.

9. *Historical Statistics of the United States*, 7, 9, 11, 13, 14, 24; Edwin G. Burrows and Mike Wallace, *Gotham: A History of New York City to 1898* (New York, 1999), 435; Thomas M. Doerflinger, *A Vigorous Spirit of Enterprise: Merchants and Economic Development in Revolutionary Philadelphia* (New York, 1986), 342; Joyce Appleby, *Inheriting the Revolution: The First Generation of Americans* (Cambridge, Mass., 2000), 64.

10. Wood, *Radicalism of the American Revolution*, 313, 340.

11. Appleby, *Inheriting the Revolution*, 27; Pasley, "1800 as a Revolution in Political Culture," in Horn, *Revolution of 1800*, 127.

12. Freeman, *Affairs of Honor*, 159–98.

13. JA to Vanderkemp, Nov. 5, 1804, Feb. 5, 1805, AFP, reel 118; JA to Trumbull, Jul. 8, 1805, ibid., reel 118; JA to Charles Gadsden, Apr. 16, 1805, ibid., reel 118; JA to Richard Cranch, May 23, 1801, ibid., reel 118; JA to Benjamin Waterhouse, in *Statesman and Friend: Correspondence of John Adams with Benjamin Waterhouse, 1784–1822*, ed. Worthington C. Ford (Boston, 1927), 31; JA to Rush, Oct. 25, 1809, in Schutz and Adair, *Spur of Fame*, 159; JA to Mercy Otis Water, Jul. 20, 1807, in "Correspondence Between John Adams and Mercy Warren Relating to Her History of the American Revolution," *Collections of the Massachusetts Historical Society*, 5th Ser. (1878): 4:337.

14. TJ to JA, Sep. 12, 1821, *AJL* 2:574–75.

15. TJ to Roger Weightman, Jun. 24, 1826, *WTJ* 10:390–92.

16. Sloan, *Principle and Interest*, 13–26, 218–23; Malone, *Jefferson*, 6:123–25, 301–5, 308–15, 343–42, 448–52.

17. TJ to Vanderkemp, Jan. 11, 1825, *WTJ* 10:336–37; TJ to Giles, Dec. 25, 1825, ibid., 10:351; TJ to Nathaniel Macon, Feb. 21, 1826, ibid., 10:378; JA to Rush, Jan. 4, 1812, in Schutz and Adair, *Spur of Fame*, 263; Ferling, *Adams*, 434; TJ to JA, Nov. 13, 1818, *AJL* 2:529.

18. On their final days and hours, see Andrew Burstein, *America's Jubilee: How in 1826 a Generation Remembered Fifty Years of Independence* (New York, 2001), 255–63.

19. Merrill D. Peterson, *The Jeffersonian Image in the American Mind* (New York, 1960), 3–13. For an excellent appraisal of the numerous eulogies delivered following JA's and TJ's demise, see Burstein, *America's Jubilee*, 268–86.

20. Peterson, *The Jefferson Image in the American Mind*, 5–13. The quotations can be found on pages 6 and 10. Also see L. H. Butterfield, "The Jubilee of Independence, July 4, 1826," *Virginia Magazine of History and Biography* 61 (1953): 136; Daniel Webster, "Adams and Jefferson, Aug. 2, 1826," in *The Writings and Speeches of Daniel Webster* (Boston, 1903), 1:324.

21. Burstein, *America's Jubilee*, 242; Appleby, *Inheriting the Revolution*, 264–65.

Index

Page numbers in *italics* refer to photographs and tables. Page numbers in **bold** refer to entire chapters.

Printed in the USA/Agawam, MA
May 4, 2022

792578.030